David Foster Wallace and Religion

David Foster Wallace and Religion

Essays on Faith and Fiction

Edited by Michael McGowan and Martin Brick

BLOOMSBURY ACADEMIC
NEW YORK • LONDON • OXFORD • NEW DELHI • SYDNEY

BLOOMSBURY ACADEMIC
Bloomsbury Publishing Inc
1385 Broadway, New York, NY 10018, USA
50 Bedford Square, London, WC1B 3DP, UK
29 Earlsfort Terrace, Dublin 2, Ireland

BLOOMSBURY, BLOOMSBURY ACADEMIC and the Diana logo
are trademarks of Bloomsbury Publishing Plc

First published in the United States of America 2020
This paperback edition published in 2021

Volume Editors' Part of the Work © Michael McGowan and Martin Brick, 2020

Each chapter © of Contributors

For legal purposes the Acknowledgements on p. xv constitute an extension
of this copyright page.

Cover design by Eleanor Rose
Cover photo © Kacey Crawford

All rights reserved. No part of this publication may be reproduced or transmitted
in any form or by any means, electronic or mechanical, including photocopying,
recording, or any information storage or retrieval system, without prior
permission in writing from the publishers.

Bloomsbury Publishing Inc does not have any control over, or responsibility for,
any third-party websites referred to or in this book. All internet addresses given
in this book were correct at the time of going to press. The author and publisher
regret any inconvenience caused if addresses have changed or sites have ceased
to exist, but can accept no responsibility for any such changes.

Library of Congress Cataloging-in-Publication Data
Names: McGowan, Michael, editor. | Brick, M. (Martin), editor.
Title: David Foster Wallace and religion : essays on faith and fiction /
edited by Michael McGowan and Martin Brick.
Description: New York : Bloomsbury Academic, 2020. |
Includes bibliographical references and index. |
Summary: "Scholars of literature, religion, and philosophy
explore the subject of religion in the life and writings of
David Foster Wallace."– Provided by publisher.
Identifiers: LCCN 2019026330 (print) | LCCN 2019026331
(ebook) | ISBN 9781501345289 (hardback) | ISBN 9781501345296 (epub) |
ISBN 9781501345302 (pdf)
Subjects: LCSH: Wallace, David Foster–Criticism and interpretation. |
Wallace, David Foster–Religion. | Religion in literature.
Classification: LCC PS3573.A425635 Z6618 2019 (print) |
LCC PS3573.A425635 (ebook) | DDC 813/.54–dc23
LC record available at https://lccn.loc.gov/2019026330
LC ebook record available at https://lccn.loc.gov/2019026331

ISBN:	HB:	978-1-5013-4528-9
	PB:	978-1-5013-8148-5
	ePDF:	978-1-5013-4530-2
	eBook:	978-1-5013-4529-6

Typeset by Integra Software Services Pvt. Ltd.

To find out more about our authors and books visit www.bloomsbury.com
and sign up for our newsletters.

CONTENTS

Notes on Contributors   vii
Preface   xi
Acknowledgments   xv
Abbreviations   xvi

Understanding Seeking Faith: An Introduction to Religion in David Foster Wallace's Life   1
Martin Brick

1 Came to Believe: The Religion of Alcoholics Anonymous in *Infinite Jest*   13
Rob Short

2 A Less "Bullshitty" Way to Live: The Pragmatic Spirituality of David Foster Wallace   25
Robert Bolger

3 "Not Another Word": Nietzsche, Wallace, and the Death of God   45
Michael McGowan

4 In G.O.D. We Trust: The Desert of the Religious in *The Broom of the System*   69
Vernon W. Cisney

5 "Saying *God* with a Straight Face": Towards an Understanding of Christian Soteriology in *Infinite Jest*   83
Dave Laird

6 *Infinite Jest*, C.S. Lewis's *Tao*, and Religious Community   99
Peter Spaulding

7 "Somewhat Lost and Desolate Inside": Overcoming Acedia in *The Pale King* 113
Michael O'Connell

8 "The Moral Equivalent of War": Fungible Transcendentals in *The Pale King* 125
Robert Hamilton

9 A Spoon, Some Eskimos, and the Wise Old Fish: Religion and the Evolution of Wallace's Kenyon Commencement Address 137
Matt Bucher and Martin Brick

10 David Foster Wallace and Postsecularism 149
Ryan Lackey

11 "There's Always a Mormon Around When You Don't Want One": What Wallace Can Teach the Church Media Machine 163
Jessica E. Sagers

12 Zen Buddhist Philosophy Lurking in the Work of David Foster Wallace 175
Krzysztof Piekarski

Conclusion: The Religious Worlds of David Foster Wallace—Both Fiction and Not 187
Michael McGowan

Index 202

NOTES ON CONTRIBUTORS

Editors

Martin Brick is Associate Professor of English at Ohio Dominican University. He earned his Ph.D. from Marquette University. His research focuses on religion in Modern and Postmodern literature. He has published on James Joyce, Virginia Woolf, D.H. Lawrence, David Foster Wallace, and Mark Z. Danielewski in venues such as *James Joyce Quarterly*, *Virginia Woolf Miscellany*, *Christianity and Literature*, and several edited collections.

Michael McGowan is Professor of Philosophy and Religion at Florida Southwestern State College. He earned graduate degrees from Yale University, University of South Florida, Claremont Graduate University, and Malone University. He is the author of *The Bridge: Revelation and Its Implications* and has written for Blackwell's "Philosophy and Pop Culture" series. His work also appears in *Christianity Today*, *Journal of Religion and Film*, *Christian Scholar's Review*, *Journal of Human Rights*, *Theological Book Review*, *Teaching Ethics*, *International Journal of Systematic Theology*, and *Pastoral Psychology*.

Contributors

Matt Bucher is Founding President and member of the board of the International David Foster Wallace Society. He is the co-host of *The Great Concavity* podcast and editorial director of Sideshow Media Group Press, which has published several books on David Foster Wallace. His work has appeared in *Publishers Weekly*, *The Austin Chronicle*, *MEL Magazine*, *The Scofield*, among others. He lives in Austin, Texas.

Robert Bolger has an M.A. in Theology from Union Theological Seminary and a Ph.D. in Philosophy of Religion and Theology from Claremont Graduate University, where he studied with D.Z. Phillips. He is the author of *Kneeling at the Altar of Science: The Mistaken Path of Contemporary Religious Scientism* (Pickwick Press, 2012) and editor (with Scott Korb) of *Gesturing*

Toward Reality: David Foster Wallace and Philosophy (Bloomsbury Press, 2014). His book, *Religious Language, Meaning and Use: The God Who Is Not There*, came out in 2019 (Bloomsbury Press). Find him online at: www.RobertBolger.com.

Vernon W. Cisney is Assistant Professor of Interdisciplinary Studies at Gettysburg College in Pennsylvania. His areas of research are contemporary continental philosophy, philosophy of literature, and philosophy of film. He is the author of *Deleuze and Derrida: Difference and the Power of the Negative* (Edinburgh University Press, 2018), as well as *Derrida's Voice and Phenomenon: An Edinburgh Philosophical Guide* (Edinburgh University Press, 2014). He is also the co-editor of *Biopower: Foucault and Beyond* (University of Chicago Press, 2015); *The Way of Nature and the Way of Grace: Philosophical Footholds on Terrence Malick's Tree of Life* (Northwestern University Press, 2016); *Between Foucault and Derrida* (Edinburgh University Press, 2016); and Pierre Klossowski's *Living Currency, Followed by Sade and Fourier* (Bloomsbury, 2017), for which he also co-translated the titular essay.

Robert Hamilton is Assistant Professor of English at Temple College in Temple, Texas. He has published on David Foster Wallace in The *Arizona Quarterly*, and has written and presented widely on post-1960 American novelists such as Louise Erdrich and Cormac McCarthy. His dissertation considers the preservation of trace elements of religious thought in the fiction of Donald Barthelme, David Foster Wallace, and Jennifer Egan. He also writes creative work, and his first chapbook of poetry was published by Ghost City Press in 2018.

Ryan Lackey is a Ph.D. student at the University of California, Berkeley. He received an M.A. from Oregon State University and a B.A. from George Fox University. He serves on the diversity committee of the International David Foster Wallace Society, and he has taught at several institutions in the Pacific Northwest. His research interests include modern and contemporary American literature and the intersections between religion and the post-45 period.

Dave Laird is the co-host of *The Great Concavity*, a podcast about David Foster Wallace, and a board member of the International David Foster Wallace Society (Membre du Conseil, Division de Convexité). He was also a weekly guide for the Infinite Winter online group read of *Infinite Jest* in 2016, and has presented three times at the Illinois State University DFW Conference, on Jonathan Lethem's *Chronic City* and its relation to *Infinite Jest* (2015), the theological significance of Mario Incandenza (2016), and his personal experiences doing the Wallace podcast, titled "Scaling the

Lucite Wall: Relational Convexities and *The Great Concavity*" (2017). He has an M.A. in English (thesis on *Infinite Jest*), a B.Ed., and a B.A., each from The University of British Columbia. Dave teaches senior-high school Humanities, and (usually) lives in Victoria, BC. He is a proud proponent of the term "Convexity."

Michael O'Connell is Associate Professor of Humanities at Siena Heights University in Adrian, Michigan. He earned his Ph.D. from Loyola University in Chicago, his M.A. from Boston University, and his B.A. from the University of Notre Dame. His essays on the intersections of contemporary literature and faith have appeared in a number of scholarly journals, including *Christianity and Literature, Renascence, Religion and the Arts*, and *American Catholic Studies*. He is currently working on a study of violence in contemporary American Catholic fiction.

Krzysztof Piekarski earned his Ph.D. in English Literature at the University of Texas in Austin, where his dissertation explored Buddhist philosophy in the work of David Foster Wallace. He currently teaches "The Non-Argumentative Rhetoric of Zen" and "The Rhetoric of Animals" in UT's Rhetoric department. Piekarski is a Council Member at Appamada Zen Center and trained in the Hakomi Method, a mindfulness-based therapy. Working to find the most skillful ways of helping people transform their consciousness, Piekarski created www.CharacterByDesign.org to articulate what it means for a person to both wake up and grow up in contemporary times. In less virtuous moments, he practices jiu-jitsu, goes on far-flung adventures with his partner Circe, and splashes around with his dog Bunk in Austin's swimming holes.

Jessica E. Sagers holds a Ph.D. in auditory neuroscience from the Division of Medical Sciences at Harvard University and a bachelor's degree in Linguistics from Brigham Young University. Her research involves identifying and testing new and existing drugs to control the growth of the fourth most common intracranial tumor, vestibular schwannoma. She grew up as a member of the Church of Jesus Christ of Latter-Day Saints and served as a missionary in Daejeon, South Korea. Outside of her scientific career, she is an ardent reader, writer, and Wallace enthusiast.

Rob Short earned his Ph.D. at the University of Florida in 2017. His dissertation is titled *Big Books: Addiction and Recovery in the Novels of David Foster Wallace*. His work on Wallace has appeared in *Normal 2015: Selected Works from the Second Annual David Foster Wallace Conference* and on the website for James Ponsoldt's film *The End of the Tour*. He serves as the president of The International David Foster Wallace Society and on the board of *The Journal of David Foster Wallace Studies*.

Peter Spaulding is a doctoral student at Marquette University, where he works on Milton's motivations and rhetoric in *Paradise Lost*, as well as debates surrounding Milton's orthodoxy, theodicy, and the character of Satan. He is also interested in the overlap of the epic tradition and Christianity/religion, Early Modern and Metaphysical poets, Shakespearean Drama, contemporary poetry, and creative writing. Peter received his M.A. in English Literature from Marquette University and B.A. from John Brown University. His non-scholarly interests are generally much more lighthearted: going to Miller Park and tailgating on warm summer afternoons, listening uncritically and unironically to pop music, and taking walks with his wife, Erin.

PREFACE

David Foster Wallace reportedly once commented to his friend Jonathan Franzen that he considered his own thoughts on religion "banal."[1] The contributors to this collection would beg to differ. Interest in Wallace and spirituality has been percolating for years. The editors of this volume began to notice a healthy representation of religiously themed panels at the annual conferences dedicated to Wallace's writing, thus far consistently hosted at Illinois State University. Many of these chapters, in fact, were first presented in Normal, IL, at a DFW conference. With this observation, the time felt right for a collection dedicated to the many nuances of Wallace's spirituality. From his earliest literature onward, Wallace's writing has expressed an interest in the "big questions": What guides us? What gives us fulfillment? How do we understand human existence? How do I know it isn't all just inside my head? What are examples of good living? Beyond his writing, numerous interviews, biographical accounts, and his own notes and papers housed at the Harry Ransom Center in Austin, Texas, reveal that these questions reverberated throughout his life.

Some contributors see overtones of Christianity while others look to Eastern religions. Some look closely at the man behind the words while others take a more Reader-Response approach and examine what audiences experience through his literature. Some see comfort and guidance while others see doubt and anxiety.[2] Surely no consensus on Wallace's faith exists, but it also seems clear that there is substance to this inquiry.

Articles in scholarly journals and online magazines dedicated to religion have perhaps not been bountiful, but they have been consistently appearing since Wallace's death in 2008. Still, to date, few books have been published on the subject. One of the earliest books released with the explicit goal of exploring Wallace's philosophy was *Gesturing Toward Reality*.[3] While several chapters do address religious themes, overall the collection deals with metaphysical problems of a more philosophical bent: identity, consciousness, freedom, ethics, and language. Similarly, but more recently, we have *David Foster Wallace: Presences of the Other*. However, the essays in this book deal primarily with philosophies of identity and selfhood and only peripherally mention religious issues in Wallace's work.[4] Adam Miller's *The Gospel According to David Foster Wallace* is one of the few monographs overtly dedicated to Wallace and religion.[5] His work is written in thirty short but thoughtful chapters, almost meditations on various themes, and differs in intention from his volume. Wallace's religion has also garnered some negative attention, most notably the chapter in Hubert L. Dreyfus and Sean Dorrance Kelly's *All Things Shining*, which reads Wallace as a postmodern nihilist who feels the "need to create meaning ex nihilo out of the individual."[6] Not surprisingly, many of the chapters in this collection take issue with Dreyfus and Kelly's conclusions.

Interest in religion and Wallace has swelled to such a state that the editor of the *Cambridge Companion to David Foster Wallace* saw fit to include a chapter on "Wallace, Spirituality, and Religion," written by Matthew Mullins.[7] This chapter presents a good overview of state of the subject, finding that a few scholars tend to push toward overtly Christian readings, and a few toward nihilism or a dismissal of Wallace's faith, but most fall somewhere between, and further they gravitate toward three prominent themes: conversion, worship, and community. Little wonder, then, that these themes make frequent appearances in the chapters here. Readers will also recognize that certain passages recurrently resonate with those who explore Wallace's faith. Chris Fogle's conversion narrative, taking up a healthy 100 pages of *The Pale King*, echoes through these chapters. Similarly, expect to find frequent nods to *This Is Water*'s interrogation of how to combat solipsism and Don Gately's clumsy yet devoted attempt to find a high power in Boston's Alcoholics Anonymous (AA) circuit. Nevertheless, this volume also teases out religion and spirituality in less frequently explored corners of Wallace's oeuvre – *Broom of the System*, "Westward the Course of Empire Takes Its Way," "Octet," and some of his essays such as "E Unibus Pluram."

The collection opens with a series of chapters that address the topic from a biographical point of view. Martin Brick provides an Introduction that examines Wallace's life-long search for faith that consistently came up short. It is frequently reported that Wallace toyed with Catholicism but backed out due to his doubts, and this trend of overintellectualizing faith affected all of his attempts at seeking transcendence, from AA to Buddhism. Next, Rob Short argues that Wallace's first serious engagement with religion, and the strongest and most persistent, lies in his personal experience in AA. He provides a keen comparison of the nature of "higher power" in both *Infinite Jest* and AA's Big Book. Robert Bolger's contribution also owes much to Wallace's AA experience, but explores the ontological and epistemological underpinnings of religious belief. The "Pragmatic Spirituality" of his subtitle involves not reason or evidence, but a commitment to live the stories into which we are born. Michael McGowan's essay on Wallace and Nietzsche specifically argues against Dreyfus and Kelly's interpretation of Wallace as a nihilist. McGowan shows that Wallace's solution to the problem of existential angst is fully capable of providing transcendent meaning to a world reeling after the "death of God."

A second section of the collection includes contributions that primarily address a single work, in most cases the novels. Vernon Cisney tackles *Broom of the System*, the novel Wallace wrote as an undergraduate student and the least intuitive place to look for religious content. Nevertheless, the novel contains G.O.D.—the Great Ohio Desert—a manmade wasteland that Cisney uses to open a Kierkegaardian exploration of the relationship between "god" and "self." Next Dave Laird explores soteriology, or the Christian doctrine of salvation, in *Infinite Jest*. Mario Incandenza, Don Gately, Barry Loach, and Lyle are used to guide us through the tripartite fascination with three core tenets of the orthodox Christian metanarrative: humanity's innate value, our fallen state, and redemption through grace. Another take on *Infinite Jest* is presented by Peter Spaulding, who reads it in tandem with C. S. Lewis's *The Abolition of Man*. Spaulding argues that both works offer, as a solution to the problems of our age, the subjection of the individual will to a greater body for their concerns about a growing cultural trend toward solipsism.

We also have two treatments of *The Pale King*. The first comes from Michael O'Connell who treats the topic that the novel is popularly said to be about—boredom—through the lens of the Christian monastic tradition, specifically the concepts of Acedia, or the "noonday demon." O'Connell looks both to Christian mystics such as the Desert Fathers and Walker Percy in his examination of how Wallace approaches our modern condition. Secondly, Robert Hamilton offers "Fungible Transcendentals"; spirituality in *The Pale King*, he argues, is characterized by active tension, productive dissonance, and is often limited in its presentation to empirical and subjective vantage points.

The final single-work examination treats Wallace's most widely known piece of writing, *This Is Water*. Matthew Bucher and Martin Brick take a genetic approach examining the array of parables that move in and out of the progression of drafts of the Kenyon Commencement Address, as well as source material he referenced while composing it, suggesting that the speech may function as our clearest portal to viewing Wallace's own spirituality.

The remaining four chapters address particular religions or religious themes. Taking as a launching off point Amy Hungerford's and John McClure's explication of the postsecular, Ryan Lackey reappraises Wallace's spirituality. He argues that Wallace illuminates and problematizes the notion of the postsecular, particularly in "Octet," concluding that Wallace's work has an abiding fundamental mystical spirituality. Jessica Sagers takes a small, comic moment—a disparaging remarks about Mormons in "Westward"—and develops a compelling comparison of the missionary media machine of the Church of Jesus Christ of Latter-Day Saints and the advertising industry of the 1980s. She takes a deep examination of LDS teachings, film, and music, then applies Wallace's criticism of media to argue that, despite altruistic intentions, their teaching feels too much like advertising.

While we have no reason to believe Wallace had much experience with Mormonism, we do have evidence of an interest in Buddhism. Krzysztof Piekarski analyzes how Wallace, in his writing, intuitively stumbled upon the same spiritual concerns of the Buddha. Specifically, both offer similar insights regarding the identifications of the stumbling blocks of life and the way we ought to live.

In his Kenyon Commencement Address, Wallace tells a joke about an atheist in the Alaskan Wilderness. Trapped in a blizzard he decides to pray and a couple of Eskimos appear, guiding him back to camp. Recounting the events later, to a believer, he dismisses the will of God. As he nears the conclusions of his speech and reinforces the call for awareness, Wallace circles back with this remark: "These Eskimos might be much more than they seem" (*TIW* 134). So too, Wallace's spirituality may be more than it seems to the lay reader. These contributions represent but a small glance at the far-from-banal theme of religion in Wallace's writing and life.

Notes

1. D.T. Max, "Questions for D. T. Max," *The New Yorker*, February 27, 2009. Available online: https://www.newyorker.com/books/ask-the-author/questions-for-d-t-max.
2. The diversity of approaches is echoed by the diversity of contributors. The editors wanted to avoid constructing the typical collection of essays from literature professors, and brought in scholars from many fields, and further, looked to those outside of academia altogether. Here you will find theologians, philosophers, and even a neuroscientist. You will find tenured faculty and graduate students, scholars and fans, religious people and nonreligious people, men, women, and different races. Wallace Studies is still an emerging field, and thus it is particularly exciting to help many young voices shape this field.
3. *Gesturing Toward Reality: David Foster Wallace and Philosophy*, ed. Robert Bolger and Scott Korb (New York: Bloomsbury Academic, 2014).
4. *David Foster Wallace: Presences of the Other*, ed. Beatrice Pire and Pierre-Louis Patoine (Eastbourne, UK: Sussex Academic Press, 2017).
5. *The Gospel According to David Foster Wallace: Boredom and Addiction in an Age of Distraction* (New York: Bloomsbury Academic, 2016).
6. *All Things Shining: Reading the Western Classics to Find Meaning in a Secular Age* (New York: Free Press, 2011), 204.
7. "Wallace, Spirituality, and Religion," in *The Cambridge Companion to David Foster Wallace*, ed. Ralph Clare (Cambridge: Cambridge University Press, 2018), 190–203.

ACKNOWLEDGMENTS

Martin Brick would like to thank his co-editor Michael, who chaired his panel at DFW17 and said, "Oh, I've already started work on that," when Brick said, "Someone ought to put together a collection about religion and Wallace." Without Mike's pre-emptive hard work and expertise this collection would not have emerged. Thanks as well to Paul Niesen for passing along his stories about "Dave" at ASU. Martin would also like to thank his wife Heather and children, Simon and Eilsih, for their patience with his boring academic endeavors. And thanks to his colleagues at Ohio Dominican for their support and kindness. He could not have imagined a better group of co-workers.

Michael McGowan would like to thank Florida Southwestern State College, who provided generous funding to research this project, the staff of the Harry Ransom Center at the University of Texas at Austin, who were incredibly helpful, and the International David Foster Wallace Conference organizers at Illinois State University, who offered a forum in which the ideas in this book took shape. Special thanks go to the contributors to this book, without whom the book would not have been possible. Michael also wants to thank his co-editor, Martin, who joined the project at a crucial moment and moved it forward with diligence and excellence. Finally, he would like to thank his wife, Magdey, who has heard all too often of a phrase or idea that reminds him of something David Foster Wallace once said or wrote.

Additionally, the editors would like to thank everyone at Bloomsbury Academic for their assistance, especially Haaris Naqvi and Amy Martin. Thanks to Bloomsbury, also, for the rights to reprint Robert Bolger's chapter, "A Less 'Bullshitty' Way to Live: The Pragmatic Spirituality of David Foster Wallace," originally published in *Gesturing Toward Reality: David Foster Wallace and Philosophy*. Thanks as well to the journal *Christianity and Literature* for their agreement to allow an adaptation of Michael O'Connell's "'Your Temple Is Self and Sentiment': David Foster Wallace's Diagnostic Novels," and adaptations of Martin Brick's "A Postmodernist's Progress: Thoughts on Spirituality across the David Foster Wallace Canon." Finally, the editors wish to thank Mark Costello and other people in Wallace's life for sharing their memories and stories about Wallace's perspective on religious issues.

ABBREVIATIONS

Quotations from books by David Foster Wallace and are cited parenthetically by the following abbreviations:

BOS   *Broom of the System*

SR   *Signifying Rappers: Rap and Race in the Urban Present*

GCH   *Girl with Curious Hair*

IJ   *Infinite Jest*

SFT   *A Supposedly Fun Thing I'll Never Do Again*

US   *Up, Simba! 7 Days on the Trail of an Anti-Candidate*

BI   *Brief Interviews with Hideous Men*

EM   *Everything and More: A Compact History of Infinity*

CL   *Consider the Lobster*

O   *Oblivion*

PK   *The Pale King*

TIW   *This Is Water*

BFN   *Both Flesh and Not*

CW   *Conversations with David Foster Wallace*

Understanding Seeking Faith: An Introduction to Religion in David Foster Wallace's Life

Martin Brick

In his five days of conversation with David Lispky at the close of his *Infinite Jest* book tour, David Foster Wallace describes the limited radio options in Bloomington, Illinois. He admits to reluctantly listening to "a lot of shitty country music."[1] But he also suggests that he ultimately finds value in it: "I remember just being real impatient with it," until he asked whether "this absent lover they're singing to is just a metaphor? And what they're really singing is to themselves, or to God, you know."[2] Upon reflection, he describes the music as "existential," filled with pathos, and about feeling complete. Looking for a means to classify his experience with country music in terms with which both he and Lipsky would be familiar, he asserts that it is "very Flannery O'Connorish," invoking the dark, Catholic author that Wallace so greatly admired.

Wallace avoids being overtly religious in this illustration. It is not he but the singers of country songs who seek God, while he remains an anthropological observer, as if religion is something he witnesses but does not practice. This analysis should not come as much of a surprise to Wallace aficionados since he frequently called upon religious metaphors, particular the idea of "worshiping," in his explorations of art and life. In a discussion of metafiction with Larry McCaffrey, he declares, "This is so fucking American, man; either make something your God and cosmos and then worship it, or else kill it" (CW 45). An oft-quoted line from his Kenyon commencement address goes, "there is no such thing as atheism. There is no such thing as not worshiping" (*TIW* 98–9). He describes Roger Federer's tennis as a "religious experience."[3] Of his own youthful tennis ability, he cites a "Taoist ability to control via non-control" among downstate Illinois's "true religious-type wind" (*SFT* 12, 5). One could argue that Wallace uses all of these terms in a fairly secular manner, but the themes in his writing and his biography would suggest that Wallace was always searching for a genuinely fulfilling type of worship, that he unironically hoped to find a god (of whatever sort or type) that he could worship and feel a satisfying return on investment.

To paraphrase a country lyric by Johnny Lee, perhaps Wallace was "looking for faith in all the wrong places." An examination of his various spiritual experiences arguably reveals a series of unsuccessful or, at best, semi-successful attempts to find transcendent fulfillment. But then again, perhaps these attempts offer more than one might first assume. Some approaches to faith, such as process theology, would value the act of seeking truth over the end result—a telos (ends) over terminus (ending) approach. Theologian Jurgen Moltmann, who often explores concepts of evil and eschatology from a process perspective, observes that in a postmodern world, individuals rarely have direct experiences, but rather often live through media. Moltmann argues that such practice leads us to have a "glorified and dualistic" view of Good and Evil; simply put, we imagine vast forces of light and dark battling for our souls, and further that evil exists "over there" and good "over here."[4] We thus overlook that evil exists everywhere, is inside of us, and arises out of our experiences. Surely this worldview bears some similarity to Wallace's thoughts on media in *Infinite Jest* and essays like "E Unibus Pluram," as well as the general life advice offered in *This Is Water*. In this light, Wallace may be one of the great theological writers of the late twentieth and early twenty-first centuries, but with a twist. Theology is often defined as "faith seeking understanding"; Wallace displayed considerable trouble accepting the faith part of this equation. Rather, he attempted to use his mind, his understanding, to seek faith.

Wallace went to many wells in this endeavor to find peace and order: philosophy, self-help books, the "higher power" of Alcoholics Anonymous (AA), as well as traditional religious systems such as Catholicism and Buddhism. One observation to be noted is a distinct desire or need for a movement away from using his head as his primary tool of spiritual engagement, as we see with his early reliance on philosophy. When he first entered AA, Wallace reportedly invoked Aristotle and Wittgenstein when attempting to determine his higher power.[5] Soon, however, he turned to a stronger reliance on the heart, or at least that is what he aspired to. The influence of the head proved difficult to shake. A recurring theme in his spiritual pursuits was his desire to excel via intellect, or as biographer D.T. Max puts it in a reference to Wallace finding his higher power and beating his substance abuse, "when he took a class, he wanted to ace it."[6] Wallace himself used academic terminology when discussing his spiritual journey. Regarding his inability to integrate into the Catholic faith he explained, "I always flunked the period of inquiry" (*CW* 99). Doubt consistently bothered Wallace; his default setting was to strive for a full, rational understanding. It appeared that Wallace was not following his own advice offered in his Kenyon address: "Probably the most dangerous thing about an academic education, at least in my own case, is that it enables my tendency to over-intellectualize stuff, to get lost in abstract thinking instead of simply paying attention to what's going on in front of me" (*TIW* 48).

The reliance on his intellect is understandable given Wallace's upbringing. His philosophy professor father and English professor mother made their values clear. Max reports, "His parents refused to let him or his sister go to church because it would contaminate the rigor of their thought."[7] He told Patrick Arden in a 1999 interview, "My parents are atheists of the '60s brand. You know, religion for them equals central suppression from authority. But their parents—so my grandparents—were very, very religious," going on to note that "I think religion kind of skips a generation" (*CW* 99). Despite his awareness of the lingering effects of his parents' influence, Wallace recognized the limits of the intellect. It becomes tempting, then, to read something like "All That," a short story published posthumously in *New Yorker*, autobiographically, or rather as a metaphor shaped by his relationship with his parents. In the story a young boy receives a toy cement mixer as a gift and his mother, "in a moment of adult boredom or whimsy," tells him that the toy is magic and the drum rotates, but only when he is not watching it.[8] The story clearly operates as an allegory about faith, a concept the parents find comically amusing. The boy later comes to accept religion despite his "devoutly atheist" parents. Compellingly, the story references "Talk Time" that the boy received with his parents before bed, a detail consistent with Wallace's own childhood.[9] Further, the father in the story is "an intellectual" who "had not yet even received tenure," which would have been true of James Wallace in David's early childhood.

In real life, Wallace appeared to be on track to emulate his father. At Amherst College, his father's alma mater, he studied philosophy, developing a particular interest in Ludwig Wittgenstein. Although not yet showing any religious inclination, a concept that would become the crux of his spiritual journey emerged and influenced his study of philosophy: solipsism. James Ryerson suggests in his introduction to *Fate, Time, and Language*, the publication of Wallace's undergrad philosophy thesis, that "Wallace's own anxieties about being 'trapped' in his own head colored or confused his reading of Wittgenstein."[10] Wallace made much of the differences between Wittgenstein's early *Tractatus Logico-Philosophicus* (1922) and later *Philosophical Investigations* (1953), claiming, erroneously, that the philosopher aimed to overthrow his earlier work because it so coldly dismissed the social aspects of language.[11]

This experience factors into the larger arc of Wallace's spiritual growth in a number of ways. It represents the first of a series of investigations that promised serenity but failed to fully deliver; philosophy could not calm his anxieties. Neither would self-help books.[12] AA would help, but not entirely. Catholicism. Buddhism. All had limits, and as a result Wallace spent much of his adult life shifting attention, while literature acted as an ever-present thread through his life "making heads throb heart-like" and addressing "what it is to be a fucking human being" (*BFN* 74, *CW* 26). The philosophical misreading of Wittgenstein marks an early recognition of the limits of Wallace's intellect and his general fear of his head. This is a paradox that dogs Wallace his whole life. On the one hand, he had been brought up and trained to use his mind, as he told David Lipsky: "I had flourished in an academic environment," and his study of philosophy would enhance his writing. "It's the only thing that I've gotten, you know, food pellets from the universe for."[13] Thus, in almost all of his religious explorations he displayed his tendency to try to "ace" things like a class. This personal experience, however, is countered by the messages running through his literature, frequently tackling the pitfalls of overthinking.

The late 1980s brought Wallace's introduction to recovery programs, and with it, the need to accept a higher power.[14] As already noted, he first looked to philosophy to fill this role, but with little success. As always, he approached AA like an academic course. One can imagine that Wallace had himself in mind when creating the character of Geoffrey Day, a junior college professor living in *Infinite Jest*'s Ennet House and a complete contrast to Don Gately. Day questions everything, especially the plethora of clichés, and wants to understand how AA works. He wants to attack his addiction with his intellect, or as the text puts it, people like him "identify their whole selves with their head" (*IJ* 272). The young Wallace did mock the clichés and logic of AA; Mary Karr's memoir *Lit* describes her first encounter with someone she dubs "philosophy Dave" who pointed out "It's a logical fallacy to say that I have a disease whose defining symptom is believing you don't have the disease," essentially the same argument Day presents to Gately during Informal Interface Hours.[15]

It is tempting to consider, however, that AA itself, or at least the community that AA created, came to serve as the higher power that Wallace needed. In a *Boston Globe* interview with Matthew Gilbert, Wallace explains his relationship to religion (at least as it stood in 1997): "I'm interested in religion only because certain churches seem to be a place where things can be talked about. What does your life mean? Do you believe in something bigger than you?" He goes on to note, "I don't know that I'd call myself a religious person," but "One place where I discovered stuff was being talked about was AA meetings" (*CW* 79–80). It appeared that AA functioned as a sort of stand-in for church in Wallace's life, and further, that he used that very term for it—church. In his September 11 reaction article published in *Rolling Stone*, "The View from Mrs. Thompson's," Wallace describes "the church I belong to" and Mrs. Thompson, "one of the world's cooler seventy-four year olds" as being a fellow member of the church (*CL* 135). In actuality, his "church" was his AA group, which met at St. Matthews Episcopal Church in Bloomington. Mrs. Thompson was the mother of fellow 12-stepper, Francis B.[16] According to Charlie Harris, Wallace's department chair at Illinois State University and a close friend, any of his public references to "church" actually means his recovery group.[17] Interestingly, it would appear that he maintained this practice privately as well. In one of Wallace's notebooks, now held at the Harry Ransom Center, he created a list labeled "What balance would look like." In addition to items like "2–3 hours a day in writing" and "Daily exercise" he includes "5 AA/week Church."[18] Even in safe, intimate environments (the notebook entry also included fears that *Infinite Jest* might have been a fluke and musing about a woman named Mary Ann) he conflates his recovery meetings with the idea of "church."

In addition to AA, another influence on Wallace's faith were the women in his life. The adult Wallace was always popular with women,[19] and Max reports the damage that this inflicted on his recovery, entering relationships with fellow addicts, an act called "thirteenth stepping" in AA.[20] His most publicized affair was with the poet and memoirist Mary Karr. Her memoir, *Lit*, chronicles her conversion to Catholicism, which paralleled her recovery from alcohol. Wallace's fervent (and abusive) dedication to Karr likely explains his interest in Catholicism (although his Amherst roommate and *Signifying Rappers*, coauthor Mark Costello was also Catholic). Arden's article on Wallace for *Book* notes that the 1991 edition of *Contemporary Authors* listed "Catholic" under "religion" in the author's profile (*CW* 99). Subsequent editions listed no religious preference. Wallace also told Arden, as well as David Streitfeld for a 1996 *Details* magazine piece, that he twice attempted RCIA (Rights of Christian Initiation for Adults), the process the Catholic Church uses to educate initiates about their faith (*CW* 69).

Several years later, Wallace would cohabitate with a Catholic in his Bloomington home. He became engaged to Julianna Harms in 1998, and the couple explored his conversion to Catholicism. Max's description of this moment raises a curious conundrum. He writes, "Wallace ... never lost his hope that he could find faith."[21] What Max is likely alluding to is Wallace's desire to find a church, a formal community and set of beliefs, but taken too literally one could interpret this line to mean that he did not possess faith, that he had not been able to bring himself to believe in anything, but always wanted to. Some would argue that the very desire to find and understand something larger than oneself constitutes faith. Faith cannot be certain, but rather requires trust. The crux of Wallace's problem, however, was that he could not trust in "faith." He always wanted something more concrete, something he could fully wrap his head around.

Looking to one of Wallace's favorite reference sources, the *Oxford English Dictionary* does not help to clarify the nature of his faith.[22] Dismissing more secular definitions alluding to trust, assurance, and credibility, the most straightforwardly religious definition of "faith" is the fifth entry:

> 5. Belief in and acceptance of the doctrines of a religion, typically involving belief in a god or gods and in the authenticity of divine revelation. Also (Theology): the capacity to spiritually apprehend divine truths, or realities beyond the limits of perception or of logical proof, viewed either as a faculty of the human soul, or as the result of divine illumination.[23]

In this sense, Max strikes a chord. Wallace clearly longed for a Church to belong to, but had trouble with "acceptance of the doctrines of a religion." On the other hand, looking a bit further into the definition, Wallace's writings display a rather strong "capacity to spiritually apprehend divine truths," and thus he might be said to possess a tremendous amount of faith.

At any rate, Harms's influence sought to address the head/heart discrepancy. She encouraged him to sign up for a Catholic program called "Cursillo," which, by their definition, "attempts from within the Church, to give life to the essential Christian truths in the singularity, originality and creativity of the person"[24] or "to bring God from the head to the heart."[25] Such a program would aspire to repair Wallace's foremost religious handicap, his tendency to overintellectualize faith. Once again, Wallace balked at giving himself over to something intangible, and doubt led him to back away.

A Catholic influence outside of his romantic partners can be found, naturally enough, in the books he read. One notable example is *Everything Belongs: The Gift of Contemplative Prayer*, by the Franciscan priest Richard Rohr.[26] The idea of "being awake" to truth or to God appears to have been a topic of growing interest for Wallace in his later life. *Infinite Jest* obviously plays with this theme via AA, as Gately and the other recovering addicts are required to live in the moment, to pay attention and give thanks. But later works, such as *This Is Water* and particularly Chapter 22, the Chris Fogle section, of *The Pale King*, rather overtly addresses the question of what it means to "be awake" to God or some other spiritual concept. Wallace's copy of *Everything Belongs* is heavily annotated; he clearly read it with some care and attention. Many of the passages he underlined or marked pertain to the concept of awareness of God's presence, and often, as reflected in the thesis of his Kenyon speech, awareness despite the distractions of modern western culture. One passage Wallace highlights notes that western civilization is too "goal oriented," expecting every action to "get us something," but God's presence is not something we attain; rather it is something we are "already totally in."[27] Similarly, Wallace underlined a passage explaining, "Spirituality is about seeing. It's not about earning or achieving."[28] Beyond a warning against materialism and type-A ambition, Rohr's book, like much of Wallace's writing, promotes an awareness and acceptance of being human, particularly the more unpleasant, trying aspects of existence. The premise of Rohr's book is that only through awareness, or contemplation, can we become full, and we can only become fully aware through God.

A final significant influence on Wallace was Buddhism. Max notes that Wallace was drawn to it early, while living in Syracuse in the early 1990s. After moving to Bloomington, he retained this interest, giving his girlfriend Kymberly Harris books on the subject.[29] He began practicing yoga and meditation, and even traveled to France to attend a meditation retreat with the famed Zen master Thich Nhat Hanh.[30] But of course, in classic Wallace fashion, he struggled with this form of spirituality as well. He grew bored with the retreat and left early, ironically as he was working on a novel chronicling boredom at the time. In the later years of his life he struck up a correspondence with a young man named Christopher Hamacher, who became his go-to resource for questions about Buddhism. Mostly, Wallace worried that he was doing things incorrectly, sitting improperly or not reading the proper books. Once again, Wallace fell into the mental trap that demanded he intellectually understand and perfect his spiritual practice.

In some respects, Buddhism should have been a good fit for Wallace. Its focus on practice and the process of initiating change in the self likens it to AA. Buddhism did not ask him to believe in something intangible and unprovable, as Catholicism did. But then again, one aspect of spirituality that Wallace appeared most attracted to was the ability to give oneself wholly over to something else, something bigger than oneself. In his Kenyon commencement address, he urged graduates to adopt "some sort of god or spiritual type thing" (in short, something external and big) to worship, because all alternatives were solipsistic and would "eat you alive" (*TIW* 102). Perhaps the best analogue to this aspect of Wallace's faith is Don Gately, who freely admits the limits of his understanding of God, religion, and prayer, but practices and has faith simply because he knows it works. At an AA meeting Gately "revealed publicly about how he was ashamed that he still as yet had no real solid understanding of a Higher Power" (*IJ* 442). After ten months of "ear-smoking concentration" he had not been able to construct a god concept he felt he understood, but nevertheless prays "whether he believes he's talking to Anything/-body or not, and somehow gets through that day clean" (*IJ* 443). Similarly, Mario Incandenza admires the Ennet House residents for their genuineness, because "he once heard someone say *God* with a straight face" there (*IJ* 591). Wallace clearly admired the faithful, those who could overcome doubt and allow religion to improve their lives, though he was never able to bring himself to their level of commitment.

So, although the question of Wallace's spirituality may be complex and difficult to define, what remains clear in his writing is the respect he develops for people of faith. Warren Cole Smith of *Christianity Today* attributes that attitude to AA, writing, "If these experiences did not lead Wallace to religion, or Christianity in particular, they did lead him to admire and respect Christians, many of them 'ordinary Joes' he met in church basements."[31] In contrast, Max suggested in a question and answer forum published on the *New Yorker*'s website that Wallace's religion may have been a maneuver to construe himself as "A middle-class Midwesterner."[32] Although we may not be able to assert with great certainty the role that religion played in Wallace's life, we may perhaps safely draw three conclusions: 1) he opposed people who were utterly dismissive of religion, 2) he displayed a concrete interest in moral and ethical issues that aligned him with religious traditions, and 3) his attention to the second point has caused a great number of Christians and readers of other faiths to see his fiction as a touchstone of faith.

Wallace's writing is littered with examples of smug atheists. The Kenyon speech includes a joke about an Alaskan nonbeliever who resorts to prayer when caught in an abrupt blizzard. When a couple of Eskimos appear and lead him back to camp, he denies the possibility that their presence could be connected to God and his prayer. Wallace calls out the atheist's "arrogance, blind certainty, [and] a close-mindedness that's like an imprisonment so complete that the prisoner doesn't even know he's locked up" (*TIW* 32). Or take Chris Fogle's dismissal of his roommate's girlfriend's evangelical conversion story in *The Pale King*, only to ultimately conclude, "I actually liked despising the Christian because I could pretend that the evangelical's smugness and self-righteousness were the only real antithesis or alternative to [my] cynical, nihilistically wastoid attitude," and in hindsight, "I was much more like the Christian than either of us believed" (*PK* 211). Similarly, portions of *The Pale King* manuscript published in *New Yorker*, "Good People" and "All That," paint evangelicals in a rather sympathetic light.[33]

While not synonymous with spirituality, Wallace has consistently expressed concern for axiological matters, leading some to view him as an old-school moralist.[34] His attention to moral and ethical issues ranges from the very secular to the overtly religious. He praises dedication to civic responsibility and traditional work ethic across the span of his career, from "Westward the Course of Empire Takes Its Way," to the father's endurance of a boring insurance job in "The Soul Is Not a Smithy," and the accountants in *The Pale King*. Wallace is probably best known for calling out the evils of false idols, be that television, controlled substances, or our own egos. In *Infinite Jest* in particular, the path to overcoming these idols is marked by the very Christian concept of grace, unmerited assistance from God. And one might say that the handling of "Good People" reveals a pro-life-leaning outlook. Smith notes that many Christian readers have likely been drawn to Wallace because he shares their values and "embraced co-belligerency on issues such as the corrosive effects of television, advertising, and addiction of all types on American culture." Smith goes on to suggest that Wallace is to postmodernism what T.S. Eliot was to modernism, someone who "drank from the fountains of the zeitgeist only to spew it out as a warning to others."[35]

But to return to the question this chapter poses, was Wallace looking for faith in all the wrong places? He does demonstrate a lifelong search for something bigger than himself that he could feel a part of, but nothing fully sticks. AA is the most concrete example of a "church" that honestly worked for him, since he was able to participate in the community for twenty years of his short life. Still, he searched for something more, a true sense of God that he could get behind, but repeatedly his intellect got in the way. "Faith" in the sense of believing in something that could not be proven consistently hampered his ability to find peace. But we as readers are left with the evidence of his search. In an interview, Wallace describes how these themes interacted with his signature writing style; he uses "postmodern techniques ... to discuss or represent very old traditional human verities that have to do with spirituality and emotion and community and ideas that the avant-garde would consider very old-fashioned."[36] Thus Wallace straddles two worlds—a definitive "voice of a generation" author, but also an old-fashioned moralist in the vein of Dostoevsky.

Notes

1. David Lipsky, *Although Of Course You End Up Becoming Yourself: A Road Trip with David Foster Wallace* (New York: Broadway Books, 2010), 198.
2. Ibid.
3. David Foster Wallace, "Roger Federer as Religious Experience." *New York Times*, August 20, 2006. Subsequently anthologized "Federer: Both Flesh and Not" (*BFN* 5–33).
4. Jurgen Moltmann, "'Deliver Us from Evil' or Doing Away with Humankind," in *World without End: Christian Eschatology from a Process Perspective*, ed. Joseph A. Bracken, S.J. (Grand Rapids [MI]: William B. Eerdmans Pub., 2005), 14.
5. D.T. Max, *Every Love Story Is a Ghost Story: A Life of David Foster Wallace* (New York: Penguin Books, 2012), 114.
6. Ibid.
7. Ibid.
8. David Foster Wallace, "All That," *New Yorker*, December 14, 2009.
9. Max, *Every Love Story*, 2.
10. James, Ryerson, "Introduction: A Head That Throbbed Heartlike: The Philosophical Mind of David Foster Wallace," in *Fate, Time, and Language: An Essay on Free Will*, ed. Stephen M. Cahn and Maureen Eckert (New York,

Columbia University Press, 2010), 32. To be fair, Wittgenstein does contribute to theological thinking, most notably "postliberal theology," which grew out of Yale through George Lindbeck, Hans Frei, and David Kelsey. In a postliberal theology attitude, religions are less about belief systems that they are about "forms of life." Wallace's undergraduate philosophy thesis does not address this subject, but it does resonate with Wallace's own search for transcendence.

11 Wallace was still making this argument in 1993 when he sat down for an interview with Larry McCaffrey. He explains, "Wittgenstein ... realized that no conclusion could be more horrible than solipsism. And so he trashed everything he'd been lauded for in the *Tractatus* and wrote the *Investigations*, which is the single most comprehensive and beautiful argument against solipsism that's ever been made" (CW 44).

12 Maria Bustillos explored and catalogued the plethora of annotations marked within self-help books soon after Wallace's personal library was made available at the Harry Ransom Center. See "Inside David Foster Wallace's Self-Help Library," *The Awl*. April 5, 2011. https://www.theawl.com/2011/04/inside-david-foster-wallaces-private-self-help-library/.

13 Lipsky, *Although You End Up*, 62.

14 For a detailed examination of the spirituality of AA as it affected Wallace, see "Came to Believe: The Religion of Alcoholics Anonymous in Infinite Jest" by Rob Short, Chapter 1 of this collection.

15 Mary Karr, *Lit: A Memoir* (New York: HarperCollins, 2009), 195. Day's conversation with Gately is presented in fn. 90: "By AA's own professed logic, everyone ought to be in AA. If you have some sort of substance-problem, then you belong in AA. But if you say you do not have a substance-problem ... why then you're by definition in *denial*, and thus you need the denial-busting Fellowship of AA" (IJ 1002).

16 Max, *Every Love Story*, 263.

17 Charles Harris, personal discussion with the author, June 9, 2017.

18 David Foster Wallace Personal journal pages, 1996, undated, handwritten, Box 31.14. David Foster Wallace Papers. Harry Ransom Humanities Research Center, Austin, TX.

19 Email conversation with Paul Niesen, an Arizona State University classmate. May 11, 2018.

20 Max, *Every Love Story*, 233.

21 Ibid., 251.

22 Matthew Mullins also notes the potentially troublesome nature of language surrounding this topic. He attempts to use terms as Wallace would, grouping "spirituality, belief, and faith" together as "denote[ing] a kind of vague transcendence beyond the physical or commitment to such a transcendence" while "religion" signifies "specific, usually a particular, historical, organized tradition." See "Wallace, Spirituality, and Religion," in *Cambridge Companion to David Foster Wallace*, ed. Ralph Clare (Cambridge: Cambridge University Press, 2018), 190–203; 191.

23 "faith, n. and int." OED Online. December 2018. Oxford University Press. http://www.oed.com.worthingtonlibraries.idm.oclc.org/view/Entry/67760?rskey=nrMBMr&result=1.

24 "Welcome to the National Cursillo Movement." *National Cursillo Movement USA*, 2016, https://www.natl-cursillo.org/.

25 Max, *Every Love Story*, 251.

26 A copy of this book was given to Wallace by Robert Bolger, author of Chapter 2: "A Less 'Bullshitty' Way to Live: The Pragmatic Spirituality of David Foster Wallace."

27 Richard Rohr, *Everything Belongs: The Gift of Contemplative Prayer*. Revised ed. (New York: Crossroad Pub, 2003), 28–9.

28 Ibid., 33.

29 Max, *Every Love Story*, 79, 181.

30 Ibid., 231.

31 Warren Cole Smith, "David Foster Wallace Broke My Heart," *Christianity Today*, September 12, 2018. Available online: https://www.christianitytoday.com/ct/2018/september-web-only/david-foster-wallace-broke-heart-suicide.html.

32 D.T. Max, "Questions for D. T. Max." *Ask the Author: New Yorker*. March 1, 2009. This assumption by Max is a claim that I argue against in an article published elsewhere. See, Martin Brick, "A Postmodernist's Progress: Thoughts on Spirituality across the David Foster Wallace Canon," *Christianity and Literature* 64, no. 1 (September 2014): 65–81.

33 Christopher Douglas aptly notes the "transgressive" nature of such publications, given that most *New Yorker* readers would likely distance themselves from the ideology and politics of the evangelicals. See "David Foster Wallace's Evangelicals: The Other Postsecularism," *Christianity and Literature* 67, no. 3 (June 2018): 548–58.

34 For an excellent examination of this subject see Jeffrey Severs, *David Foster Wallace's Balancing Books: Fictions of Value* (New York: Columbia University Press, 2017).

35 Smith, "David Foster Wallace Broke My Heart."

36 David Foster Wallace, "Le Conversazioni 2006 David Foster Wallace sub ita," YouTube Video, 1:17, August 24, 2015, https://www.youtube.com/watch?v=JXdXZeIQwyw.

1

Came to Believe: The Religion of Alcoholics Anonymous in *Infinite Jest*

Rob Short

In his introduction to the twentieth-anniversary edition of *Infinite Jest*, Tom Bissell writes: "While I have never been able to get a handle on Wallace's notion of spirituality, I think it is a mistake to view him as anything other than a religious writer. His religion, like many, was a religion of language."[1] While I agree with Bissell that to understand Wallace (at least from *Infinite Jest* on) as anything other than a religious writer is a mistake, I am surprised by Bissell's confession that he has difficulty understanding Wallace's spiritual motivations, especially given the context. Wallace mentions spirituality and religion in numerous places—from interviews with Brian Garner and Larry McCaffery, to the commencement speech at Kenyon College, to nonfiction essays like "The Nature of the Fun."[2] However, nowhere in Wallace's output is spirituality discussed more frequently or at greater length than in *Infinite Jest*. What's more, Wallace is reasonably consistent about what he says. This spiritual consistency, I would argue, stems from Wallace's first serious engagement with religion: his participation in Alcoholics Anonymous (AA).

The presence of AA in *Infinite Jest* has not gone critically unnoticed. However, given the many long stretches of the novel that are set in Boston AA meetings, the amount of secondary literature that reads Wallace through AA is scant, especially since D.T. Max's biography[3] has made obvious the overlaps between the twelve-step programs in Wallace's personal history and his fiction. Although a handful of critics have published shorter pieces[4] considering addiction or recovery in Wallace's writing, there exists no monograph-length study of the enormous importance of twelve-step recovery programs across the larger body of his work, nor any sustained study of the way that Wallace's religious attendance of AA meetings or his rigid adherence to AA's doctrine informs his fiction. Wallace considered himself an addict; failure to read him as one is to forego one of the most productive critical lenses at our disposal.

Among the aforementioned handful of Wallace critics, Timothy Aubry, the author of "Selfless Cravings: Addiction and Recovery in Wallace's *Infinite Jest*," comes closest to my approach. In "Selfless Cravings," Aubry argues that AA's function in *Infinite Jest* is to provide a narrative counterweight to the dispassionate aesthetic that prevailed in American literature at the time, serving as a kind of Trojan horse by which Wallace could smuggle his more sentimental tendencies into the novel. I contend rather that Wallace's adoption and internalization of twelve-step doctrine is what made *Infinite Jest* possible at all.

Wallace began having bouts of anxiety and paranoia—symptoms he would later recognize as the onset of his mental illness—at the age of ten.[5] During his freshman year of high school, he started self-medicating these symptoms with alcohol and marijuana. Over the next fifteen years, what began as coping mechanisms grew into dependency, and at twenty-eight, Wallace's excessive substance abuse and a concomitant mental health crisis landed him in a series of hospitals, state-run mental health facilities, and halfway houses. As a recovering addict, he joined twelve-step recovery programs for both narcotics and alcohol, maintaining his sobriety with regular attendance at Narcotics Anonymous and AA meetings until his death in 2008.

Wallace's initial participation in AA was not an entirely volitional affair; regular attendance at meetings was a requirement for all residents of the halfway houses where he lived for nearly two years. The idea that a group of addicts huddled in smoke-filled church basements sharing personal stories of addiction with one another could somehow solve his substance-abuse problem was an affront to his intelligence. Wallace found the program's clichéd vernacular and its insistence on members' belief in a higher power too hokey to be taken seriously, a sentiment we see portrayed frequently in *Infinite Jest*.

In the Big Book,[6] the only indispensable text for all AA members and the one that officially outlines AA's doctrine, alcoholism is presented as a self-inflicted problem, and that "self" is understood as a tripartite construction comprising the "mind," "body," and—crucially—the "spirit" of the alcoholic. This spiritual side of the self is basically the human capacity for numinous or religious experiences—something like the feeling of being moved emotionally by the sublime. The Big Book proposes this spiritual component of the self as an explanation for the preponderance of religion in so many disparate cultures, for the "persistence of the myth"—whether it be true or not. But most importantly, the Big Book's authors see this innate spiritual capacity as something that is exceptionally and singularly human. In Chapter 4, "We Agnostics," they elaborate on how this third component, the alcoholic's spiritual or metaphysical aspect, must be reformed.

"We Agnostics" relates the difficulty some of the earliest members of AA had with following the second step. This amounts to a fairly big problem for someone in AA because the rest of the twelve steps hang on the acceptance of the first two: "1. We admitted we were powerless over alcohol—that our lives had become unmanageable" and "2. Came to believe that a Power greater than ourselves could restore us to sanity."[7] Writing as former agnostics who had been able to overcome their skepticism, the authors are "at pains to tell why we think our present faith is reasonable, why we think it more sane and logical to believe than not to believe, why we say our former thinking was soft and mushy when we threw up our hands in doubt and said 'We don't know.'"[8] When the agnostics looked closely at what held them back from being "restored to sanity" through belief in a "Power greater than [them]selves,"[9] they found it was another belief—a belief in their own ability to reason, or a faith in their reasonable faculties:

> Let us think a little more closely. Without knowing it, had we not been brought to where we stood by a certain kind of faith? For did we not believe in our own reasoning? Did we not have confidence in our ability to think? What was that but a sort of faith? Yes, we had been faithful, abjectly faithful to the God of Reason. So, in one way or another, we discovered that faith had been involved all the time!
>
> We found, too, that we had been *worshippers*.... Had we not variously *worshipped people, sentiment, things, money, and ourselves?* ... Who of us had not loved something or somebody? How much did these feelings, these loves, these *worships*, have to do with pure reason? Little or nothing, we saw at last. Were not these things the tissue out of which our lives were constructed? Did not these feelings, after all, determine the course of our existence? It was impossible to say we had no capacity for faith, or love, or *worship*. In one form or another we had been living by faith and little else.[10]

The authors go on to explain that the matter of their conversion was no small thing; if they had not been primed to accept the necessity of handing over their wills to a higher power, they probably would not have been able to do it—save that they had recently experienced a particular event in the narrative common to all addicts: hitting bottom. And at the point in David Foster Wallace's life when the Big Book crossed his path, he was already on a steep downward trajectory.[11]

Even so, Wallace could not simply accept what AA said about spirituality on faith; he had to do his own research. At least one of the texts Wallace consulted was Huston Smith's *The World's Religions: Our Great Wisdom Traditions*.[12] I mention this here because I think it goes a long way toward helping us "get a handle on Wallace's notion of spirituality." In his copy of Smith's text, Wallace annotated the following passage:

> Might not becoming a part of a larger, more significant whole relieve life of its triviality? That question announces the birth of religion. <u>For though in some watered-down sense there may be a religion of self-worship, true religion begins with the quest for meaning and value beyond self-centeredness. It renounces the ego's claims to finality.</u>
>
> But what is this renunciation for? The question brings us to the two signposts on the Path of Renunciation. <u>The first of these reads "the community," as the obvious candidate for something greater than ourselves.</u> In supporting at once our own life and the lives others, the community has an importance no single life can command. Let us, then, transfer our allegiance to it, giving its claims priority over our own.
>
> This transfer marks the first great step in religion. It produces the religion of duty, after pleasure and success the third great aim of life in the Hindu outlook. Its power over the mature is tremendous. Myriads have transformed the will-to-get into the will-to-give, the will-to-win into the will-to-serve. Not to triumph but to do their best—to acquit themselves responsibly, whatever the task at hand—has become their prime objective.[13]

And in the margin next to his underlining is Wallace's note: "AA."

I do not mean here to equate the underscoring of a passage with its unequivocal or uncritical endorsement, but neither do I think it a stretch to say that Wallace had read the Big Book closely enough to see in this passage from Smith the core principles of "spirituality" as they are presented in AA: the relinquishment of the will to a power greater than oneself and the consequent undertaking of work in service of others. As the Big Book (cribbing the *KJV*) cautions: "faith without works is dead."[14]

This notion of "service" and its relation to self-centeredness is one that crops up again and again in AA's Big Book: "Never was I to pray for myself, except as my requests bore on my *usefulness* to others. Then only might I expect to receive.... Simple, but not easy; a price had to be paid. It meant the destruction of *self-centeredness*."[15] In fact, the concept of service work— "passing it on," as it is codified in one AA maxim—is directly and repeatedly correlated with the chances of a successful recovery:

For if an alcoholic failed to perfect and enlarge his spiritual life through *work and self-sacrifice for others*, he could not survive the certain trials and low spots ahead. If he did not *work*, he would surely drink again, and if he drank he would surely die. Then faith would be dead indeed. With us it is just like that.... Faith has to *work* twenty-four hours a day in and through us, or we perish (14–16); Our very lives, as ex-problem drinkers, depend upon *our constant thought of others* and how we may help *meet their needs* ... ; Whatever our protestations, are not most of us concerned with ourselves, our resentments, or our self-pity? *Selfishness—self-centeredness*! That, we think, is the door of our troubles.... So our troubles, we think, are basically of our own making. They arise out of ourselves, and the alcoholic is an extreme example of *self-will run riot,* though he usually doesn't think so. Above everything, we alcoholics must be rid of this *selfishness*. We must, or it kills us![16]

Ultimately, the mere abstention from drinking is not finally the point; it is rather a means to another rehabilitation—the restoration of the capacity for service: "At the moment we are trying to put our lives in order. But this is not an end in itself. *Our real purpose is to fit ourselves to be of maximum service* to God and the people about us."[17]

I am inclined to read all of Wallace's writing from *Infinite Jest* on as a function of "working the steps." Because although Wallace's status as an addict was a large part of what defined his identity, so too was his status as a writer. As an addict, Wallace knew AA had saved his life; as a writer, he saw an opportunity to be of service by passing on what he had learned through his fiction. Wallace's sobriety enabled him to write his own big book, the impetus for which, Wallace explained to David Lipsky, was a need to address what he saw as a uniquely American condition:

[The] most distinctively American [things] right now [...] had to do with both entertainment and about some kind of weird addictive, um ... wanting to give yourself away to something [that] was kind of a distorted religious impulse. And a lot of the AA stuff in the book was mostly an excuse [...] to talk about people's relationship with any kind of God.[18]

Wallace understood American culture as fundamentally addicted, whether to substances like alcohol or to its own entertainment. And while an "entertainment addiction" sounds comparatively harmless, the point for Wallace was that being truly addicted to anything necessarily means choosing the object of one's addiction at the cost of everything else. For Wallace, the real danger of addiction was the way that it turned the addict inward, making it easier to justify selfish and self-destructive choices and to ignore those choices' consequences. And what Wallace prescribed was a paradigm of other-directedness, which, it turns out, is the ultimate goal of

AA's recovery program: to overcome a toxic and crippling self-centeredness in order to live in service of something larger than the self. Even AA's foundational insistence on anonymity reinforces this goal; the erasure of members' surnames minimizes the individual for the sake of the larger whole. And as the passage from Smith's text argues, this enlargement of identity—understanding oneself primarily as a member of a community rather than an autonomous individual—is a radical shift in self-understanding common to all religious worldviews.

Religion in *Infinite Jest* is a matter of orthopraxy ("right actions") rather than orthodoxy ("right beliefs"), though to pick a side here is to ignore the ways that belief and practice in the novel function as a dialectic, one side enriching and informing the other. It is perhaps more accurate to say that religion in *Infinite Jest* takes orthopraxy as its necessary starting point, the practice of which leads organically to belief.

The Boston AA section's narrator explains how AA's sloganeering orthopraxy leads to a kind of orthodoxy of salvation:

> This doesn't mean you can't pay empty or hypocritical lip-service, however. Paradoxically enough. The desperate, newly sober White Flaggers are always encouraged to invoke and pay empty lip-service to slogans they don't yet understand or believe—e.g. 'Easy Does It!' and 'Turn It Over!' and 'One Day At a Time!' It's called 'Fake It Till You Make It,' itself an oft-invoked slogan. Everybody on a Commitment who gets up publicly to speak starts out saying he's an alcoholic, says it whether he believes he is yet or not; then everybody up there says how Grateful he is to be sober today and how great it is to be Active and out on a Commitment with his Group, even if he's not grateful or pleased about it at all. You're encouraged to keep saying stuff like this until you start to believe it, just like if you ask somebody with serious sober time how long you'll have to keep schlepping to all the goddamn meetings he'll smile that infuriating smile and tell you just until you start to *want* to go to all these goddamn meetings. (IJ 369)

What is unsaid in this passage is the underlying belief that allows the AA member with "serious sober time" to say with conviction that, eventually, the new AA member's forced attendance of meetings will in time become a genuine desire to attend. This underlying confidence is predicated on a belief in human commonality—a set of characteristics shared by all human beings—or at least those who are addicted to alcohol. It is a belief in the power of ritual and of community, and it is a belief borne out by the longtime-member's own experience and reinforced by the experiences of other sober members. The "right actions" of AA's praxis are not ones that proceed from "right belief." In AA, one's right actions—whether the member sincerely buys into in the program's putative reasons for going through the motions or not—lead to a belief in the salvific "higher power" of the program, a salvation made possible by the handing over of the individual's will to something larger than oneself, which, in many cases, is the community of AA fellowship itself.

In the America of *Infinite Jest*, so many of its characters—finding no other viable coping models available and nothing worth giving themselves away to—respond to the problem of solipsistic isolation with drug use and, eventually, addiction. But Wallace, not content to simply fictionalize the darker parts of his culture, offers the reader a possible alternative to addiction through the AA sections of the narrative—and especially through one of the two principal characters, Don Gately. Although Wallace's early drafts contained a comparatively small amount of material about him, as Wallace's sober time increased, so did the number of pages in the novel concerned with Gately, the recovering Demerol addict and reformed felon turned halfway-house counselor.[19]

Toward the end of *Infinite Jest*, Gately's character steps in to defend another member of a halfway house, Randy Lenz, who is being chased by a neighborhood resident after catching Lenz killing his (the neighborhood resident's) dog. Although Lenz is probably guilty of whatever he is being accused of, Gately nevertheless defends his halfway-house ward in a street fight that turns into a shooting in front of Ennet House.[20] We rejoin Gately later in the narrative as he regains consciousness in a hospital. Although he is suffering from severe trauma and struggling to speak because of a breathing tube, he refuses the pain medication offered by doctors for fear of jeopardizing his sobriety (Gately's drug of choice before recovery was oral narcotics). Wallace explains the recovering addict's difficult feat of restraint by letting us in on Gately's coping technique: "Abiding. No one single instant of it was unendurable. Here was a second right here: he endured it. What was undealable-with was the thought of all the instants all lined up and stretching ahead, glittering" (*IJ* 860). This technique is one that Gately learned during a forced detox in jail:

> Gately remembered some evil fucking personal detoxes.... Feeling the edge of every second that went by. Taking it a second at a time.... Any one second: he remembered: the thought of feeling like he'd be feeling this second for 60 more of these seconds—he couldn't deal. He could not fucking deal. He had to build a wall around each second just to take it. (*IJ* 859–60)

Said another way: the period of his withdrawal, like the pain he is experiencing in the hospital, when conceptualized as a continuous, uninterrupted expanse of time, amounts to experiencing the entire aggregate effect of each moment simultaneously.

The fourth edition of AA's Big Book stresses the importance of taking sobriety "one day at a time" in ten separate places.[21] But the passage that best explains the material reality of the adage appears in a section titled "The Missing Link":

> A couple of members, realizing I was there for my first meeting, took me downstairs and sat down with me and outlined the program.... I remember telling these members that AA sounded like just what I needed, but I didn't think I could stay sober for the rest of my life. Exactly how was I supposed to not drink if my girlfriend breaks up with me, or if my best friend dies, or even through happy times like graduations, weddings, and birthdays. They suggested I could just stay sober one day at a time. They explained that it might be easier to set my sights on the twenty-four hours in front of me and to take on these other situations when and if they ever arrived. I decided to give sobriety a try, one day at a time, and I've done it that way ever since.[22]

Like the anonymous author of "The Missing Link," Gately's solution is to *choose* to understand or idealize time as a series of static moments, separate from one another like the individual frames of a film reel. Paradoxically, during this exercise, Gately realizes that he had "never before or since felt so excruciatingly alive. Living in the Present between pulses. It's a gift, the Now: it's AA's real gift: it's no accident they call it *The Present*" (*IJ* 860, italics original). The phrasing of Gately's technique may sound familiar. Its source is taken from another work whose title is mentioned earlier in the narrative. The original formulation is from William James's *Gifford Lectures*, later published under the title *The Varieties of Religious Experience*.[23]

The conceptualization of time that Gately learned in AA derives from James's description of a religious adherent who has achieved a certain kind of inner peace, one who is "never anxious about the future, nor worr[ied] over the outcome of the day; [she] took cognizance of things, only as they were presented to her in succession, *moment by moment*." For her, "the divine moment was the present moment ... and when the present moment was estimated in itself and in its relations, and when the duty that was involved in it was accomplished, it was permitted to pass away as if it had never been, and to give way to the facts and duties of the moment which came after".[24]

Gately is not the only character in the novel to profess the usefulness of this divide-and-abide method of enduring otherwise-unendurable stretches of time. Joelle van Dyne tells Gately that without a mindset capable of living in the present, she is not surprised that her previous attempts at staying sober had failed:

> This was why I couldn't get off and stay off. Just as the cliché warns. I literally wasn't keeping it in the day. I was adding the clean days up in my

head.... I'd throw away the pipe and shake my fist at the sky and say As God is my fucking witness NEVER AGAIN, as of this minute right here I QUIT FOR ALL TIME.... And I'd bunker up all white-knuckled and stay straight. And count the days. I was proud of each day I stayed off.... I'd add them up. Line them up end to end. You know? ... And soon it would get ... improbable. And the rest of the year, looking ahead, hundreds and hundreds ... Who could do it? How did I ever think anyone could do it that way? (*IJ* 859)

Ultimately, it was Wallace's entry into recovery that allowed his writing to progress into an ethical dimension marked by a focus on forging connections with readers. Wallace's mature, recovery-inspired fiction, in D.T. Max's phrasing, "h[olds] out a hope rarely signaled in Wallace's earlier work but dear to his recovery experiences: the possibility that telling a story can heal."[25] Recovery had changed not only the way Wallace wrote, it had fundamentally altered the reason he continued to write anything at all.

The process of writing *Infinite Jest*, then, can be seen as Wallace working the later steps of AA, endeavoring to transfer the gift he received in AA to his reader. In a way, *Infinite Jest* is structured like a postmodern version of AA's Big Book: while the Big Book comprises neatly a direct reader-address section wherein the program is explained in detail and then followed up by narrative accounts of AA members' recoveries, *Infinite Jest* contains these same two basic elements: didactic sections (the Marathe and Steeply conversations, the Boston AA passages, and the section titled "Tennis and the Feral Prodigy"—the last of which is almost catechistic in its structure) and the narrative accounts of addicts—both those in recovery and those "out there." The sum of which is a novel that functions as an update to the Big Book, or perhaps a Trojan horse for it. The novel is the product of Wallace's "service to others"—it is his gift. It paints a grim picture of our culture and yet does not stop there—it points toward a way out. It wakes the reader up to the fact that he or she is even addicted in the first place, pushes the reader to locate the precise nature and object of his or her addiction, and then offers a path forward, one already begun in the self-examination of what it is he or she has been unconsciously addicted to.

Infinite Jest offers its readers an antidote to the numbness and complacency induced by our immersion in a culture of unceasing distraction—a condition Wallace referred to as "total noise."[26] He was acutely aware of fiction's unique ability to allow us access to another's consciousness in ways that deepen our capacity for identification and empathy, that focus our attention on similarity rather than difference. In a 1993 interview for *Whiskey River Magazine*, Hugh Kennedy asks Wallace flatly, "What would you like your writing to do?" And in a rare instance of brevity, Wallace replies,

> I think all good writing somehow addresses the concern of and acts as an anodyne against loneliness. We're all terribly, terribly lonely. And there's a way, at least in prose fiction, that can allow you to be intimate with the world and with a mind and with characters that you just can't be in the real world.... I think what I would like my stuff to do is make people less lonely. (CW 16)

But insofar as Wallace's fiction affords us a vantage point outside our own, it provides escape in order to demand engagement.

Notes

1. Tom Bissell. "Foreword: Everything about Everything: Infinite Jest, Twenty Years Later," in *Infinite Jest: 20th Anniversary Edition* (Boston: Back Bay, 2016), xiii.

2. Bryan Garner, *Quack This Way: David Foster Wallace & Bryan A. Garner Talk Language and Writing* (Dallas: Rosepen, 2013). For McCaffrey's interview see *CW* 21–52. The Kenyon address has been published as *This Is Water*. For "The Nature of Fun" see *BFN* 193–202.

3. D.T. Max, *Every Love Story Is a Ghost Story: A Life of David Foster Wallace* (New York: Viking Penguin, 2012).

4. These include Timothy Aubry's, "Selfless Cravings: Addiction and Recovery in Wallace's *Infinite Jest*," in *American Fiction of the 1990s: Reflections of History and Culture*, ed. Jay Prosser (New York: Routledge, 2008), 206–19; Robert Bolger's "A Less "Bullshitty' Way to Live: The Pragmatic Spirituality of David Foster Wallace," in *Gesturing Toward Reality: David Foster Wallace and Philosophy*, ed. Robert Bolger and Scott Korb (London: Bloomsbury, 2014), 31–51; Elizabeth Freudenthal's, "Anti-Interiority: Compulsiveness, Objectification, and Identity in *Infinite Jest*," *New Literary History* 41, no. 1 (Winter 2010): 191–211; Casey Michael Henry's, "'Sudden Awakening to the Fact That the Mischief Is Irretrievably Done'": Epiphanic Structure in David Foster Wallace's *Infinite Jest*," *Critique* 56, no. 5 (2015): 480–502; Emily Spalding's "The Addiction Spectrum: An Analysis of the Three Branches of Addiction in David Foster Wallace's *Infinite Jest*," in *Normal 2015: Selected Works from the Second Annual David Foster Wallace Conference*, ed. Carissa Kampmeier et al. (Gilson [IL]: Lit Fest, 2016), 119–23; and Petrus van Ewijk's "'I' and the 'Other': The Relevance of Wittgenstein, Buber and Levinas for an Understanding of AA's Recovery Program in David Foster Wallace's *Infinite Jest*," *English Text Construction* 2, no. 1 (2009): 132–45.

5. Max, *Every Love Story*, 8.

6. A colloquial title for the basic text of AA, written by AA founder William G. Wilson (Bill W.). *Alcoholics Anonymous: The Story of How Many Thousands of Men and Women Have Recovered from Alcoholism*, 4th ed. (New York: Alcoholics Anonymous World Services, 2001).

7   Ibid., 79.
8   Ibid., 53.
9   Ibid., 59.
10 Ibid., 53–4, emphasis added.
11 According to D.T. Max, Wallace first started attending "weekly sobriety meetings" in February of 1988 (106). And although Wallace's own personal "bottoming out" would not happen until October of 1989, the intervening time was marked by an increasingly heavy regimen of drugs and alcohol and a suicide attempt. It was not until after his admission to the facilities at McLean and Appleton House in October–November of 1989 that a supervised and fully detoxed Wallace began taking seriously the AA clichés that had initially chafed him.
12 By the time Wallace read it, the work had been re-issued and re-titled; Wallace's annotated copy, with its original title, *The Religions of Man*, is available for viewing at the Harry Ransom Center in Austin.
13 Huston Smith, *The World's Religions: Our Great Wisdom Traditions* (New York: HarperCollins, 1991). Underlining by Wallace.
14 James 2:14–26.
15 Bill W., *Alcoholics Anonymous*, 13–14, emphasis added.
16 Ibid., 20, 62, emphasis added.
17 Ibid., 77, emphasis added.
18 David Lipsky, *Although of Course You End Up Becoming Yourself: A Road Trip with David Foster Wallace* (New York: Broadway, 2010), 82.
19 Max, *Every Love Story*, 190.
20 See Dave Laird's "Saying God with a Straight Face: Towards an Understanding of Christian Soteriology in *Infinite Jest*," Chapter 5 in the present volume, for further treatment of this scene.
21 Bill W., *Alcoholics Anonymous*, 255, 286, 287, 288, 333, 345, 346, 401, 451, 528.
22 Ibid., 286–7.
23 A fictional edition that combines James's *Gifford Lectures* and *Principles of Psychology* appears earlier in the novel's narrative. (Its owner, the character Randy Lenz, has hollowed out its midsection to use as a cocaine stash.)
24 William James, *The Varieties of Religious Experience: A Study in Human Nature* (New York: Modern Library, 1994), 317–318.
25 Max, *Every Love Story*, 193.
26 David Foster Wallace, "Deciderization 2007: A Special Report." *The Best American Essays 2007* (Boston: Mariner, 2007), xiii.

2

A Less "Bullshitty" Way to Live: The Pragmatic Spirituality of David Foster Wallace

Robert Bolger

> *All men seek happiness. This is without exception ... This is the motive of every action of every man, even of those who hang themselves.*
> – BLAISE PASCAL

Email from Wallace: March 7, 2007

R: Your second paragraph basically sums up my own fidelity to AA. I feel, think better; I'm less hypersensitive. I'm nicer to people. I'm less depressed ... I wish I could get it as well in other ways (exercise helps, too, slightly).

/dw/[1]

Philosophical reflection, when it does occur, takes place in the midst of the warp and woof of everyday life. Much like building a fence in a hurricane the philosopher, *qua* human, must construct arguments with their whole life whirling and buzzing around them. Even when, as Descartes famously managed, we can slow life down to practice our philosophical musing alone by a fire, our past worries and future concerns tend to come along for the ride. This claim does not simply amount to the simplistic fact that thinking is done by living rational beings (of course that's true); it is rather the substantive claim that all we are, all we fear, and all we hope for, is brought to bear on what we think is valid, believe is advantageous, and argue is true. Philosophy, for better or worse, is a human endeavor, and this fact must not be forgotten when we are reflecting on an individual's intellectual achievements. I think something like this must be what the Spanish philosopher Miguel de Unamuno had in mind when he wrote:

> In most of the histories of philosophy that I know philosophic systems are presented to us as if growing out of one another spontaneously, and their authors, the philosophers, appear as mere pretexts. The inner biography of the philosophers, of the men [and woman] who philosophized, is assigned a secondary place. And yet it is precisely that inner biography which can mean most to us.[2]

Like all intellectuals—and, in fact, like all of us who are, to use Wallace's term "flesh-sacs"—David Foster Wallace had a life to live. While he was indeed an impressive walking lexicon and accomplished postmodern prophet adored by the literarily savvy Northeast intelligentsia, he was also a friend (of mine), husband, depressed person, lover of tennis, and Alcoholics Anonymous (AA) member. Wallace, at least since his undergraduate days at Amherst, eschewed the pristine world of logic and rationality for descriptions of the contingencies and vicissitudes of human life. His writing oozed the pus of life in all its variety and grossness from consumerism to recovery to depression to boredom. It is this sort of literary pluralism that makes it nearly impossible to ascertain clearly where Wallace's own human stain bleeds into the lives of his fictional characters.[3] As with most fiction, the authorial Wallace tends to hide in the shadows with only occasional peeps and pokes through the curtain of language. But that is how it should be, right? The writer creates the fiction, which in turn re-creates the writer ... (repeat till death).

Happily, Wallace's inner biography was not always shrouded behind linguistic subterfuge or poststructuralist word games; there are times when Wallace thrusts *himself* to the forefront, allowing all to view (or listen). This is kenspeckle in his Kenyon College commencement address, later published as *This Is Water*. It is in this work that Wallace presents not only a spiritual way of living, but *his* own spiritual philosophy of life, a philosophy that I believe he tried to live out in his day-to-day existence. A philosophy that also represents his attempt to try and squeeze some modicum of peace from a life that was often fraught with self-doubt and a torturous desire to please. Sadly, his neurotransmitters made maintaining such a view impossible at the end.

While *This Is Water* is couched in the folksy language of a quaint commencement address delivered on a hot summer day in a picturesque Ohio town, it contains an account of the process of self-realization that, in some key ways, resembles a fairly straightforward and orthodox explanation of the religious path from self to God. Wallace, in a linear and serial manner, which betrays his wordy and circuitous stylistic tendencies, presents a sort of tripartite theology that begins with an account of the innate problem of human selfishness (an interpretation of the "sinful" human condition), presents a practical way to begin to overcome this "fallen state" (an interpretation of "conversion") and finally offers suggestions on how we can begin to see the divine presence in the mundane stuff of the world—including in the other people we regularly bump up against (an interpretation of "salvation"). If we wanted to be a bit more medieval, we could interpret *This Is Water* as a modern account of the mystical path to God that was spelled out by Dionysius (or maybe Bernard of Clairvaux with some latter emendations by Ignatius) and codified in the concepts of *purgation, illumination,* and *unification*.[4] More probably, however—and as a way of forcing me away from theological speculation—what Wallace offers in *This Is Water* is a sort of practical/theological account of the program of AA. The recognition of selfishness, the need to learn to turn away from self-obsession and turn toward others, and the traversing of a path that culminates in an ongoing practical experience of a higher power, is something Wallace knew well as an active member of AA, sober for more than fifteen years and the sponsor of many other addicts. Of course, because AA arose out of the context of the Christian holiness movement known as the Oxford Group and under the direct influence of many of the ideas outlined in William James's *Varieties of Religious Experience*, it's no wonder that Wallace's tone is somewhat religious in nature. Whatever Wallace's actual influences, what should not be overlooked is the fact that what he is offering is a set of practical steps (*his* practical steps) that must be applied rather than a series of beliefs that must be assented to.

The speculative nature of the origins and influence of *This Is Water* is not, for better or worse, my concern here[5]; my goal is simply to present Wallace's pragmatic approach to spirituality in a clear way that dissects it into its philosophically and theologically interesting component parts. In doing this, I hope to show the practical reasons for taking Wallace's theology seriously.

Email From Wallace: October 18, 2005

Work is not going well, and some days I get very depressed and anxious about it. The AA stuff is about the only thing that helps when my thoughts get in obsessive, boring, anxious fear-loops ... I find myself REALLY praying instead of just saying words ...

X, Dave W.[6]

Email From Wallace: January 6, 2006

I have not written on religion per se—don't know how I would, since even the kimndergarten [*sic*] stuff in AA seems mindbendingly [*sic*] complex to me.[7]

Stage setting: Two parables one point

Wallace begins *This Is Water* with a set of parables that, taken together, lay the foundation for the entirety of his argument (if argument is the appropriate term, maybe *presentation* would be more apt). For the sake of simplicity, I will refer to the two parables as the "Fish Parable" and the "Eskimo Parable" ("Inuit Parable" for our Canadian friends). First the fish:

> There are these two young fish swimming along and they happen to meet an older fish swimming the other way, who nods at them and says, "Morning, boys. How's the water?" And the two young fish swim on for a bit, and then eventually one of them looks over at the other and goes, "What the hell is water?" (*TIW* 3–4)

Wallace tells us "clearly" what this parable means: "the immediate point of the fish story is merely that the most obvious, ubiquitous, important realities are often the ones that are hardest to see and talk about" (*TIW* 8). This hermeneutical helpmate, while sufficiently clear (at least as an English sentence goes), is still a bit unsatisfying because we are not yet told what these "most obvious, ubiquitous, important realities" are? What is it that is as close to us as water to fish, so close, that is, that we do not easily recognize its existence? As it turns out, what is so close is not one thing but a variety of things, but more about this as we progress.

Now the Eskimo Parable:

> There are these two guys sitting together in a bar in the remote Alaskan wilderness. One of the guys is religious, the other's an atheist, and they're arguing about the existence of God … And the atheist says, "Look, it's not like I don't have actual reasons for not believing in God. It's not like I haven't ever experimented with the whole God-and-prayer thing. Just last month, I got caught off away from the camp in that terrible blizzard, and I couldn't see a thing, and I was totally lost, and it was fifty below, and so I did, I tried it: I fell to my knees in the snow and cried out, 'God, if there is a God, I'm lost in this blizzard, and I'm gonna die if you don't help me!'" And now, in the bar, the religious guy looks at the atheist all puzzled: "Well then, you must believe now," he says. "After all, here you are, alive." The atheist rolls his eyes like the religious guy is a total simp: "No, man, all that happened was that a couple Eskimos just happened to come wandering by and they showed me the way back to the camp." (*TIW* 17–23)

Wallace, recognizing that his audience is composed of a bunch of freshly minted graduating college kids from one of America's premier liberal arts colleges (what old people and the middle-aged like to call "know-it-alls"), is keenly aware that some may simply take this parable as another hackneyed example of the fact that a single event is open to multiple interpretations ("my truth is not your truth," "everything is relative," yadda, yadda). Wallace responds that such an interpretation is fine, "except we also never end up talking about just where these individual templates and beliefs come from, meaning, where they come from *inside* the two guys ... As if how we construct meaning were not actually a matter of personal, intentional choice, of conscious decision. Plus, there's the matter of arrogance" (*TIW* 26-9, emphasis original). This little, seemingly insignificant, response to the liberal arts simp (to use Wallace's shortened version of simpleton) actually turns out to be quite important for Wallace's overall project, for it is in this response that Wallace shows the intimate link between the possibility of epistemological freedom (the freedom to choose how we interpret certain events, i.e., the Eskimo Parable) and the ontological price we pay for being human (the things that are hardest to recognize while being the "most obvious, ubiquitous, important realities", i.e., human arrogance).[8] Here is the same point made with a bit more perspicuity.

If constructing meaning is a matter of forming beliefs about the world by peering through an inner "interpretive filter," and if we are *free* to choose (with certain normative constraints) which beliefs we are going to entertain and which beliefs we are going to ignore, then it appears that we can *both* freely choose to see the world in a variety of ways (some ways being less stress-producing than others) and we can disregard (or change) our "interpretive filter." This freedom to choose how we interpret certain aspects of reality is the *epistemological* point Wallace is making in the Eskimo parable. However, this is not the whole story. It may be that there is something that is part and parcel of being human, something so close to our nature that—like our noses—we rarely notice, but something that is also capable of frustrating and thwarting our *actual* freedom to choose how we interpret reality. This is the *ontological* point of the Fish parable. Wallace's whole argument, as well as his move toward a pragmatic spirituality, rests on these two issues: epistemological freedom and ontological constraint. And it is, according to Wallace, when we recognize the latter (ontological constraint) that we begin to learn to practice the former (epistemological freedom). So what is as close to us as water to a fish? It is our *ability* to choose and our *inability* to choose how we interpret the things that happen around us every day. It is this paradox that must be investigated.

Email From Wallace: April 26, 2006

I don't take rejection well, either. My ego is very large and fragile. I think one idea behind AA is that it helps make our egos slightly smaller and also slightly denser, more resilient and immune to Shattering from the rejections/criticisms that come to everyone at times, i.e., the end goal is Reduced Suffering.

/dw/[9]

The epistemic effects of a life curved inward

In his book *Saving God*, Mark Johnston describes the propensity of humans to preference their own needs and desires over those of others by referencing Kant's concept of "radical evil." Johnston writes:

> Kant's doctrine that we are radically evil is not the doctrine that we are bad to the bone, bad through and through; it is the manifestly true claim that there is something at the root of human nature that disposes each one of us to favor himself or herself over the others ... this is something in the very structure of our consciousness, a profound asymmetry of the evaluational affect, which privileges what is HERE over those things THERE.[10]

In *This Is Water*, Wallace presents a view of human selfishness that has some affinities with Kant's idea of "radical evil." The initial challenge in Wallace's discussion is getting clear about just what he is claiming because he, like Kant, is actually making two different but intimately related points. Wallace writes:

> Think about it: There is no experience you've had that you were not the absolute center of. The world as you experience it is there in front of you, or behind you, to the left or right of you, on your TV, or your monitor or whatever. Other people's thoughts and feelings have to be communicated, but your own are so immediate, urgent real. You get the idea. (*TIW* 39–42)

I do indeed, but this does not yet get us anywhere near "radical evil"; it only describes a cursory and obvious fact about what it means to be human. A simple statement about the privacy of personal experience (or what Lynne Rudder Baker refers to as the "first-person perspective"[11]) does not *entail* that the conscious person having the experience is selfish. These first-person statements are true for all human beings, but it is also obviously true that I may use my first-person point of view to help meet others' needs. I may decide to give my life in service for others or even die trying to save another person's life with absolutely no regard for my own well-being. Again, the mere fact that human consciousness *essentially* entails a first-person perspective does not itself *necessitate* selfishness (if it did, handicapped parking spaces would be fruitless). Wallace seems to understand this fact in *This Is Water* when he notes, "Everything in my own immediate experience supports my deep belief that I am the absolute center of the universe, the realest, most vivid and important person in existence" (*TIW* 36). Much like Kant's account of radical evil, Wallace's selfishness, while being parasitic on the fact of human consciousness, also claims that such a privileged point of view lends itself quite naturally to bending all of our thoughts and interests inward on themselves (*incurvatus in se*). We begin to think that *our* interests, *our* wants, and *our* needs are *the most important* things in the world. We may call this idea *innate selfishness*, "innate" because as Wallace describes it, this is the "default setting" (*TIW* 38) most human beings operate on. Here is how Wallace describes the situation: "It's the automatic, unconscious way that I experience the boring, frustrating, crowded parts of adult life when I'm operating on the automatic, unconscious belief that I am the center of the world and that my immediate needs and feelings are what should determine the world's priorities" (*TIW* 83). Here is the same sort of thing in the words of *AA*: "Selfishness—self-centeredness! That, we think, is the root of our troubles. Driven by a hundred forms of fear, self-delusion, self-seeking, and self-pity, we step on the toes of our fellows and they retaliate."[12]

This account of selfishness is not benign; it rather has very real and practical consequences for the way we live our lives. Here is how this works. Wallace asks us to imagine a seemingly normal trip to the grocery store, one that adults living in the humdrum, déjà vu-like repetitive nature of day-to-day existence tend to experience *ad infinitum*. Wallace then points out a variety of ways in which this seemingly mundane trip to the market can, if we are aware of our thoughts, reveal to us just how automatic, how annoyingly natural, and how cunningly ubiquitous our selfish thinking tends to be. Wallace's description of shopping for supper ("supper" being Wallace's homey Midwest synonym for what coastal people call "dinner") involves a litany of normal activities: bad traffic, crowds at the store, aisles filled with tired people, and kids blocking the aisle way. When we finally do make it to the checkout, we are met with a hideously long Disneyland-like line, people talking on their cell phones and, at the end, a cashier's farewell that Wallace describes as "a voice that is the absolute voice of death" (*TIW* 71). The point is that if we let our "default setting" do the job of interpreting these events (and it does so quite effortlessly), we end up focusing endlessly on "I" and "me" and "mine," the end result being certain frustration and anger. Wallace continues:

> If I don't make a conscious decision about how to think and what to pay attention to, I'm gonna be pissed and miserable every time I have to food shop, because my natural default setting is that situations like this are really all about *me*, about my hungriness and my fatigue and my desire to just get home, and it's going to seem, for all the world, like everybody is just *in my way*, and who the fuck are all these people in my way? (*TIW* 77, emphasis original)

Wallace's point is interesting because he makes a distinction between how the world is and how we perceive it to be when we look at it through the lens of selfishness. It is not that everyone else is *actually* in my way or *really* out to make my trip miserable, it is just that when my focus is on my own little plans and desires, this is how things appear; these are the beliefs I automatically form. My beliefs create a reality, a reality that drives me to frustration, but these beliefs are not necessarily true; they are just beliefs filtered through a selfish narrative.

In Wallace's first novel *The Broom of the System*, Jay asks, "The truth is that there's no difference between a life and a story? But a life pretends to be something more? But it really isn't more?" Wallace, in *This Is Water*, answers Jay in the affirmative (*BOS*, 120). Wallace writes,

> If you're automatically sure that you know what reality is and who and what is really important—if you want to operate on your default setting—then you, like me, probably will not consider possibilities that aren't pointless and annoying. But if you've really learned how to think, how to pay attention, then you will know that you have other options. (*TIW* 91–2)

Our lives are lived through the filter of stories that we have either been born into, been educated into, or simply come to accept as true, but the stories can always be changed. Stories themselves are not true or false; they are rather the contexts in which statements are judged as true or false. It is not that other possibilities are not possible; it is just that given the apparatus that is helping form some of our beliefs—that is, our own selfishness—these other possibilities are simply not available without some story-changing work being done. The Buddhist scholar David Loy writes, "concepts in themselves are fragments, meaningful as parts of stories ... We do not see our stories as stories because we see through them: the world we experience is constructed with them."[13] We may call these stories "life-orienting stories" (following philosopher David Holley), "forms of life" (following Wittgenstein), or simply "world-views"; the important point is to remember that it is from these stories that our beliefs about the world arise. Loy writes, "Our joys and sorrow, laughter and tears, pleasures and pains, loves and fears, epiphanies and despairs—all are storied. They are meaningful within the context of a narrative."[14] In a more overtly theological context, David Holley writes,

> people who believe in God are convinced, not by a process of reasoning from publicly available evidence to the conclusion that God exists, but by a *narrative* vision in which the idea of God plays a fundamental role. When they are able to use this *narrative* to orient themselves in life by discerning the kinds of significance it highlights, the conception of reality it presupposes become believable.[15]

When we operate from within a default setting of selfishness, other epistemic possibilities become difficult at best and impossible at worst. Selfishness has epistemic consequences because we naturally have a narrative in place telling us that we are "the absolute center of the universe, the most real, most vivid and important person in existence."[16]

But that is not all; innate selfishness also has pragmatic effects, effects that I refer to as *practical solipsism*. If we take solipsism to be the belief that we are the only things in the world that really exist and all else is a mere figment of my (*really real*) mind, then I submit that there are probably very few real solipsists. But solipsism can be more sinister. If I believe that my needs are more important than the needs of others and that others are simply obstacles in my way then I have, for all practical purposes, cut myself off from being able to see others as *really real*. When we operate on our default setting, other people become mere objects: obstacles to be overcome and babbling entities to be endured. What we have lost is the ability to see other people as people. I, as the *really real*, am alone in a world of objects, objects that are constantly thwarting my plans. This type of judgment about the worth of others alienates us from them. Richard Rohr writes, "The small 'I' [ego] knows itself by comparison … As long as we're comparing and differentiating from the other, we can't love the other. We judge it."[17] This is why Wallace can tell the group of graduating students assembled in front of him that the real "no-shit value of your liberal arts education is supposed to be about: How to keep from going through your comfortable, prosperous, respectable adult life dead, unconscious, a slave to your head and to your natural default setting of being uniquely, completely, *imperially alone*, day in and day out" (*TIW* 60, emphasis added). This type of aloneness is existential, not ontological, and it is something that probably should be overcome if we are going to live fulfilling happy lives.

Wallace instinctively seemed to recognize the importance of welcoming other people into our lives. In an email where I had mentioned how much I liked the Philip Larkin poem "Aubade," Wallace wrote, "Larkin is often bleaker 'on the surface' than he really is (for instance, what do you make of the last line? Notice that the dreadful fear of death afflicts him most when he is *alone*. Is there some suggestion that "treatment" for the fear (not for the death, which is unstoppable) consists of interhuman connection? Is the last line not hopeful, in some way?"[18] Connecting with others, however, is impossible until we can restore a relationship whereby we look upon them with a certain amount of care, respect or even love. In order for this to happen, a certain conversion away from selfishness must take place.

Email From Wallace: 17 January 2006

We're quite alike, so I know it's true: you have them [T.S. Eliot-like "tremors of bliss"] all the time. The trick is noticing them, which requires thinking less and trying to notice more. It's very hard. This kind of awareness appears to me to be the real goal (and perhaps the promised "4th Dimension") of the sort of spirituality with which AA is concerned. But they really are there all the time; think about it: The anglre [sic] of light through a bus window at certain times, the feeling of the the [sic] first swallow of water when you're thirsty, the [sight of our wives] doing something small that delights you without her knowing, etc. All sorts of tremors. The good days are the days I'm awake and aware enough to feel them.[19]

Overcoming the epistemic obstacle: Or, how to care about the stranger

Wallace's suggestion for overcoming the epistemological and solipsistic effects of innate selfishness is twofold. First, we must learn to be aware enough of our thoughts to recognize that some of our beliefs are utterly selfish and, quite possibly, wrong. This involves an act of attentive awareness to what we think and a certain amount of epistemic humility about what we think we are certain of. Second, we must be able to *make up* (or construct) a set of new and "plausible" stories about other people that acknowledges not only their right to exist but also explains why they justifiably do the things they do and act the way they act.[20] In short, we must develop *compassion* for other people. This sort of stuff—humility and compassion—is rarely an act of simple ratiocination but more likely the product of our will. Because these ideas form the guts of Wallace's way of overcoming the browbeating effects of selfishness, I should say a bit more about them.

When Wallace talks of "paying attention," he is not simply referring to concentrating harder on what is going on around us but rather paying attention to what is going on inside of us. He says, "Probably the most dangerous thing about an academic education, at least in my own case, is that it enables my tendency to over-intellectualize stuff. To get lost in abstract thinking instead of simply paying attention to what's going on in front of me. Instead of paying attention to what's going on *inside me*" (*TIW* 48–9, emphasis original). Of course, we have already seen that the type of thinking going on inside us is (often) tainted by innate selfishness; nevertheless, it is good to remember that innate selfishness is also something arising from our storied lives and is therefore under our volition. So, paying "attention" for Wallace is not simply some sort of New Age *faux-Buddhism*; it is not the "attention for attention's sake" stuff like feeling the heat of the mug of tea we are drinking or being acutely and painfully aware of each and every bite of our food. Wallace is talking about being on the lookout for thoughts that automatically and ferociously preference our desires and our needs over those of others. If we recognize these beliefs as selfish by-products of our humanity, then we may be able to *will* other beliefs in their place.

What we are being asked to do is no less than "die to ourselves." It is learning to practice a little bit of epistemological humility. We are being asked to jettison our cocksureness that we are absolutely correct and entertain the possibility that we may not know everything (even things we are sure we know). Wallace explains, writing:

> The point here is that I think this is one part of what the liberal arts mantra of 'teaching me how to think' is really supposed to mean: to be just a little less arrogant, to have some 'critical awareness' about myself and my certainties ... because a huge percentage of the stuff that I tend to be automatically certain of is, it turns out, totally wrong and deluded. (*TIW* 33)

If we can recognize—really recognize—our epistemic fallibility, we will begin to open the door to considering other possibilities, considering that there just may be some really good explanations for why other people are shopping, driving, walking their dog, and working out at the exact moment I decide to do the same. Our attentiveness to our beliefs permits us to be open to a plurality of epistemic possibilities; that is, we can tell stories that explain and justify others' actions, and, if we can consider some of these stories as if they are *really* possible (but not necessarily true), we may be able to short-circuit our selfish default setting allowing us to reboot (to keep the computer analogy going) the system as a whole (BTW: does anybody *reboot* anything anymore?).

In *Everything Belongs*, Richard Rohr writes:

> As we observe our mental and emotional flow over a period of disciplined time, we recognize that we largely create our own experiences ... We have the power to decide what the moment means and how we will respond to it. We have the power when we have the ability to respond freely. We can decide if we're going to respond to something hatefully or lovingly.[21]

Compare Rohr's ideas to the following two statements from Wallace:

> "Learning how to think" really means learning how to exercise some control over *how* and *what* you think. It means being conscious and aware enough to choose what you pay attention to and to choose how you construct meaning from experience.
>
> The really important kind of freedom involves attention, and awareness, and discipline, and effort, and being able truly to care about other people ... (*TIW* 53–4, 120, emphasis original)

If the freedom to choose a new story is within our capabilities, then, simply on pragmatic grounds (e.g., choosing a belief for its advantageous results), we may want to begin to change the way we think about others. David Loy, employing a version of the Fish parable, writes, "Like the proverbial fish who cannot see the water they swim in, we do not notice the medium we dwell within. Unaware that our stories are stories, we experience them as the world. But we can change the water. When our accounts of the world become different the world becomes different."[22]

Now let us harken back to the drudgery of the people who had the nerve to cohabit with us at the supermarket making our life (at least momentarily) miserable. Wallace, recognizing that his opinion of their existence flows from his own selfishness, realizes he can freely choose to change the story.

> [I]f you're aware enough to give yourself a choice, you can choose to look differently at this fat, dead-eyed, over-made-up lady who just screamed at her kid in the checkout line—maybe she's not usually like this; maybe she's been up three straight nights holding the hand of her husband, who's dying of bone cancer, or maybe this very lady is the low-wage clerk at the motor vehicles department who just yesterday helped your spouse resolve a nightmarish red-tape problem through some small act of bureaucratic kindness. Of course, none of this is likely, but it's not impossible—it just depends what you want to consider. (*TIW* 89)

Regarding the traffic problems encountered on the freeway and the maddeningly gigantic gas-guzzling vehicles that race through traffic with little care for basic safety, Wallace writes,

> In this traffic, all these vehicles stuck and idling in my way: It's not impossible that some of these people in SUV's have been in horrible auto accidents in the past and now find driving so traumatic that their therapist has all but ordered them to get a huge, heavy SUV so they can feel safe enough to drive; or that the Hummer that just cut me off is maybe being driven by a father whose little child is hurt or sick in the seat next to him, and he's trying to rush to the hospital. (*TIW* 85)

This sort of "self-deception" is Wallace's Eskimo parable in practice. If we realize that those beliefs that separate us from others are simply the manifestation of innate selfishness, then we can begin to tell ourselves new stories that not only respect others' right to exist but also release us from the petty frustrations that consume us at a gut level.

Although this suggestion appears trivial and simplistic, it is not. Our selfishness is so ingrained and natural that thinking in a new, nonselfish way takes an act of the will. This is made even more difficult by the fact that we do not choose most of our beliefs. But Wallace is not simply proposing that we reinterpret the events of life in order to create beliefs we can *justify* as true. He is asking us to create sensible epistemic possibilities (tell ourselves new stories) *that could be true for all we know*. These are possibilities that, if true, would allow us to be less frustrated and more peaceful. This is close to what William James has in mind when he writes:

> Pragmatism, on the other hand, asks its usual question. 'Grant an idea or belief to be true,' it says, 'what concrete difference will its being true make in anyone's actual life? How will the truth be realized? What experiences will be different from those that would obtain if the belief were false? What, in short, is the truth's cash-value in experiential terms?'[23]

The conversion that Wallace is advocating is conversion *away* from ourselves, but it is also a conversion that we bring about volitionally and possibly circularly; we create new beliefs and change our inner narrative, which changes our beliefs, which ... you get the idea. This process is an acceptance of what many in AA call "life on life's terms," and it may have repercussions for our sanity. An earlier defender of AA, the psychiatrist Henry Tiebout writes:

> When an individual surrenders, the ability to accept reality functions on the unconscious level, and there is no residual of battle; relaxation with freedom from strain and conflict ensues. In fact, it is perfectly possible to ascertain how much acceptance of reality is on the unconscious level by the degree of relaxation that develops. The greater the relaxation, the greater the inner acceptance of reality.[24]

Email From Wallace: October 22, 2005

I think this is it; I think you've got it. It's not overcoming the in[d]ividual ego's terror of annihilation. It is somehow cathecting enough other people and enough of the world that we identify, less and less, with the individual ego—that we literally care more about the universe than about our own flesh-sac and its needs. Cath[e]xis of and identification with God yiel[d]s "immortality," since the part of us that is or is—in God can clearl[y] not be a[n]nihilated the way the individual ego can.

It's like the old joke: Q: What did the mystic say to the hot dog vendor? A: Make me one with everything.

Very, very hard to actually do, in my experience. Especially because it's not intellectual but rather attitudinal, existential. But each minute bit of progress yields hugely disproportionate gains in terms of less fear, less depression, less loneliness. And minu[t]e bits of progress appear to be what we're in AA to make, once physical sobriety is accomplished.

X, Dave W.[25]

Seeing and the sacred

In *The Brothers Karamazov*, Dostoevsky writes,

> Love people even in their sin, for that is the semblance of Divine Love and is the highest love on earth. Love all of God's creation, the whole and every grain of sand of it. Love every leaf, every ray of God's light. Love the animals, love the plants, love everything. If you love everything, you will perceive the divine mystery in things. Once you perceive it, you will begin to comprehend it better every day. And you will come at last to love the whole world with an all-embracing love.[26]

In an earlier book of mine, *Kneeling at the Altar of Science*, I called this sort of view of religious belief a "religious stance" writing that:

> The religious stance can be defined as an attitude taken towards the facts of existence whereby the believer interprets the facts of science as being imbued with grace and love. In a sense this is a way of seeing the world *sub specie aeternitatis*. The religious believer sees the whole of existence as interrelated, not because science has proven this to be so, but because the world, with all its foibles, is still God's world. The direction of seeing is reversed. We do not passively *see* what is there; rather we *interpret* what is there ...[27]

These quotations appear to be at odds. Dostoevsky is claiming that learning to take a stance of love toward others is a sort of precondition for perceiving the divine mystery in things, whereas I am claiming that we love others *because* we see the world already imbued with divinity. I think both of us are correct, and to see why, let us turn back briefly to Wallace.

In the section above, I mentioned that a Wallacian theology sees that one way we can begin to burrow out of our selfishness is to begin to tell another story about the people we plod around with on this planet. Again, these stories need not be true—who cares about truth when our peace of mind is on the line? The main thing is that such stories should create a sort of "meta-narrative" that justifies other individual's existence and actions. We tell ourselves stories of compassion.

Let us call the attitude we take in these "self-deceptive" stories "faux-love" (or fluv for short). Now fluv is not love but a temporary substitute for love. We tell stories of compassion that involve our fluving others; that is, we tell stories that look and sound as if we care for others' needs and concerns at least as much as we care about our own. What we are really doing is bypassing our default setting. Now here is the rub, if we continue to tell fluving stories about others, we may actually be able to transform our fluv into something like real love (or at least real compassion).[28] Here is how this might work.

Pretend you are a hypochondriac who believes every ache, every little pain, and every small twinge that occurs in your body is a sign of a heart attack, terminal cancer, or some other disease that will result in your demise.[29] After years of therapy your doctor convinces you to speak to your pains and body aches as if they were alive, letting them know that you are on to their trick to scare you and declaring that you know their pranks are harmless and ineffective (you are then to let out two hardy chuckles "Ha Ha!"). While you think this makes you look somewhat sicker than you were when you started therapy, you begin to take the doctor's advice.

At first with some trepidation you tell the mild ache in your chest that you are not fooled nor are you scared, "Ha, Ha." As the months go by, you get better and better at this "Ha-Ha-ing." You continue it whenever you feel the crushing anxiety that death is imminent—in the car, at work, at church, in a boat, on a goat, etc. One day you realize you have had a variety of twinges and pangs *without* the debilitating anxiety. No anxiety, no fear! You feel better and you no longer interpret or believe that pain = death/disease. Now of course, your real cure started with a fake story (a lie even, since pains cannot hear you talking to them!), a story that got ingrained into your belief system and changed your world.[30]

Couldn't the same type of thing happen with the fluving stories we tell about others? Wallace says, "The really important kind of freedom involves attention, and awareness, and discipline, and effort, and being able truly to care about other people and to sacrifice for them, over and over, in myriad petty little unsexy ways, every day" (*TIW* 119). Earlier he notes that if we learn how to think compassionately "[i]t will actually be within your power to experience a crowded, hot, slow, consumer-hell-type situation as not only meaningful, but sacred, on fire with the same force that lit the stars—compassion, love, the subsurface unity of all things" (*TIW* 93). But these things are instances of real love (not fluv); they are instances where we sacrifice for others on a regular basis and where we feel unified with all reality (including other people). These types of actions and feelings, however, can only manifest if the ego is deflated, if our default setting is short-circuited. If we feel alienated and angry with others, it is going to be very hard to sacrifice for them and nearly impossible to feel we are a part (with them) of something greater. Now let us revisit my earlier dispute with Dostoevsky.

Earlier I said that it seemed that Dostoevsky in *The Brothers Karamazov* encourages us to begin to love other people and in this state of constantly choosing to love we will begin to "perceive the divine mystery in things." In an earlier work, I seemed to insist that if we already believe in a divine presence that imbues reality, we would (as part of this belief) take a religious stance toward all of creation. While these seem incompatible, they really are not. It may simply be that Dostoevsky is admonishing us to take an attitude of love toward others even if we do not really love them (he is asking us to fluv them), and in that process (over a period of time), the fake love may just be replaced with real love, which leads, ultimately, to seeing them as the divine does. My discussion, on the other hand, begins with the presumption that someone has taken a religious stance toward reality and then suggests that this stance is partly manifested in our "loving our neighbors as ourselves." Either way, what we get is a spiritual point of view that involves an active choice to look at reality in a certain way, and this, I contend, is also what we get in Wallace. This is not a religion of believing certain propositions; it is not doctrinal and not metaphysical. It is an interpretive spirituality, a sort of "seeing-as" (following Wittgenstein).[31]

Before anyone thinks that Wallace is just being cute or pithy presenting a sort of folk-spirituality, they should think again. In her book *Practical Mysticism*, Evelyn Underhill writes, "Mysticism is the art of Union with Reality. The mystic is a person who has attained that union in greater or less degree; or who aims at and believes in such attainment."[32] The key is not getting too caught up in what a unified reality amounts to; this is mysticism after all, not metaphysics. Later, attempting to explain what the novice mystic is committed to, Underhill writes:

> All that he is asked to consider now is this: that the word "union" represents not so much a rare and unimaginable operation, as something which he is doing, in a vague, imperfect fashion, at every moment of his conscious life; and doing with intensity and thoroughness in all the more valid moments of that life. We know a thing only by uniting with it; by assimilating it; by an interpenetration of it and ourselves.[33]

Finally, Richard Rohr, considered by many a contemporary mystic,[34] writes, "In Mature Religion, the secular becomes sacred. There are no longer two worlds. We no longer have to leave the secular world to find sacred space because they've come together."[35] If this sort of unification of reality is part of the historic mystical tradition, then I think it is clear that Wallace is presenting a sort of practical mysticism that places him squarely in a long tradition. To think otherwise is to misread (or misrepresent) what he is saying.[36]

The fish prequel

Wallace's use of the Fish Parable in *This Is Water* is not the story's first appearance. In *Infinite Jest*, the parable is told in a context that may be enlightening for our purposes here.

The telling of the parable in *Infinite Jest* is preceded by Don Gately appearing at the podium in an AA meeting telling others how difficult of a time he is having finding a "God of his own understanding." Wallace writes,

"His [Gately's] sole experience so far is that he takes one of AA's very rare specific suggestions and hits the knees in the A.M. and asks for Help and then hits the knees again at bedtime and says Thank You, whether he believes he's talking to Anything/body or not, *and he somehow gets through that day clean*" (*IJ* 443, emphasis added). He later continues, "when he [Gately] tries to go beyond the very basic rote automatic get-me-through-the-day-please stuff, when he kneels at other times and prays or meditates or tries to achieve a Big-Picture spiritual understanding of a God as he can understand Him, he feels Nothing—not nothing but *Nothing*" (*IJ* 443, emphasis original). It is in the context of Gately's apparent inability to make intellectual sense of the "God thing" while, oddly enough, experiencing the practical success of sobriety as the result of following rote religious practices, that Wallace inserts the Fish parable. After the meeting is over, a biker guy thanks Gately for his share[37] and asks if "he's heard the one about the fish" (*IJ* 445). The biker then says, "This wise old whiskery fish[38] swims up to three young fish and goes, 'Morning boys, how's the water?' and swims away; and the three young fish watch him swim away and look at each other and go, 'What the fuck is Water?' and swim away" (*TIW* 4–5). This all seems a bit cryptic and gnostic because Wallace does not further comment on this tale. The biker just shrugs and drives off. But I think given the context in which the parable is placed, no further comment is necessary. Gately's struggle was to find a Higher Power that existed *outside* of his life; that is, outside of the rote religious actions he performed. He desired a higher power that was more than the simple rote stuff *plus* the benefit of daily sobriety. But he was looking too far away. If Gately had noticed what was right in front of him— that is, the fact that the rote prayers had the pragmatic effect of keeping him sober—he would have seen his higher power in action; Gately did not have a God-finding problem, he had a God-concept problem.

In the appendix titled "Spiritual Experience" in the book *Alcoholics Anonymous*, the author writes:

> Most of our experiences are what the psychologist William James calls the "educational variety" because they develop slowly over a period of time. Quite often friends of the newcomer are aware of the difference long before he is himself. He finally realizes that he has undergone a profound alteration in his reaction to life; that such a change could hardly have been brought about by himself alone. What often takes place in a few months could seldom have been accomplished by years of self-discipline. With few exceptions, our members find that they have tapped an unsuspected inner resource which they presently identify with their own conception of a Power greater than themselves.[39]

This is exactly what Wallace presents in Gately, and it is exactly what the biker was trying to get Gately to see by relating to him the fish parable.

The lesson seems to be that the further we look for the divine, the harder it is to locate. There are times when Wallace equates water with our own innate selfishness or our ability to change our meta-story; we may, however, justifiably begin to see that a spiritual life lived in the presence of God and in union with reality is as close to us as water is to a fish. What we need is to be told just where and how to look. Maybe *This Is Water* is Wallace's secular equivalent of "The Kingdom of God Is Within You" or his form of secular mysticism. Whatever it is, I think it is certainly a less "bullshitty" way to live.

Notes

1. Message to Robert Bolger. March 7, 2007. Email.
2. Miguel de Unamuno, *The Tragic Sense of Life in Men and Nations* (Princeton: Princeton University Press, 1971), 4.
3. This is true with a bit of a caveat. Surely Wallace's personal life can be seen in some of the recovery and tennis stuff in *Infinite Jest,* and we also probably see parts of the philosophy of the real Wallace in the boredom theme in *The Pale King*. The difficulty is that Wallace is so topically diverse that it is hard to tell what is autobiographical to some extent and what is pure fiction (I imagine it is usually an admixture of both).
4. For a nice discussion of these ideas, see Jean-Marc Laporte, S.J., "Understanding the spiritual journey: from the classical tradition to the Spiritual Exercises of Ignatius," 2009. http://www.jesuits.ca/orientations/stages%20in%20the%20spiritual%20journey.pdf.
5. For a thorough exploration of Wallace's influences, motivations, and process of composing *TIW*, see Chapter 9 of this collection: "A Spoon, Some Eskimos, and the Wise Old Fish: Religion and the Evolution of Wallace's Kenyon Commencement Address," by Brick and Bucher.
6. Message to Robert Bolger. October 18, 2005. Email.
7. Message to Robert Bolger. January 6, 2006. Email.
8. There is a lot of philosophical dispute swimming in these waters; at the forefront are issues about whether or not we can freely choose our beliefs.
9. Message to Robert Bolger. April 26, 2006. Email.
10. Mark Johnston, *Surviving Death* (Princeton: Princeton University Press, 2010), 157–8.
11. See, Lynne Rudder Baker, *Naturalism and the First-Person Perspective* (Oxford: Oxford University Press, 2013).
12. Bill W., *Alcoholics Anonymous*, 4th ed. (New York: Alcoholics Anonymous World Services Inc., 2009), 62.
13. David Loy, *The World Is Made of Stories* (Somerville, MA.: Wisdom Publication, 2010), Loc. 17. Kindle Edition.

14 Ibid., Loc. 225. Kindle Edition.
15 David M. Holley, *Meaning and Mystery: What It Means to Believe in God* (Malden, MA: Wiley-Blackwell, 2010), 5. Emphasis added.
16 Op. cit. See note 12 above.
17 Richard Rohr, *Everything Belongs* (New York: The Crossroad Publishing Company, 1999), 55.
18 Personal email dated October 20, 2005. In the quote, the first parenthesis never closes since this is how the email appears.
19 Message to Robert Bolger. January 17, 2006. Email.
20 Of course, these types of stories will have their limits. We do not want to justify all acts to the point where there is no real culpability for behavior that is truly harmful.
21 Rohr, *Everything Belongs*, 91.
22 Loy, *The Word Is Made of Stories*, Loc. 59. Kindle Edition.
23 William James, *Pragmatism* (New York: Barnes and Noble, 2003), 87–8.
24 Henry M. Tiebout M.D., "The Act of Surrender in the Therapeutic Process," http://www.thejaywalker.com/pages/tiebout/actofsurrender.html.
25 Message to Robert Bolger. October 22, 2005. Email.
26 Fyodor Dostoevsky, *The Brothers Karamazov* quoted in Rohr, *Everything Belongs*, 27.
27 Robert Bolger, *Kneeling at the Altar of Science: The Mistaken Path of Contemporary Religious Scientism* (Eugene, OR: Wipf and Stock Publishers, 2012), Loc. 2781–5. Kindle Edition. Emphasis in the original.
28 Obviously, this is not meant to apply to cases where a loving relationship is already presumed to exist. I take it that most of us don't fluv our spouse on our wedding day and hope that after some time of telling fluving stories about them to ourselves we will come to love them.
29 Alright, since we are being honest here I should admit that this part is autobiographical. For whatever reason I have been afraid of death since I was a child and, due to this fear of death, I have never been a fan of ailments that could bring about my own demise.
30 Incidentally, something like this sort of "fake it till you make it" philosophy is what Wallace describes as happening to Don Gately when Gately one day realizes he no longer is craving drugs. See *IJ* 349.
31 See Ludwig Wittgenstein, *Philosophical Investigations*, trans. G.E.M. Anscombe, ed. P.M.S. Hacker and Joachim Schulte, revised 4th ed. (Chichester, West Sussex: Wiley-Blackwell, 2009), Part II.
32 Evelyn Underhill, *Practical Mysticism: A Little Book for Normal People* (Seattle, WA: Amazon Digital Services, 2011), Loc. 105. Kindle edition.
33 Ibid., Loc. 112. Kindle Edition.
34 See his book, *The Naked Now: How to See as the Mystics See* (The Crossroads Publishing Company, 2009).

35 Rohr, *Everything Belongs*, 134.

36 I think something like this is what is happening in the chapter on Wallace in *All Things Shining: Reading the Western Classics to Find Meaning in a Secular Age* by Hubert Dreyfus and Sean Dorrance Kelly (Free Press, 2011). In this book, Wallace's spiritual insights are presented as being out of touch with other historically significant religious thinkers. He is shown as a sort of pop-culture self-help simpleton. I take this as another instance (much like Richard Dawkins, Sam Harris and the other "new atheists") of intellectuals believing they are experts in fields outside of their own. The authors simply auditing a class in "Introduction to Theology" at Harvard Divinity School would have corrected this error.

37 The use of "share" is important since it invokes the personal nature of what Gately had to say from the podium. Gately was not giving a talk, he was sharing his experience.

38 Interestingly in *This Is Water*, Wallace clearly states he is not the wise old fish. I take it he knew his audience well enough to know that the students at Kenyon did not want (or need) to be told what to do by this disheveled, nervousy-type author from Pomona College.

39 Bill W., *Alcoholics Anonymous*, 567.

3

"Not Another Word": Nietzsche, Wallace, and the Death of God

Michael McGowan

One of the only book-length treatments on David Foster Wallace and religion before the present volume is Adam Miller's *The Gospel According to David Foster Wallace*. As Miller mentions in the Afterword,[1] his book is in direct response to Hubert Dreyfus's and Sean Kelly's assertion in *All Things Shining*[2] that Wallace was a Nietzschean nihilist.[3] The term "nihilism" has been variously defined, but the general idea is that when old convictions no longer convict, when old beliefs seem simply unbelievable, and old patterns of life are unlivable, people are left with no reason to choose one worldview over another.[4] In part, Dreyfus and Kelly blame Nietzsche for our contemporary nihilism, because on their reading, "Nietzsche thought that nihilism was a great joy, since it frees us to live any life we choose."[5] They read Wallace to be promoting a similar approach, the view that "we are the sole active agents in the universe, responsible for generating out of nothing whatever notion of the sacred and divine there can ever be."[6] Miller reads the same passages as Dreyfus and Kelly, but comes to drastically different conclusions. Miller argues that Dreyfus and Kelly fail to understand Wallace's conception of "worship," which unfortunately results in an uncharitable reading of Wallace at best, and at worst, a "cartoonish" one.

In this chapter, I will address whether Wallace was, in fact, a Nietzschean nihilist. That is, I suggest a winner in this literary and philosophical debate. Miller's book is a great introduction to Wallace's attempts to deal with the consequences of nihilism (boredom, addiction), but he does not interact a great deal with Nietzsche, who is only mentioned twice in the text. In what follows, I provide support for Miller's conclusion that Wallace was *not* a Nietzschean nihilist, but I will also extend the argument to claim that Wallace's attempts to find meaning in a nihilistic world are more capable than Nietzsche's of resolving some of the existential crises in which twenty-first-century thinkers find themselves. To my knowledge, no serious comparative work other than *All Things Shining* exists on the relation between Nietzsche's brand of nihilism and Wallace. This chapter, therefore, seeks to fill this lacuna by bolstering Miller's conclusion through a close reading of both Nietzsche and Wallace on the problem of nihilism.[7]

Whether Wallace possessed only a cursory understanding of Nietzsche or a more sophisticated one is a matter of some debate. Wallace's father, James, tells me that he does not recall any conversations with his son about Nietzsche, nihilism, or the work of James's close colleague at Illinois State University, Richard Schacht, who has written a great deal about Nietzsche. However, on March 1, 1989, Schacht gave the young Wallace a book he had written on *Alienation*,[8] which includes an introductory essay by famed Nietzsche scholar, Walter Kaufmann. (Wallace's copy can be found at the Harry Ransom Center archives in Texas.) Schacht's inscription to Wallace mentions that his work on alienation and Wallace's *Broom of the System* were "sort of on the same general topic." In Schacht's book, Wallace underlined passages having to do with Nietzsche,[9] the themes of which eventually made their way into Wallace's subsequent work, like the following: "Long before the days of television, Nietzsche inveighed against the *Verhummung*, or moronization, of his people, and today moronization is widely associated with our mass media."[10] Wallace revisited Schacht's *Alienation* as preparation/research for *The Pale King*, as evidenced by "Drinion" and "boredom of jobs" making their way into Wallace's handwritten notes in the text. He also used the book on alienation as a tool for self-reflection, as evidenced by the "DW" notes next to passages about depression, competitiveness, and creativity.[11]

Why Nietzsche and Wallace

I am certainly not the first to explore nihilism in Nietzsche's work, but its relation to Wallace is a new development.[12] For a host of reasons, however, a conversation between the two seems long overdue. Much to the chagrin of Miller, Dreyfus and Kelly take as a data point some biographical details in their interpretation of Wallace's message. And while I am sympathetic to Miller's reluctance to do so, there are important similarities worth mentioning. Although Nietzsche and Wallace lived in different centuries on different continents, both are geniuses in the estimation of their interpreters.

Stylistically, both were purposefully oblique at times, and insofar as Nietzsche and Wallace "allow themselves to be unriddled—for it belongs to their nature to *want* to remain riddles at some point—these philosophers of the future may have a right—it might also be a wrong—to be called *attempters*."[13] To call them "attempters" is to recognize that they were both *daring* in their written work; at times they discussed novel ideas and at other times discussed traditional ideas in novel ways. As both Wallace scholars and Nietzsche scholars well know, interpretive diversity is one of the goals of both authors: Nietzsche did "not wish to be understood by 'just anybody'"[14] and Wallace could have subtitled *Infinite Jest* "A Book for All and None" (*Zarathustra's* subtitle) due to the complexity of Wallace's diction, prose, and plot.

There are other stylistic similarities worth mentioning. Both Nietzsche and Wallace present distinctively literary personae who stand in stark contrast to their real-life counterparts. Nietzsche's authorial voice does not ask for the reader's attention. He demands it. Nietzsche's uncompromising strongman on the page, who penned such memorable lines as "Listen to Me!"[15] and "I am Dynamite!"[16] hid a sickly and relationally frustrated man behind the scenes,[17] much as his mustache acted as a mask behind which his real face could hide.[18] Wallace, too, had mechanisms for navigation of social situations that allowed him to hide his real "self" from others (e.g., the infamous bandana,[19] the towel and tennis racket,[20] etc.). And like Nietzsche, there are times when Wallace's "maximalism"[21] and hyperbolic "hysterical realism"[22] leap from the page, showing no signs of the timid author. In addition to hyperbole, Wallace also used many of the literary strategies Nietzsche used: their writings are often undecidable in meaning, resistant to paraphrase, embody the concepts for which they argue (i.e., "tokening"[23]), demand the reader's full attention, and contain self-consuming concepts.[24]

Moreover, both Nietzsche and Wallace considered fiction to be their best work. Reflecting on *Thus Spoke Zarathustra*, Nietzsche says, "Among my writings *Zarathustra* stands alone. With it I have given humanity the greatest gift it has ever been given."[25] A philologist by training, Nietzsche writes about philosophical issues in his nonfiction work, but he views his only novel with singular fondness. Wallace is also a master of nonfiction, but, like Nietzsche, he most prizes his fiction work. Their processes of writing, however, were quite different. Nietzsche describes writing *Zarathustra* as a process of inspiration,[26] even *revelation*, but Wallace's writing comes much less easily. Borrowing from DeLillo, Wallace describes "a book-in-progress as a kind of hideously damaged infant that follows the writer around … " (*BFN* 193). The effort is worth it for Wallace, however, because, although he was trained in philosophy (e.g., symbolic and modal logic[27] for which Wallace entered Harvard's Ph.D. program in philosophy[28]), Wallace believes good storytelling can do things that standard philosophical argumentation cannot.[29]

Finally, the careers of both men ended in their mid-forties, well before one would expect. After a wildly productive year, 1888, in which Nietzsche wrote *Twilight of the Idols, The Case of Wagner, The Antichrist,* and his version of an autobiography, *Ecce Homo,* Nietzsche's mental illness took irrevocable hold of him after he witnessed a horse being whipped in Turin, Italy. As the story goes, Nietzsche rushed outside, threw his arms around the horse, wept and cried, "I understand you!", and dropped to his knees, never to fully recover.[30] He was forty-four years old. Wallace's death was also precipitated by mental illness,[31] which culminated in his suicide on September 12, 2008, in Claremont, California. Dreyfus and Kelly remind us that "he was forty-six years old."[32]

Both men were "once in a generation" figures, but both died early, tragically, from the consequences of mental illness. Nietzsche and Wallace both left large bodies of in-process work—notes, manuscripts, comments written on scraps of paper—which family members would attempt to assemble into some coherent whole. Nietzsche's unfinished work became *The Will to Power* and Wallace's *The Pale King*,[33] both of which are major accomplishments but neither was authorized or released by its author. Nietzsche is, perhaps, the most literary of the philosophical figures and Wallace, perhaps, the most philosophical of the literary figures.[34] Whereas Nietzsche was raised religious and left the faith in adulthood, Wallace was raised by atheists and, if the essays in this volume are correct, sought faith later in life. But both Nietzsche and Wallace are defined in relation to the same historical era; they stand at opposite ends of postmodernity: Nietzsche, the proto-postmodern thinker, and Wallace, the post-postmodern advocate of a "new sincerity."[35]

The "death of God" and its fallout

Dreyfus and Kelly present Nietzsche's view of nihilism just before their chapter on Wallace, so some background on Nietzsche's philosophy will help set the stage for how Wallace addressed similar concerns in a different and *better* way.

Nietzsche is the author of a number of now-famous aphorisms (e.g., "What does not kill me makes me stronger"[36]). One of these memorable lines—"God is dead"—is introduced by a fictional figure Nietzsche calls "*The madman.*"[37] Nietzsche's madman cried "I seek God!" in front of a crowd of atheists laughing at him. He elaborates on what happened to God: "*We have killed him—you and I. All of us are his murderers.*" Nietzsche introduces the death of God not to claim that there used to exist an infinite being who is now dead, but rather to illustrate how the idea of God will increasingly struggle to exert moral influence in the future. For Nietzsche, much that is wrong with the world is due to the Christian faith. Nietzsche concedes that Christianity provided a source of moral and social stability for centuries,[38] but he foresees a time when confidence in Christianity's message erodes. The effect will be staggering, Nietzsche warns, when all previously held values simply collapse. It is a seismic event comparable to untethering the earth "from its sun."[39] In short, the Christian faith will cease to convict hearts and minds. In response, humanity will plunge "continually ... Backward, sideward, forward, in all directions." We may ask "Is there still any up or down?" as we stray "through an infinite nothing."[40]

One reason Christianity will lose its power is that its morality is based on insecure foundations. The way Christianity understands "right" and "wrong" is wrongheaded, according to Nietzsche. He presents this as a distinction between "noble" morality and "slave" morality, the former of which is good because it is self-assertive, confident, and strong; the latter of which is bad because it is vulgar, unsatisfied, reactionary and weak. Rather than embracing those parts of humanity that are strong, rather than embracing the ego and trying to expand its power in the world, Nietzsche says Christianity values weakness: qualities such as meekness, self-sacrifice, and poverty become virtues while acting on natural inclinations becomes evil. This is not life-affirming, for it creates a strong sense of guilt and a "bad conscience." One comes to resent oneself in the face of the ultimate noble/master, God. Sin results in punishment, not only in this life but the next. One of Nietzsche's central goals throughout his career was to expose "the shabby origin of these values."[41]

Paradoxically, the Christian tradition is presented to adherents as a quest for truth, but it is in actuality a will to untruth. That is to say, in Nietzsche's view, Christian dogma cannot withstand close scrutiny or lived reality. Schacht has argued that this is not primarily an epistemological claim but rather a practical one: "What is ultimately decisive for Nietzsche in his assessment of forms of religion is not their truth-value or epistemic plausibility as belief-systems, but rather their impact upon the quality of the lives of those whose lives they do or might touch and affect."[42] Or, as Nietzsche expressed in *The Will to Power*, the advent of nihilism is "The end of Christianity—at the hands of its own morality (which cannot be replaced), which turns against the Christian God. The sense of truthfulness, developed highly by Christianity, is nauseated by the falseness and mendaciousness of all Christian interpretations of the world and of history."[43]

The recognition that dogmatic Christian ideas are unpersuasive and unlivable is but one stage in Europe's transition to *nihilism*, where humanity simply gives up. In *The Will to Power*, Nietzsche says, "nihilism comes into being" when humanity has "disbelief in any metaphysical world and forbids itself any belief in a *true* world."[44] Although Nietzsche was not the first thinker to deal with nihilism,[45] his understanding of it in *The Will to Power* is unique. "What does nihilism mean? *That the highest values devalue themselves.* The aim is lacking; 'why?' finds no answer."[46] Eventually, people will see the meaninglessness of their long-wasted search, recognize that they cannot recover or regain their composure, and come to resent themselves.[47] Nietzsche's brand of nihilism should not be seen as a reversal of Christianity *per se*, as Simon Critchley has noted, "but its *consequence*."[48]

Contrary to Dreyfus and Kelly's reading of Nietzsche, the death of God is cause for grave concern for Nietzsche, as it will inevitably leave a vacuum which gives birth to dread.[49] Nihilism is that stage in which everything lacks meaning, and a nihilist is he who "judges of the world as it is that it ought *not* to be, and of the world as it ought to be that *it does not exist*. According to this view, our existence (action, suffering, willing, freedom) has no meaning: the pathos of 'in vain' is the nihilists' pathos."[50] The nihilist does not accept reality.

The type of man who will recognize the futility of his efforts is "the most contemptible," whom Nietzsche's *Zarathustra* refers to as "the last man,"[51] who represents the worst of humanity, a "poor and domesticated" person who, ever blinking in the face of his own worthlessness, "is no longer able to despise himself."[52] Craving the warmth of relationships, hopelessly codependent on others, exerting himself only minimally if at all, the last man is a full member of the herd.

Dreyfus and Kelly are not only unfair to Wallace; they are also unfair to Nietzsche, who attempts to present a way out of the problem of nihilism in *Thus Spoke Zarathustra*. The solution to nihilism is seen in the figure of the Übermensch, or "overman," who illuminates the way forward like lightening against dark skies by redefining what it means to be human. Once older values have ceased to persuade, Zarathustra says the overman will create *new* values. Only a revolutionary figure will be able to create new values, a god-like figure, as he mentioned earlier in *The Gay Science*: "Must we not become gods simply to appear worthy" of atonement for killing God?[53] The first step on this journey—like the first step in Wallace's recovery program—is to convince people of the problem. "I beseech you," Zarathustra says, "remain faithful to the earth, and do not believe those who speak to you of otherworldly hopes!"[54] Humanity improves, evolves, when it abandons the illusion that God exists, and this recognition alone will benefit future generations. The answer to nihilism, says Nietzsche, is this: "*I teach you the overman.* Man is something that shall be overcome ... The overman is the meaning of the earth. Let your will say: the overman *shall be* the meaning of the earth!"[55] Zarathustra's "overman" is the "man of the future" about whom Nietzsche speaks in subsequent work.[56] "This man of the future," writes Nietzsche,

> will redeem us not only from the hitherto reigning ideal but also from that which was bound to grow out of it, the great nausea, the will to nothingness, nihilism; this bell-stroke of noon and of the great decision

that liberates the will again and restores its goal to the earth and his hope to man; this victor over God and nothingness—*he must come one day*.[57]

The broader moral and metaphysical import of the death of God, the last man, and the Übermensch relates to Nietzsche's all-encompassing doctrine of the *will to power*.[58] For Nietzsche, reality is governed by this one immutable law, a "tablet of good [which] hangs over every people," according to which all beings strive to increase their power. Nietzsche sums up the whole of the teaching this way: *"This world is the will to power—and nothing besides! And you yourself are also this will to power—and nothing besides."*[59] Rather than being an occasion to negotiate with or suppress natural inclinations of the "self," as he finds in Christianity and Kant's *Prolegomenon*, Nietzsche advocates for the full embrace of the self's goals, projects, and ambitions. This is the meaning of humanity, *full* humanity, as he puts into the mouth of Zarathustra: "Whatever makes them *rule* and *triumph* and *shine*, to the awe and envy of their neighbors, this is to them the high, the first, the measure, the meaning of all things."[60] This is also why, although Nietzsche recognizes asceticism as a means of preserving one's existence,[61] he faults it for being self-defeating and psychologically destructive. Asceticism does not accept reality and instead is weak-willed. As noted by R. Lanier Anderson, the ascetic ideal is a tool "for self-medication"[62] (a major theme occurring in Wallace as well). So strong is the drive to exert power that humanity "would rather will *nothingness* than *not* will."[63] Only the Übermensch will exercise his will to power in exemplary ways.

In sum, Nietzsche seeks to overcome the nihilism that threatens to unhinge European society by calling into question their most cherished beliefs about the value of Christian morality. On the road to overcoming nihilism, Nietzsche passed through the death of God, the last man, and finally found a solution in the figure of the Übermensch, whose creation of new values demonstrates the will to power.

Toxic freneticism and its fallout

The problems faced by Wallace are eerily similar to those faced by Nietzsche, but their responses to it are very different. There are, I would suggest, five "stages" in Wallace's struggle with nihilism: loneliness/angst, self-medication, recovery, boredom, and finally, endurance.

First, as Wallace discusses the audience he imagined for *Infinite Jest*, he tells David Lipsky in 1996 that the book was "about loneliness."[64] Literature, Wallace thinks, can mirror a person's inner life back at them, and in the process, make them feel less alone. There is "the relief of knowing that I wasn't the only one … who felt this way, [who] worried that perhaps the reverse of paranoia was true: that nothing was connected to anything else."[65] Like Nietzsche, Wallace does not address the problem conventionally but rather creatively. Unlike traditional philosophers, "I don't have a system of prescriptions," he tells Lipsky; "I don't have [a list of] four things that I think are wrong."[66] But something is wrong, Wallace thinks, and one question keeps begging him for an answer: "Why are we—and by 'we' I mean people like you and me: mostly white, upper middle class or upper class, obscenely well educated, doing really interesting jobs, sitting in really expensive chairs ... watching the most sophisticated electronic equipment money can buy—why do we feel empty and unhappy?"[67] There is a disconnect between the expectations one has of life and the feelings one receives when one achieves the goals one set for oneself. In light of the inconsistency in our achievements and the emotional payoff, Wallace takes stock of the cultural context and how that context informs his authorial choices: "Reality is fractured right now, at least the reality that I live in ... "[68] The results of a relentless drive for pleasure and achievement mask "sort of a sadness for people" when they realize there is "a kind of emptiness at the heart of what they thought was going on."[69] This places Wallace squarely in the realm of the existentialists, and the problem one of debilitating existential angst.[70] "Where am I? I feel very far away," Wallace writes to himself in the margins of an early draft of one of his stories.[71]

If the first stage is existential angst, the second attempts to self-medicate pain in any way possible. Fans of Wallace know that the three plot lines of *Infinite Jest* are full of characters who attempt to minimize their suffering through self-medication. In one plot line, people lose themselves in the seductive power of entertainment, illustrated by the film from which the book gets its name: "Infinite Jest" is the title of a movie so compelling that viewers—a medical attaché, hotel staff that checks on the attaché, and anyone else who enters the attaché's room—are enthralled, transfixed, and unable to stop watching. So enticing is the film that it becomes weaponized and used as a tool of terrorism, and the victims of it, not unlike Nietzsche's "last man,"[72] are complacent and immovable, even to the point of death. Rather than feel the angst, many prefer to entertain themselves to death.[73] In another plot line—the competitive world of junior tennis—students like Hal Incandenza frenetically compete against one another to the point of viewing winning as an end in itself; an isolated Hal medicates himself by getting high in the basement of the school while another student kills himself (*IJ* 430–3). The third plotline takes place at the Ennet House Drug and Alcohol Recovery House, where residents share vile and abhorrent stories about the lengths to which they would go to self-medicate, remain in Denial, and feed their addiction. A pregnant woman, for example, refuses to stop her cocaine habit and, after her baby was stillborn, she carries it around with her for a long time, making those in proximity to her wince at the stench (*IJ* 376–8).

If angst is the problem, self-medication is the initial solution. Echoing Nietzsche's comments about the value of willing nothingness rather than not willing, Marathe describes the bondage: when one can exercise one's will but has no reason to do so or no higher, unchanging set of values in line with which to choose, those are "the chains of not choosing" (*IJ* 780–1). And for people struggling to cope, trying to find meaning in a world bombarded by this sort of frenetic activity, Wallace hoped "that parts of [*Infinite Jest*] will speak to their nerve endings a little bit."[74]

Wallace could write about these stories with great passion and perspicacity because his own life attests to the futility of self-medication in response to existential angst. When Wallace entered Harvard's graduate program in philosophy, he felt that he was too old for graduate school. Although his fiction was published at a young age and he entered a world-renowned graduate program at Harvard, neither could fill the void,[75] and his alcohol and drug use increased: "That felt really bad, and I didn't want to feel it … I really sort of felt like my life was over at twenty-seven or twenty-eight."[76] When he did not use alcohol or drugs, Wallace self-medicated in other ways: "I would f*ck strangers … [or] I'd run ten miles every morning. You know, that kind of desperate, like very American, 'I will fix this somehow, by taking radical action.'"[77]

Lurking behind the efforts to self-medicate was a deep and insatiable need to find meaning in the world as a ballast against self-doubt. "If I could just achieve X and Y and Z, everything would be okay," Wallace confesses, but achieving one's goals was ultimately unsatisfying. He tells Lipsky, "It's worse than any kind of physical injury … it may be what in the old days was called a spiritual crisis or whatever. It's just feeling as though … every axiom of your life turned out to be false, and there was actually nothing, and you were nothing."[78] Wallace and many of his characters fight the same dilemma as Nietzsche's "last man," the debilitating and "constant gnawing sense of having had and lost some infinite thing" (*TIW* 123). In Wallace's copy of Anthony DeMello's book, *Awareness*, at the Harry Ransom Center, he emphasized this passage in which DeMello says, "you'll have to deal with the big villain, and that villain is self-condemnation, self-hatred, self-dissatisfaction."[79]

In a third stage, the early Wallace found a solution to the freneticism that masks existential angst in recovery from drugs and alcohol.[80] The solution is paradoxical, according to Wallace: surrender to a Higher Power, even if one doubts that the Higher Power exists. Wallace was a longtime member of Alcoholics Anonymous, whose step 2 reads: "Came to believe that a Power greater than ourselves could restore us to sanity."[81] In step 3 he submitted his will to this Power. Wallace's characters in *Infinite Jest* similarly wrestle with submission of their will, especially to God. For example, Gately feels strange praying as an agnostic,[82] but he was told by older members of his fellowship that "all that mattered was what he *did*. If he did the right things, and kept doing them for long enough, what Gately thought and believed would magically change." Strangely enough, Gately and Wallace found that it worked; "the Desire and Compulsion had been Removed" (*IJ* 466–7). Neither Wallace nor Gately understood *how* it worked, only that it worked. By handing their wills over to the care of God as they understood God, as well as submitting to the wisdom and experiences of seasoned veterans (i.e., the "Crocodiles") in "the Program," Wallace and Gately were now capable of long lengths of sobriety. They no longer needed to self-medicate their existential angst through substance abuse.

In response to extreme loneliness (stage 1), the initial solution of self-medication proved deadly (stage 2) and the solution was the surrender of the will to a higher power (stage 3); however, after surrendering the will to a higher power, one still needs to deal with the underlying existential angst that the substance abuse was intended to medicate. A fourth stage, then, becomes apparent in Wallace's work, in which one must live within the full weight of the negative emotions in their totality (stage 4). For Wallace, as for the characters in his last unfinished novel, *The Pale King*, this new problem is "crushing, crushing boredom" (*PK* 546). In a particularly boring section about a boring profession (IRS auditors), Wallace presents a number of boring characters doing the most boring activity one can imagine: "Chris Fogle turns a page. Howard Cardwell turns a page. Ken Wax turns a page. Matt Redgate turns a page … Ann Williams turns a page. Anand Singh turns two pages at once by mistake and turns one back which makes a slightly different sound. David Cusk turns a page. Sandra Pounder turns a page …" (*PK* 310). The page turning continues for several pages. This mirrors the boredom Wallace dealt with in his own life. As he scribbled a working thesis of the novel in one of his notebooks, he says,

> Maybe dullness is associated with psychic pain because something that's dull or opaque fails to provide enough stimulation to distract people from some other, deeper type of pain that is always there, if only in an ambient low-level way, and which most of us spend nearly all our time and energy trying to distract ourselves from feeling, or at least from feeling directly or with our full attention.[83]

Wallace's frustration in the writing itself was palpable: "I've brooded and brooded about all this till my brooder is sore," he told Jonathan Franzen.[84] Wallace's stated goal for the novel was to "show people a way to insulate themselves from the toxic freneticism of American life," but the insulation was difficult to both live (for Wallace) or dramatize (for his characters).

A solution to these deeper issues is found, however, in Wallace's work if not his life. The fifth and final stage on the way to release is to endure, abide,[85] hold on, remain "in it" until it passes. Maturity means getting "above" these negative emotions. In one of Wallace's books housed in the Harry Ransom Center, Wallace underlines this passage: "As we become older we should develop a perspective that allows us not to be quite so engulfed by the passing fluctuations of fortune."[86] Some of Wallace's characters were able to make this a reality. In *The Pale King*, Drinion "is happy" because he has the "ability to pay attention" (*PK* 546) to the minutia and tedium of life. Wallace recognizes the payoff of abiding:

> It turns out that bliss—a second-by-second joy and gratitude at the gift of being alive, conscious—lies on the other side of crushing, crushing boredom … A boredom like you've never known will wash over you and just about kill you. Ride these out, and it's like stepping from black and white into color. Like water after days in the desert. Constant bliss in every atom. (*PK* 546)

Similarly, another character in *The Pale King*, Chris Fogle, overcomes his nihilistic boredom. The Fogle story is discussed in other chapters of this book, so here I will not burden the reader by recounting the story. Suffice it to say, the later Wallace of *The Pale King*, like the early Wallace of *Infinite Jest*, believed that self-medication is no answer to the problem of existential angst, but whereas the early Wallace highlighted turning one's will over to the care of God to calm the unrest in one's soul, the later Wallace adds to that relationship with a higher power the importance of mindfulness, paying attention, and being *present*. Wallace observed that just as the word "boring" connotes both a state of mind and a verb describing the impact of the state of mind on the mind itself, so too does "present" have several meanings, one of which is a state of mind and the other of which is the result of that state of mind (a gift).[87] Embracing monotony, looking to the structure provided by the past and those whose lives have given them wisdom (whether they be "Crocodiles" or Jesuit Priests), these are the solutions to nihilism, according to Wallace.

The broader message of Wallace's encounters with nihilism are in sharp disagreement with Nietzsche's. Whereas Nietzsche encouraged a full embrace of the ego, which would separate an individual from the herd, Wallace advocated a renunciation of the ego and submission to something larger than oneself. In a sense, this puts Wallace's response to nihilism among the post-Kantian but pre-Nietzschean philosophers. "If the highest upon which I can reflect, what I can contemplate, is my empty and pure, naked and mere ego," said Jacobi to Fichte, "with its autonomy and freedom: then rational self-contemplation, then rationality is for me a curse—I deplore my existence."[88] For Wallace, defining himself against the era Nietzsche helped instantiate, the way to overcome nihilism is to be sincere, to return to a culture of honor and honesty, structure and stability, provided by historical institutions, viz., to look to the *past*:

> The old postmodern insurgents risked the gasp and squeal: shock, disgust, outrage, censorship, accusations of socialism, anarchism, *nihilism*. Today's risks are different. The new rebels might be artists willing to risk the yawn, the rolled eyes, the cool smile, the nudged ribs, the parody of gifted ironists, the "Oh how banal" ... The next real literary "rebels" in this country might well emerge as some weird bunch of anti-rebels, born oglers who dare somehow to back away from ironic watching, who have the childish gall actually to endorse and instantiate single-entendre principles. (*SFT* 81)

That Wallace looked to the past for wisdom and sought to bring its insights to the present is not mere speculation. He is quite clear that this was his way of responding to contemporary problems, the "American disease." In 2006, when interviewed in Capri, Italy at La Conversazioni, Wallace says: "Many of the writers that I admire – I don't know whether I'm one of them – are interested in using postmodern techniques, the postmodern aesthetic, but... using that to discuss or represent very old, traditional human verities that have to do with spirituality and emotion and community and ideas that the avant garde would consider very old fashioned... It's using postmodern formal techniques for very traditional ends... If there's a group... that's the group I want to belong to."

Contrasting higher powers and human nature

Nietzsche tried to eradicate the notion of a transcendent, objective reality so that we would be able to embrace that which we truly are and *create* the values that will sustain us. Nietzsche sees his efforts as life affirming. Belief in God as an ultimate objective force has been "perhaps the greatest danger that has yet confronted humanity"[89] because it caused humans to stagnate, to give up their will, to abandon the evolutionary drive. Only the strong—the *overman*—would be able to take upon himself the chaos of the world and the contradictions in his nature to forge his own destiny and values. The Übermensch is Nietzsche's assertive, atheistic higher power.

For Wallace, however, the major problem confronting humanity is not sacrificing one's will, but rather asserting it. The problem is self-centeredness.[90] He told the Kenyon students to disbelieve what their "default setting" would tell them, that "I am the *absolute center* of the universe; the realist, most vivid and important person in existence" (*TIW* 36, emphasis added). The great value of education, Wallace suggests, is that it can enable us to overcome this self-centeredness, to look differently at situations and people to consider the possibility that a deeper reality is at work, a "sub-surface unity" or "mystical union of all things deep down."

Wallace's understanding of the problem confronting humanity is similar to Nietzsche's: both struggle to overcome existential angst brought about by spiritual crises. But whereas Nietzsche sees self-sacrifice as a sign of moral weakness, Wallace sees self-assertion as a sign of mental weakness, an inability to discipline one's mind to consider other options. Moreover, Wallace's answer to the problem of nihilism is decidedly different from Nietzsche's. Whereas Nietzsche suggests that people embrace their individual will to power, Wallace suggests that we should subsume selfish tendencies into a larger vision of life, a grander, more life-giving goal of a "compassionate life." One of Wallace's handwritten notes addresses this well: "We tried to bombard our problems with willpower instead of bringing it into alignment with God's intention for us."[91]

Not only do Wallace and Nietzsche disagree about the solution to the human predicament, but they also disagree on how to measure the quality of one's life. Here, Nietzsche's doctrine of *eternal recurrence* is relevant, according to which a person is presented with the possibility that s/he will have to redo, relive, and re-experience every event in his/her life, exactly as it happened before for all eternity. "There will be nothing new in it," Nietzsche writes in *The Gay Science*, "but every pain and every joy and every thought and sigh and everything unutterably small or great in your life will have to return to you, all in the same succession and sequence."[92] On one interpretation,[93] eternal recurrence is a "thought experiment" of sorts, which would help assess the quality of one's life by asking whether one would repeat the same life *ad infinitum*, in which case it would be a positive thing: "My eternal lot wants it,"[94] says Zarathustra. Eternal recurrence, of course, ties into Nietzsche's doctrine of *amor fati*, the love of fate. If people can love their lot in life, their lives have meaning.

Wallace, too, deals with a sort of eternal recurrence, but he presents it as a negative, not a positive tool. In his short story, "Good Old Neon," Wallace's main character is Neal, a self-centered yet self-aware narrator who is intent on killing himself. It is Neal's experience of the afterlife that helps us see how Wallace might have viewed Nietzschean eternal recurrence as a tool for self-evaluation. In the afterlife, Neal says, time moves in unexpected ways, cyclical ways: "the fact is that this whole seemingly endless back-and-forth between us has come and gone and come again … " (O 180). Whereas Wallace at first appears to affirm Nietzschean eternal recurrence, Neal's story does not have a happy ending. Neal's story is a lesson in "what not to do," because he follows through on his promise to kill himself by swallowing pills and slamming his car into a bridge. The importance of "Good Old Neon" is what happens in the last two pages: a "David Wallace" character emerges, and tells the voices in his head, of which Neal was the manifestation, to cease, "commanding that other part to be silent as if looking it levelly in the eye and saying, almost aloud, 'Not another word'" (O 181). Wallace tells his reader that viewing reality as cyclical has detrimental consequences, among them the danger of putting off living the kind of life one should be living. For Wallace, eternal recurrence is not a helpful tool of self-reflection and should not be used to assess whether one's life has meaning. In almost existentialist vocabulary, Wallace says to the Kenyon students, "The only thing that's capital-T True is that you get to decide how you're going to see [reality]. This, I submit, is the freedom of a real education, of learning how to be well-adjusted. You get to consciously decide what has meaning and what does not. You get to decide what to worship" (*TIW* 95–101).

Another difference between Nietzsche and Wallace is that for Wallace, deciding what to worship is not tantamount to saying that there is no objective reality or that we have no reason to accept one worldview over another, contrary to Dreyfus and Kelly's *All Things Shining*. In Wallace's view, some worldviews are better than others and some things are more deserving of worship than others, as Miller shows in his book. "Everybody worships," says Wallace, and we get to choose "what to worship" (TIW 100-1). But the value of an objective object of one's worship, i.e., any "*Power greater than ourselves*,"[95] is that "pretty much anything else you worship will eat you alive" (TIW 102). Worshipping one's beauty and sexual allure leaves a person feeling ugly; worshipping one's intellect leaves a person feeling dumb; worshipping one's money leaves a person feeling poor. Wallace digs deep into narrative history to make his point, for "it's been codified as myths, proverbs, clichés, epigrams, parables; the skeleton of every great story." But the "whole trick is keeping the *truth* up front in daily consciousness" (*TIW* 107, 108). The point, for Wallace, is that nihilism is only made worse when one focuses on satisfying one's ego.

On this much Nietzsche and Wallace agree: there is a pragmatic element in living a good life. For Nietzsche, we should adopt the belief system that allows us to exercise power and dominance. "Although questions of knowledge were always secondary in his mind," writes Robert Solomon, Nietzsche's "considerations were aimed at answering the practical question *how to live a life well*. Thus one would not go far wrong in calling Nietzsche a *pragmatist* and linking his thought with that of the American philosopher William James (his near contemporary)."[96] For Wallace, who held William James in high esteem, the real value of religion, like philosophy according to a pragmatist, is "that it satisfies some fundamental need of the philosopher."[97] One does not align oneself with God in order to secure some eternal reward, but rather for the benefits it offers in the here and now. So, whereas they have similarly pragmatic moral philosophies, Nietzsche and Wallace disagree about the value of tethering oneself to an unchanging set of values. For Nietzsche, this sort of sacrifice is indicative of a dedication to objectivity we need to overcome, but for Wallace, this sort of connection is vital to living a good life in a world immersed in selfishness.

Conclusion

In the hermeneutical disagreement between Dreyfus/Kelly and Miller mentioned at the start of this chapter, I concur with Miller that Wallace was *not* a Nietzschean nihilist. To bolster Miller's argument, I have put Wallace into conversation with Nietzsche and looked at core Nietzschean doctrines. Whereas Nietzsche strives to exercise power individually, Wallace strives to live a compassionate life. Whereas Nietzsche strives to impress readers or leave them in the dark about his true intentions, limiting interpretation from unworthy readers, Wallace said the writer's job is to give "CPR to those elements of what's human and magical that still live and glow despite the times' darkness ... Fiction's about what it is to be a f**king human being,"[98] and good fiction helps readers "become less alone inside."[99]

In a manner befitting Nietzsche and Wallace, I close with a quote apropos to both. In *The Twilight of the Idols*, Nietzsche's last work published before his mental illness rendered him unaware of what was happening around him, he discusses ending life on one's own terms. Wallace's biographer says that his suicide "was not an ending anyone would have wanted for him, but it was the one he had chosen."[100] Perhaps in the final months of Wallace's life—struggling to finish his last novel, having trouble doing that which gave him significance and set him apart from the herd—his thoughts resonated with Nietzsche's:

> Dying proudly when it is no longer feasible to live proudly. Death chosen freely, death at the right time ... this makes it possible to have a real leave-taking where the leave-taker is still there, and a real assessment of everything that has been achieved or willed, a summation of life ... You are never destroyed by anyone except yourself. This is just a death under the most despicable conditions, an unfree death, a death at the wrong time, a coward's death. Out of love for life, you should want death to be different, free, conscious, without chance, without surprises ... Finally, a piece of advice for our dear friends the pessimists, and other decadents as well. We cannot help having been born: but we can make up for this mistake (because sometimes it is a mistake). When you do away with yourself you are doing the most admirable thing there is: it almost makes you deserve to live ...[101]

Notes

1. Adam Miller, *The Gospel According to David Foster Wallace: Boredom and Addiction in an Age of Distraction* (New York: Bloomsbury Academic, 2016).
2. Hubert Dreyfus and Sean Dorrance Kelly, *All Things Shining: Reading the Western Classics to Find Meaning in a Secular Age* (New York: Free Press, 2011), Ch. 2: "David Foster Wallace's Nihilism." See also Sean D. Kelley,

"Navigating Past Nihilism," *The New York Times* (December 5, 2010) for a discussion of Nietzsche's nihilism, and an interview with Kelly by Jeff Wise, "What Is Nihilism, Anyway? A Chat with Sean D. Kelly, Co-Author of All Things Shining," *Huffington Post* (January 14, 2011; updated May 25, 2011).

3. The Nietzsche texts used in this chapter include the following, and they are most often cited using section numbers rather than page numbers (unless otherwise noted): Friedrich Nietzsche, *The Gay Science, With a Prelude in Rhymes and an Appendix of Songs*, trans. W. Kaufmann (New York: Vintage Books); Friedrich Nietzsche, *Twilight of the Idols in The Anti-Christ, Ecce Homo, Twilight of the Idols, and Other Writings*, ed. A. Ridley, trans. J. Norman (Cambridge: Cambridge University Press, 2005); Friedrich Nietzsche, *Ecce Homo: How to Become What You Are*, trans. D. Large (Oxford: Oxford University Press, 2007). Friedrich Nietzsche, *The Genealogy of Morality*, ed. K. Ansell-Pearson, trans. C. Diethe (Cambridge: Cambridge University Press, 2006); Friedrich Nietzsche, *Thus Spoke Zarathustra: A Book for All and None*, trans. W. Kaufmann (New York: Penguin Press, 1966); Friedrich Nietzsche, *Daybreak: Thoughts on the Prejudices of Morality*, ed. M. Clark and B. Leiter, trans. R.J. Hollingdale (Cambridge: Cambridge University Press, 1997); and Friedrich Nietzsche, *Basic Writings of Nietzsche*, which includes *The Birth of Tragedy, Beyond Good and Evil, On the Genealogy of Morals, The Case of Wagner*, and *Ecce Homo* (trans. and ed. W. Kaufman (New York: The Modern Library, 1992).

4. Dreyfus and Kelly, *All Things Shining*, 21; "The idea that there is no reason to prefer any answer to any other … is called nihilism, and Nietzsche thought this the better description of our current condition after the death of God."

5. Dreyfus and Kelly, *All Things Shining*, 21.

6. Ibid., 57.

7. Nietzsche scholarship on nihilism is widespread, so here I only mention recent attempts to discuss Wallace and nihilism: See, e.g., Joseph F. Goeke, "'Everyone Knows It's About Something Else, Way Down': Boredom, Nihilism, and the Search for Meaning in David Foster Wallace's The Pale King," *Critique: Studies in Contemporary Fiction* 38, no. 3 (2017): 193–213; Thomas Meaney, "David Foster Wallace on Planet Trillaphon," *TLS* (March 13, 2013); Cynthia Haven, "David Foster Wallace: 'Dostoevsky wasn't just a genius—he was, finally, brave'," *The Book Haven* (Stanford University, April 1, 2013); Edwin Turner, "Is American Psycho Profound, Artistic Nihilism, or Stupid, Shallow Nihilism—Bret Easton vs. David Foster Wallace," *Bibliokept* (June 14, 2011); and James K.A. Smith, "David Foster Wallace to the Rescue: The Acclaimed Novelist's Postmodern Conservativism," *First Things* (March 2013).

8. Richard Schacht, *Alienation* (London: George Allen and Unwin, Ltd, 1971).

9. Not only in Schacht's *Alienation*, but also in a host of other books that were in Wallace's library now housed at the Ransom Center, Wallace underlined, starred, highlighted, or commented on Nietzsche's ideas. For example, in Joseph Campbell's *Myths to Live By: How We Re-Create Ancient Legends in Our Daily Lives to Release Human Potential* (New York: Random House, 1984), Wallace underlines portions dealing with Nietzsche's doctrine of *amor fati*, or

love of fate (p. 125). In his copy of Leo Tolstoy's essay, *What Is Art?* Wallace writes notes a passage in which Tolstoy differentiates true religious believers from those whose privileged backgrounds made faith difficult (p. 59). Wallace's written response in the margins of Tolstoy's book is to connect these comments to his own experience with nihilism, writing, "1980's upper-class Nihilism. Nietszchan [sic] inversion in face of inability to worship—worship evil."

10 Schacht, *Alienation*, xlv, 161.
11 Ibid., xlvii.
12 Other than Dreyfus/Kelly and Miller, another recent example is found in Josh Roiland, "Getting Away from It All: The Literary Journalism of David Foster Wallace and Nietzsche's Concept of Oblivion," in *The Legacy of David Foster Wallace*, ed. S. Cohen and L. Konstantinou (Iowa City, Iowa: University of Iowa Press, 2012), 25–52. Roiland explores connections between the two. However, Roiland's essay concentrates less on the extent to which Wallace's *fiction* work relates to Nietzsche's work and more on Wallace's *nonfiction*.
13 Nietzsche, *Beyond Good and Evil*, 42.
14 Nietzsche, *Gay Science*, 343.
15 Nietzsche, *Ecce Homo*, "Forward," section 1.
16 Nietzsche, *Ecce Homo*, "Why I Am a Destiny," section 1.
17 In "Nietzsche *ad hominem*: Perspectivism, personality, and *resentiment*," Robert Solomon argues that "There is quite a difference between the ironic genius portrayed (in the first person) in *Ecce Homo* and the Nietzsche whom his sometime companion Lou Salomé described as 'quiet, pensive, refined and lonesome.' On the one hand there are all of those volumes celebrating Homeric warrior virtues and the love of life, and on the other there is poor Nietzsche, lying lonely and sleepless, thinking about suicide as a way to get through the difficult night. There are all of those pages unmasking ressentiment in some of the greatest minds in Western thought, but they are self-evidently animated by the same unmistakable resentfulness and envy in their unloved and unappreciated author. Indeed, even so enthusiastic a defender of Nietzsche as Alexander Nehamas feels compelled to contrast the author's writings to the 'miserable little man' who wrote them. To be sure, Nietzsche hardly displayed in himself the virtues he makes us envision." See *The Cambridge Companion to Nietzsche* (Cambridge: Cambridge University Press, 1996), ch. 6.
18 Nietzsche, *Daybreak*, section 381: "The gentlest and most reasonable of men can, if he wears a large moustache, sit as it were in its shade and feel safe there—he will usually be seen as no more than the *appurtenance* of a large moustache, that is to say a military type, easily angered and occasionally violent—and as such he will be treated." Cf. Kathleen Marie Higgins, "Double Consciousness and Second Sight," in *Critical Affinities: Nietzsche and African American Thought*, ed. J. Scott and A.T. Franklin (Albany, NY: State University of New York Press, 2006), 59.
19 David Lipsky, *Although, Of Course, You End Up Becoming Yourself: A Road Trip with David Foster Wallace* (New York: Broadway, 2010), 296. Says Wallace: "I know it's a security blanket for me—whenever I'm nervous. Or

whenever I feel like I have to be prepared, or keep myself together, I tend to wear it … It's more just a foible, it's the recognition of a weakness, which is that I'm just kind of worried my head's gonna explode."

20　Max, *Every Love Story Is a Ghost Story: A Life of David Foster Wallace* (New York: Viking Penguin, 2012), 12. Wallace covered his panic/sweating attacks by walking "around school with his tennis racket and a towel" telling people he "was sweating because he was just off the court."

21　Max, *Every Love Story*, 60.

22　James Wood, cribbing a title from Nietzsche, explains in "Human, All Too Inhuman: On the Formation of a New Genre: Hysterical Realism," *The New Republic*, July 24, 2000. Available online: https://newrepublic.com/article/61361/human-inhuman.

23　Bernd Magnus, Stanley Stewart, and Jean-Pierre Mileur, *Nietzsche's Case: Philosophy as/and Literature* (New York: Routledge, 1993), 21.

24　Much more can be and has been said about the ways in which Nietzsche's and Wallace's styles are tethered to their thought; for our purposes in this chapter, stylistic similarities are less relevant than the *content* of their work. For an elaboration on ways in which Nietzsche uses hyperbolic language, see Alexander Nehamas, *Nietzsche: Life as Literature* (Cambridge, MA: Harvard University Press, 1985). For an elaboration on the other stylistic conventions of Nietzsche mentioned here, see Magnus et al., *Nietzsche's Case*, many of which he shares with Wallace. As Nietzsche himself notes in *Ecce Homo* III/4: "I have many stylistic possibilities—the most multifarious art of style that has ever been at the disposal of one man."

25　Nietzsche, *Ecce Homo*, 4.

26　See Ibid., 68–9.

27　See, e.g., Wallace's interview with Charlie Rose, in which Wallace says, "I was a philosophy major in college, but my areas of interest were mathematical logic and semantics … The stuff that I was doing was really more math than it was philosophy." Interview can be found here: https://youtu.be/mLPStHVi0SI.

28　Max, *Every Love Story*, 132–4.

29　Ibid., 193.

30　Robert Wicks, "Nietzsche's Life and Works," *The Stanford Encyclopedia of Philosophy* (Spring 2017 edition; E.N. Zalta, ed.). Available online: http://plato.stanford.edu/archives/spr2017/entries/nietzsche-life-works. Wicks gives the story: "On the morning of January 3, 1889, while in Turin, Nietzsche experienced a mental breakdown which left him an invalid for the rest of his life … Nietzsche, upon witnessing a horse being whipped by a coachman at the Piazza Carlo Alberto—although this episode with the horse could be anecdotal—threw his arms around the horse's neck and collapsed in the plaza, never to return to full sanity."

31　The details of which can be found in D.T. Max, *Every Love Story*, 297–301.

32　Dreyfus and Kelly, *All Things Shining*, 22.

33　Though not in the same sense; *Will to Power* is a collection of notes on many things.

34 David Evans calls Wallace "an intensely philosophical fiction writer" in his chapter "'The Chains of Not Choosing:' Free Will and Faith in William James and David Foster Wallace," in *A Companion to David Foster Wallace Studies*, ed. M. Boswell and S. Burn (New York: Palgrave Macmillan, 2013), 172.

35 Adam Kelly, "David Foster Wallace and the New Sincerity in American Fiction," in *Consider David Foster Wallace: Critical Essays*, ed. D. Hering (Austin, Texas: SSMG Press, 2010), 131–46.

36 Nietzsche, *Twilight*, 157. Cf. Nietzsche, *Ecce Homo*, 8–9.

37 Nietzsche, *Gay Science*, section 125. The quotes from this chapter come from this section.

38 Nietzsche, *Will to Power*, I/4: Christianity "prevented man from despising himself as man, from taking sides against life; from despairing of knowledge; it was a *means of preservation*."

39 Nietzsche, *Gay Science*, section 125.

40 Ibid., section 125.

41 Nietzsche, *Will to Power*, I/7.

42 Richard Schacht, "Friedrich Nietzsche," in *The Blackwell Guide to Modern Philosophers*, ed. S. Emmanuel (Malden, MA: Blackwell Publishing, 2001).

43 Nietzsche, *Will to Power*, "Toward an Outline," section 2.

44 Nietzsche, *Will to Power*, I/12.

45 For example, nearly one hundred years before Nietzsche, Friedrich Jacobi's 1799 *Letter to Fichte* accuses Fichte of egoistic nihilism rather than idealism in light of the fact that we cannot know metaphysical truths about God, souls, or "things in themselves." In Jacobi's estimation, this is an impoverished view of humanity in which "rationality is for me a curse" and "I deplore my existence." Quoted in Ernst Behler, *Philosophy of German Idealism: Fichte, Jacobi, and Schelling* (New York: Continuum Publishing, 1987), 135.

46 Nietzsche, *Will to Power*, I/2.

47 Ibid., I/12.

48 Simon Critchley, *Continental Philosophy: A Very Brief Introduction* (New York: Oxford University Press, 2001), 84.

49 For an elaboration on this point, see Thomas Pangle and Timothy Burns, *The Key Texts in Political Philosophy: An Introduction* (Cambridge: Cambridge University Press, 2015), Chapter 14: "Nietzsche did not promote the death of God; he saw it as the terrible fate of mankind in our time. He intended to point the way out of the ensuing crisis of nihilism, to a radically new way of thinking and being, a new form of humanity" (400).

50 Nietzsche, *Will to Power*, III/1/10.

51 Nietzsche, *Zarathustra*, Prologue, 4.

52 Ibid., Prologue, 4.

53 Nietzsche, *Gay Science*, section 125.

54 Nietzsche, *Zarathustra*, Prologue, 3.

55 Ibid., Prologue, 3.
56 Nietzsche wrote to Jacob Burckhardt on September 22, 1886, that *Beyond Good and Evil* "says the same things as my *Zarathustra*, but differently, very differently." And Nietzsche believed that the *Genealogy of Morals* could not be understood without the requisite exposure to *Beyond Good and Evil*. See Kauffman's "Translator's Preface," in *Basic Writings of Nietzsche* (New York: The Modern Library, 1992), 182 and "Editor's Introduction" to the *Genealogy of Morals*, 439.
57 Nietzsche, *Genealogy of Morals*, II/24.
58 Although I take seriously Linda Williams's assertion that "scholars who think that will to power is Nietzsche's metaphsyics or cosmology appeal almost exclusively to textual support from the writings that were never authorized for publication by Nietzsche" in *Nietzsche's Mirror: The World as Will to Power* (New York: Rowman and Littlefield, 2001), 51. I also present it in order to show a similarity later in the essay with Wallace's form of the will to power.
59 Nietzsche, *Will to Power*, 1087 (p. 550).
60 Nietzsche, *Zarathustra*, "On the Thousand and One Goals," I/15.
61 Nietzsche, *Genealogy of Morals*, III/13.
62 As noted by R. Lanier Anderson, "Nietzsche's concern is not so much to refute that view as to diagnose it. He insists that such evaluative commitments are symptoms of psychological and cultural sickness, and that the ascetic response is an 'instinctive', but ultimately self-defeating, effort at self-medication." Cf. *Genealogy of Morals*, III/13 and III/16. Anderson continues: "While asceticism imposes self-discipline on the sick practitioner, it simultaneously makes the person sicker, plunging her into intensified inner conflict" (Cf. *Genealogy of Morals*, III/15, III/20–1). Finally, therefore, "Nietzsche's fundamental objection to asceticism is that it is psychologically destructive and practically self-defeating, even for those (the sick) for whom it does its best work—and this is so even if it remains (from a certain perspective) the best they can do for themselves in their condition." See R. Lanier Anderson, "Friedrich Nietzsche" in The Stanford Encyclopedia of Philosophy (Summer 2017 edition; E.N. Zalta, ed.). Available online: https://plato.stanford.edu/archives/sum2017/entries/nietzsche.
63 Nietzsche, *Genealogy of Morals*, III/28.
64 Lipsky, *Becoming Yourself*, 273.
65 Ibid., 274.
66 Ibid., 82–3.
67 Ibid., 82–3.
68 Wallace, *Charlie Rose Interview*, available online: https://youtu.be/91ytSdSM-Kk.
69 Lipsky, *Becoming Yourself*, 274.
70 For a lengthier study of existentialism in Wallace, see Allard den Dulk's *Existential Engagement in Wallace, Eggers and Foer: A Philosophical Analysis*

of *Contemporary American Literature* (New York: Bloomsbury, 2016). For more on existentialist themes, see Steven Crowell, "Existentialism," in *The Stanford Encyclopedia of Philosophy* (Winter 2017 edition; E.N. Zalta, ed.). Available online: https://plato.stanford.edu/archives/win2017/entries/existentialism. Crowell states the problem much as Wallace did: "In anxiety, as in fear, I grasp myself as threatened or as vulnerable; but unlike fear, anxiety has no direct object, there is nothing in the world that is threatening. This is because anxiety pulls me altogether out of the circuit of those projects thanks to which things are there for me in meaningful ways; I can no longer 'gear into' the world. And with this collapse of my practical immersion in roles and projects, I also lose the basic sense of who I am that is provided by these roles. In thus robbing me of the possibility of practical self-identification, anxiety teaches me that I do not coincide with anything that I factically am."

71 "Good Old Neon," handwritten drafts, HRC, UT Austin. Viewed July 2018.

72 Here is an interesting overlap between Nietzsche and Wallace: "Humans are becoming a species that is contented by mere physical comfort and sensual pleasures together with entertainment, sports, hobbies, easygoing companionship, and petty competitions of vanity. Humanoids are emerging who look a lot like past humans, physically (though prettier and a bit artificial on account of plastic surgery), but who have lost their souls: who have lost that uniquely human need and capacity to live for the sake of demanding spiritual challenges, involving transformative self-overcoming" (Pangle and Burns, *Key Texts*, 401).

73 Compare this to Nietzsche, *Zarathustra*, Prologue, 5: "One still works, for work is a form of entertainment. But one is careful lest the entertainment be too harrowing. One no longer becomes poor or rich: both require too much exertion. Who still wants to rule? Who obey? Both require too much exertion. No shepherd and one herd. Everybody wants the same, everybody is the same: whoever feels different goes voluntarily into a madhouse."

74 Lipsky, *Becoming Yourself*, 274.

75 Ibid. In one of Wallace's books found at the Harry Ransom Center in Austin, Wallace made note of the passage that explains how people who work hard are often discontented because, when they do not accomplish all they set out to, they often feel lazy. He writes "laziness + will" in the margins of Paramandanda, *A Practical Guide to Buddhist Meditation* (New York: Barnes and Noble Books, 1996), 83.

76 Lipsky, *Becoming Yourself*, 62–3.

77 Ibid., 62–3.

78 Ibid., 67–8.

79 Anthony DeMello, *Awareness: The Perils and Opportunities of Reality* (New York: Image Books, 1990), 158.

80 For a summary of Wallace's recovery practice and its relation to spirituality/religion, see Rob Short's "Came to Believe: The Religion of Alcoholics Anonymous in *Infinite Jest*," Chapter 1 in this volume.

81 Bill W., *Alcoholics Anonymous: The Story of How Many Thousands of Men and Women Have Recovered from Alcoholism* (New York: Alcoholics Anonymous World Services, 1976), 59. For a thorough explanation of how AA figures into Wallace's novels, see Robert W. Short, *Big Books: Addiction and Recovery in the Novels of David Foster Wallace* (Ph.D. diss.; University of Florida, 2017).

82 Wallace, *IJ*, 350–1: " … how can you pray to a 'God' you believe only morons believe in, still?—but the old guys say it doesn't yet matter what you believe or don't believe, Just Do It, they say, and like a shock-trained organism without any kind of independent human will you do exactly like you're told, you keep coming and coming, nightly … and not only does the urge to get high stay more or less away, but more general life-quality-type things—just as improbably promised, at first, when you'd Come In—things seem to get progressively somehow better, inside, for a while, then rose, then even better, then for a while worse in a way that's still somehow better, realer, you feel weirdly unblinded, which is good, even though a lot of the things you see about yourself and how you've lived are horrible to have to see … and at this point you've started to have an almost classic sort of Blind Faith in the older guys, a Blind Faith in them born not out of zealotry or even belief but just of a chilled conviction that you have no faith whatsoever left in yourself; and now if the older guys say Jump you ask them to hold their hand at the desired height, and now they've got you, and you're free."

83 Harry Ransom Center archives, "David Foster Wallace Collection," personal visit, July 2018. Also quoted in Max, *Every Love Story*, 281.

84 Max, *Every Love Story*, 289.

85 Cf. Gately's abiding in *IJ*, 859–60.

86 Parmananda, *A Practical Guide*, 120.

87 Cf. Gately's abiding in *IJ*, 859–60.

88 Behler, *Philosophy of German Idealism*, 135.

89 Nietzsche, *Gay Science*, 192.

90 Bill W., *Alcoholics Anonymous*, 62: "Above everything, we alcoholics must be rid of this selfishness. God makes that possible. And there often seems no way of entirely getting rid of self without His aid."

91 "Good Old Neon" handwritten manuscript, found at the Harry Ransom Center at UT Austin. Viewed July 2018.

92 Nietzsche, *Gay Science*, section 341. See also *Thus Spoke Zarathustra*, "The Convalescent," 2.

93 Scholars are somewhat divided on whether this is the best interpretation of Nietzsche's eternal recurrence. As with many of Nietzsche's concepts, the interpretation of this doctrine is fraught with difficulties and has generated two types of interpretations. One suggests that Nietzsche uses it as a tool for self-reflection, an aid to discern whether one is living life well and whether one's life has meaning, in which case it would be an "aesthetic ideal." The second interpretation, found only in Nietzsche's unpublished notes and journals, is that eternal recurrence is a cosmological theory of the

universe in which time is cyclical, not linear. Proponents of the cosmological interpretation based their view on various "sketches" in which Nietzsche gives "scientific proofs of eternal recurrence, based on the assumptions that time is infinite while configurations of energy are finite." For more on eternal recurrence and its various interpretations, see the following: Tracy Strong, *Friedrich Nietzsche and the Politics of Transfiguration* (Berkeley: University of California Press, 1975), 270–1; Alexander Nehemas, *Nietzsche: Life as Literature* (Cambridge, MA: Harvard University Press, 1985), 141–65. Nehemas says, "Eternal recurrence is a view of the ideal life. It holds that a life is justified only if one would want to have again the same life one had already had, since, as the will to power shows, *no other life can ever be possible* [our italics]. The eternal recurrence therefore holds that our life is justified only if we fashion it in such a way that we would want it to be exactly as it had already been" (7); and Arthur Danto, *Nietzsche as Philosopher: An Original Study* (New York: Columbia University Press, 1965), 203–9.

94 Nietzsche, *Thus Spoke Zarathustra*, 221.
95 Bill W., *Alcoholics Anonymous*, 45.
96 Robert H. Solomon, "Friedrich Nietzsche," in *The Blackwell Guide to Continental Philosophy*, ed. R. Solomon and D. Sherman (Malden, MA: Blackwell Publishing, 2003), 95.
97 Evans, "The Chains of Not Choosing," 172.
98 Max, *Every Love Story*, 178.
99 D.T. Max, "The Unfinished: David Foster Wallace's Struggle to Surpass *Infinite Jest*," *The New Yorker* (March 9, 2009), Available online: http://www.newyorker.com/magazine/2009/03/09/the-unfinished.
100 Max, *Every Love Story*, 301.
101 Nietzsche, *Twilight*, 210–11.

4

In G.O.D. We Trust: The Desert of the Religious in *The Broom of the System*

Vernon W. Cisney

Whether we are Christians or atheists, in our universal schizophrenia,
we need reasons to believe in this world.
—GILLES DELEUZE, CINEMA II

The Broom of the System was David Foster Wallace's first novel, initially drafted over a period of five months in 1984 as his undergraduate honors thesis for his English major at Amherst (CW 166). Its style is undeniably absurdist, with numerous deliberate nods to Thomas Pynchon's *The Crying of Lot 49*; a female protagonist who fears two-dimensionality—that she may be nothing more than the sum total of everything that can be said about her; character names such as Judith Prietht, Peter Abbott, and the ironically named Rick Vigorous; cities outlined in the shape of Jayne Mansfield; and a suspiciously loquacious cockatiel named Vlad the Impaler. Amidst this zaniness, the presence of the Great Ohio Desert (acronym G.O.D.), a "wasteland" (*BOS* 54) in the heart of Ohio, manufactured by a company specializing in the production of "industrial deserts," can be easily overlooked as just one more absurd component, one of Wallace's "more inspired comic inventions … "[1] But to do so, one must toss aside many substantial considerations, not only of the novel itself, but also of Wallace's own remarks on spirituality and religion.

First, one must ignore the unifying role that G.O.D. plays in the novel. For, like the elusive McDonald's reunion in "Westward," G.O.D. in *Broom* serves a function that is apocalyptic, in the dual senses of teleological threat—the fatalistic sense of impending doom as the novel builds to its resolution—as well as the etymological connotations of the Greek word *apokálypsis*, having to do with revelation or disclosure. Despite the infrequency of its references, G.O.D. haunts the entirety of *Broom,* ultimately luring the characters—particularly the protagonist, Lenore Beadsman—to its sinister barrenness for the novel's climax. But perhaps more importantly, one must also set aside the ongoing spiritual or religious undercurrent in Wallace's work. Throughout *Infinite Jest,* for example, we see an abiding emphasis on the kenotic[2] efficacy of recovery programs and their "Higher Power," embodied in the oft-repeated mantra, "My Best Thinking Got Me Here." (*IJ* 1026 n135). We see the suspicion, voiced in the mouth of Joelle van Dyne, that the self-cancellation associated with substance abuse may in fact be but a deficient shortcut to the superior "self-forgetting" of the religious (*IJ* 742). We see the uncomplicated belief of Mario Incandenza in his conversations with Hal (*IJ* 40–1). But this undercurrent is made explicit in Wallace's now-famous Kenyon address, published as *This Is Water*; in which Wallace claims, "In the day-to-day trenches of adult life, there is actually no such thing as atheism. There is no such thing as not worshipping. Everybody worships. The only choice we get is *what* to worship" (*TIW* 105–8). Wallace is admittedly vague on questions of substance when it comes to this object of worship, and hence, David H. Evans is not wrong when he writes that "The question of Wallace's religious attitudes is a vexed one."[3] Moreover, *The Broom of the System* is not, in most other ways, nearly as spiritually themed as later works such as *Infinite Jest* or *The Pale King*. Nevertheless, Wallace could have designated *Broom*'s desert by any name, but he chose to christen it with the historically and philosophically complicated proper noun—G.O.D.

The task of this essay is to explore the role of G.O.D. in *The Broom of the System,* and in so doing, to examine elements of the relation, largely overlooked in the secondary literature, between Wallace and Danish philosopher, Søren Kierkegaard. In particular, I shall investigate the relation between the notions of "God" and "self" in the two, pointing to similar structures of that relation, and hence, toward the likelihood of a more prominent significance of Kierkegaard's work in the thought and writing of Wallace than has been hitherto acknowledged.[4] This analysis will also shed light on the role of the religious in Wallace's early period.

"The wasteland grows"

Of the ninety-five sections of *The Broom of the System,* only one, spanning a mere four of the novel's 467 pages, is dedicated explicitly to the Great Ohio Desert. This section is presented in the form of a transcript of a conversation dated June 21, 1972. Ohio's governor, speaking to his aides, invokes what he understands as a sense of complacency that has overtaken Ohioans (and by extension, America more generally). Modern life, he laments, has grown too comfortable and, in a word, "soft" (*BOS* 53). Absorbed by the plasticity of suburbs, cookie cutter housing developments, shopping malls, and consumer luxuries, we have forgotten "the way this state was historically hewn out of the wilderness" (*BOS* 54). The governor's proposed solution, for which he expresses deep and unprecedented personal conviction, is the creation of a *new* wilderness, a wasteland of one hundred square miles, in roughly the center of the state: "An Other for Ohio's Self. Cacti and scorpions and the sun beating down. Desolation. A place for people to wander alone. To reflect. Away from everything" (*BOS* 54). The desert is intended to be violent and unsettling, brutal and unforgiving. When the governor initially proposes white sand for the G.O.D., one of his aides suggests black instead, noting that the blackness will not only provide greater contrast with the whiteness of the majority of the state's population, but will also better absorb the heat from the sunlight, making the terrain even more intolerable. This convinces the governor, who decides that black sand is indeed worth the additional taxpayer expense. When the governor is reminded that the proposed location of the desert will completely displace the town of Caldwell, the governor responds: "Relocation. Eminent domain. A desert respects no man. Fits with the whole concept" (*BOS* 54). When one of his aides protests that the aide's mother lives near Caldwell, the governor replies: "Hewing is violence, Neil. We're going to hew a wilderness out of the soft underbelly of this state. It's going to hit home" (*BOS* 55). Moreover, the governor is insistent that construction is to begin immediately, thus executing through an unnatural (i.e., a humanly imposed) event the equivalent of a natural disaster against the residents of his own state, who will now face the unheralded and unforeseeable loss of their homes and livelihoods. But it is worth the sacrifice, according to the governor, because the purpose of G.O.D. is to facilitate the rediscovery of Ohio's lost sense of Self. To find G.O.D., in other words, is to find oneself.

Despite the fact that G.O.D. appears by name only a few times through the remainder of the novel, it is always with a sense of magnitude, even reverence. The most significant appearance of G.O.D. occurs in the climax of the novel when Rick, driven mad by his insecurities and sensing Lenore's growing attraction to Andrew Lang, insists that Lenore accompany him to G.O.D. for one last story session. Throughout the novel, Rick's narrations have been presented to Lenore under the guise of submissions that he has received as chief editor at Frequent and Vigorous Publishing; in point of fact, the stories are thinly veiled moral tales, designed to manipulate the emotions and behaviors of Lenore. The uniqueness of Rick's final story lies in the fact that the fabulistic veneer is almost completely discarded, as Rick weaves a tale of a selfless dentist who "saves" a forlorn woman from certain death in the Indiana forests, thereby securing the affection and eventually the marriage of the woman. Tragedy ensues, however, when the dentist later falls victim to a car accident, leaving the dentist deaf, blind, and nonverbal, and leaving the woman at the mercy of the sexual advances of another man who, incidentally, physically resembles Lang. The woman, starving for the carnal pleasure that the dentist cannot provide, at last succumbs to the seductions of the other man, having a coital romp with him on the floor of the hospital, just a few feet from the bed where her almost completely incapacitated and insensate husband lies. But the surprising plot twist is that the dentist in the story forgives the wife, just as Rick, in his self-perceived magnanimity, forgives Lenore for her inability to resist the charms of Lang. That so-called forgiveness, however, comes at a high price, as Rick then handcuffs Lenore to himself, with the intention of lying together (and dying together) in the black sand of G.O.D., to literally melt into oneness with her, as he says, "in negation and discipline" (*BOS* 441). Rick thus attempts to forcefully consummate Lenore's "two-dimensionality," as mere words on a page, by writing, against her will, her conclusion. At this point, Lang, who has been watching from afar, intervenes, breaking the chain of the handcuffs. But Lenore has already, in a sense, "freed" herself from the clutches of Rick, in that she has recognized that Rick is but one more component of that nexus of control that has hitherto kept her suspended in two-dimensional bondage. G.O.D. is the site where Lenore comes to realize that in order to become a self, to take possession of her own three-dimensionality,[5] she must break permanently with Rick. Lenore had gone to G.O.D. in search of Lenore (i.e., Lenore, Sr.), and instead, found Herself (and here we can hear echoes of the similar strategy from *Infinite Jest*, where Orin seeks a relationship with Himself, i.e., James Incandenza).

The outside within

G.O.D. in *The Broom of the System* is thus an exteriority or an outside—radically Other, as the governor says—but nevertheless situated at the heart of the inside, in the center of America. It is a blistering and unforgiving wasteland, lodged at the philosophical core, the "heartland," of the quintessential land of consumer comfort. It is constructed in order to liberate Ohioans from their own apathy and complacency, to strip away the superfluities of modern life and remind them of the mettle that defines them, to free them to live lives of intensity and purpose. It is to be revelatory, showing them who they *really* are, just as her time in G.O.D. shows Lenore who *she* really is or, at least, who she *can* be. How, then, are we to make sense of this desert?

In *Understanding David Foster Wallace*, Marshall Boswell negatively connects G.O.D. with the Wittgensteinian questions concerning language that run throughout the novel. He writes that G.O.D. "embodies the novel's dim view of referent-based signification,"[6] noting that Western thought—

both philosophically and religiously—has always conceptualized God (or one of God's metonymic placeholders) as the ultimate foundation of meaning.[7] Examples include, but are not limited to: Plato's form of the good beyond being; Aristotle's self-thinking thought; Plotinus's "the One"; the God of Augustine, Leibniz, and Malebranche; Anselm's being than which none greater can be conceived; the necessary being of Ibn-Sina; the infinite substance of Descartes and Spinoza; the Absolute of Hegel ... and so on. In each of these cases, *some* central concept serves as the final bedrock, the ultimate signifying foundation upon which the very possibility of meaningfulness rests—what French philosopher Jacques Derrida called the "transcendental signified"[8] holding together the Western tradition. Capitalizing on the equivocality of the Greek word "logos,"[9] Derrida crystallizes this philosophical, cultural, and theological tradition under the heading of "logocentrism."[10] But as Boswell writes, in *The Broom of the System*, "the Logos is a vast void, an emptiness—literally a desert" (*BOS* 35).

As Boswell understands it, if the Logos—the transcendental signified—is a desert or an abyss, if there *is* no ultimate foundation of meaning, then any given sign that we might use in order to *convey* meaning is based, *not* on some teleological referent, "but rather on its own volition within a system of relations,"[11] or what Wittgenstein called its position within its particular language game.[12] And while I have no bones to pick with Boswell's reading on its face, I think it does not go quite far enough in its exploration of G.O.D. in the novel. For even if the novel is indeed deeply concerned with questions of language and reference, it is so in the service of Wallace's even more fundamental concerns over what it means to be a self, what it means to be a human being[13]; and in this context, if God—the apocalyptic thread that ties together the whole of the novel—is a desert, then the question of the relation of that desert to the notion of selfhood is one that demands to be thought. It is also worth noting the significance that this notion of a constitutive and empty center plays elsewhere in Wallace's writings. Toward the end of "Westward," for example, Magda says to Mark Nechtr, "Everybody who really wants to knows what's true. Most people just don't want to. It means listening from deep inside," and a bit further down, "If you want, ... your whole life in the adult world can be like this country. In the center. Flat as nothing" (*GCH* 351–2). And it is on this point, of God as a constitutive outside at the center of the inside, that Kierkegaard enters into this discussion.

Kierkegaard's Christian God

I should note, there are really good reasons to *not* bring Kierkegaard into this discussion. For starters, Wallace does not cite Kierkegaard, in his interviews or in his fiction, with nearly the frequency with which he cites folks like Wittgenstein and Derrida. But, Kierkegaard *does* make appearances, as

Allard den Dulk's work has shown: "Kierkegaard, however, is repeatedly mentioned by Wallace."[14] Secondly, Kierkegaard is a notoriously difficult thinker to grapple with, not just with respect to his ideas themselves, but more importantly with respect to the *dramatization* of his ideas—the fact that the vast majority of his philosophical works were written pseudonymously, in the guises of specific characters at specific stages of their own spiritual and psychological development. The ideas themselves *evolve*, as the subjectivities who espouse them occupy various stages of maturity. Hence, pinning down precisely which ideas come from Kierkegaard, and which are mere expressions of pseudonymous characters is no simple task.[15] But finally, the reality is that many philosophers find themselves uncomfortable, unable, or unwilling to engage meaningfully with Kierkegaard's overtly religious language.[16]

For example, in his groundbreaking work, Allard den Dulk writes of the Wallace–Kierkegaard connection in the following way: "repetition means that choice is not just dependent on the self, but also always implies a dependence on something that is transcendent to the self," clarifying that "contrary to Kierkegaard who regards the transcendence of repetition … as vertical, as religious, as a recurring responsibility before God … I regard this limitation of repetition, to stop with the ethical …,"[17] which is to say, short of Kierkegaard's religious leap. Likewise, in his reading of *Infinite Jest*, Marshall Boswell incorporates aspects of Kierkegaard's philosophy, mostly having to do with the aesthetic sphere of existence. But Boswell hedges in his incorporation of Kierkegaard, claiming that Wallace is "much more comfortable with AA's nondenominational idea of a 'Higher Power' than with Kierkegaard's dogmatic Christian God."[18] But the limitations of these readings lie in the number of assumptions they make: it is implied that we know what "vertical" as opposed to "horizontal" transcendence means, what "dogma" means, what "Christian" means, how these adjectives characterize the noun—"God," and finally, that Kierkegaard in fact *embraces* such a "dogmatic Christian" conception of that God. It is precisely these assumptions that need to be challenged; for, however Kierkegaard understands these concepts, it must be made absolutely and abundantly clear that his conceptions of the "leap of faith in the face of the absurd" do not, in any way, conform to traditional, objective fideistic[19] religious categories. So at this time, I shall address Kierkegaard's concept of the three spheres of existence, and from there tease out the conception of God that they imply.

The three spheres of existence, for Kierkegaard, are the aesthetic, the ethical and the religious. The aesthetic stage is focused primarily on "sensation," coming from the Greek word "*aisthesis*," which means feeling or sensation. The key to the aesthetic life, for Kierkegaard, is that it craves the sort of immediacy, stimulation, and pleasure that is, of its very nature, fleeting. The aesthetic is superficial because it is unrepeatable—the existential sphere of masks and surfaces. The aesthete inhabits a spectrum that ranges from the basest modalities—the pursuit of pleasure strictly for the sake of pleasure; to more poetizing forms—where desire is conceived as a rapturous, almost spiritual passion that burns so brightly and so hot as to consume the lover, as in Shakespeare's *Romeo and Juliet*. But either way, the aesthetic is inauthentic for Kierkegaard, because it is, of its very nature, fleeting, and its eroticism entangles, *not* real human beings, but rather, poetized idealizations or abstractions of human beings. In his template for the aesthetic life, *The Seducer's Diary*, Kierkegaard writes, "Under the aesthetic sky, everything is buoyant, beautiful, transient ... "[20] Later he writes, "I am seeking immediacy."[21] But precisely because of its transience and its immediacy, the aesthetic cannot become the substance of a meaningful human life. While the aesthetic could aptly describe many of the characters in Wallace's fiction, the consummate aesthete would likely be *Infinite Jest*'s Orin Incandenza. Likewise, in *The Broom of the System*, we are given indications that the aesthetic life has exhausted itself in the character of Andrew Lang, when, as he is ending his relationship with Mindy Metalman, he says to her, "My analysis of the problem, if you want my analysis of the problem, is that you've just run out of holes in your pretty body, and I've run out of things to stick in them" (*BOS* 177).

Then we have the ethical sphere. With the ethical, the individual relinquishes her superficial desires, in subordination to her communal identity. In the case of erotic love, for instance, while the aesthete craves only the passion of the body, the ethical individual wills the intensive consummation of love, but in an ongoing repetition, repeating throughout her life the act of commitment in the form of the marriage vow. The poet's passion is thereby transfigured, from one that is essentially unrepeatable to a promise that is essentially unbreakable, rooted in a choice made on the basis of the awareness of one's duty and responsibility. This entry into the ethical brings one into a harmonious relationship with the community, with the religious order and the family, etc., subordinating the individual to the societal structure. It is the sphere of the universal, rationality, and language, very close in nature to what Jacques Lacan called "the Symbolic." Most of us, Kierkegaard thinks, live most of our lives somewhere between the aesthetic and the ethical. But for Kierkegaard, the ethical still does not encapsulate what is unique about the individual. And the reason is clear—in the ethical sphere, everything that makes one singular is subsumed or cancelled so that one may fit into the institutional frameworks of the communal order. One *chooses* to choose, but her choice is made in deference to duty, responsibility, and moral law, all of which are communal and universal. The singularity of selfhood, for Kierkegaard, is only reached in the leap to the religious sphere of existence.

Kierkegaard repeatedly and explicitly connects the leap of faith and the religious sphere to the question of selfhood. In *Fear and Trembling*, for example, Kierkegaard writes that "The paradox of faith is this, that there is an inwardness that is incommensurable with the outer,"[22] and in *The Sickness Unto Death,* "the formula for faith: in relating to itself and in wanting to be itself, the self is grounded transparently in the power that established it."[23] He characterizes this inwardness and this power in terms of "the absolute."[24]

We can think of this "absolute" in senses both absolutely *great*, and absolutely *small*—absolutely *great* in the sense of the whole of being which, as infinite, is radically external to *language* (which essentially deals only with finite bits); but the absolute is also absolutely *small*, in the sense that there is an aspect of ourselves that is *infinite* and *eternal*, insofar as it is in touch with the eternality of the absolutely great ("the power that established it"), and hence, it is also, like its counterpart, irreducible to language, insofar as it indicates an intensity of the interior life—which Kierkegaard characterizes as spirit—that is not categorizable beneath the universals of rationality. And because the religious movement toward the absolute encounters the limits of language and rationality, the movement can only be made by way of a leap, which Kierkegaard, on many occasions, refers to as a madness: "to have faith is precisely to lose one's mind so as to win God."[25] But it must be made clear that God is *not* a "being" having external, objective reality: "But God is not something external like a police constable."[26] To "win God" is to gain what is most deeply interior about selfhood itself. In Genesis 22, when Abraham offers Isaac as a sacrifice, he does it, Kierkegaard says, "For God's sake, and what is altogether identical with this, for his own sake."[27]

This leap strips away everything about the ego held together by the "externals"[28]—our possessions, our offices and reputations, our political practicalities, etc. They are, as he says, "teleologically suspended"[29] in this religious leap. We can detect echoes in Wallace's work when he writes that, "The only choice we get is *what* to worship. And an outstanding reason for choosing some sort of god or spiritual-type thing ... is that pretty much anything else you worship will eat you alive" (*TIW* 101–2). But we should also note, for Kierkegaard, this suspension includes the linguistic categories and concepts by which we rationally understand and communicate with *ourselves* as well, *everything* about the ego up to and including the term "I." So, this "leap" leaps to a space that is "outside" of the I, insofar as it transcends all of the categories, including and especially those of language, with which the "ego" cognizes itself. But it is an "outside" that is deep within the individual—it is what is most fundamentally and uniquely me. In *The Gift of Death,* Jacques Derrida writes:

> Once I have within me, *thanks to the invisible word as such*, a witness that others cannot see, and who is therefore *at the same time other than me and more intimate with me than myself*, once I can have a secret relationship with myself and not tell everything, once there is secrecy and secret witnessing within me, then what I call God exists, (there is) what

I call God in me, ... God is in me, he is the absolute "me" or "self," he is that structure of invisible interiority that is called, in Kierkegaard's sense, "subjectivity."[30]

So, this leap to this radical outside is one that puts the self into a proper relation with the "absolute," which is to say, with itself. And it is for this reason that Kierkegaard writes in *The Sickness Unto Death* that "The self is a relation which relates itself to itself ... "[31]

To transition back to Wallace and bring us back to the concerns of den Dulk and Boswell, regarding Kierkegaard's religious language, it must be made clear that whatever "vertical" transcendence might mean for Kierkegaard, it is certainly *not* a leap to some *other* world, and Kierkegaard makes this explicit on numerous occasions: "But Abraham believed and believed for this life."[32] To believe in *some other world*, which is merely the moral and logical outcome of *this* world, Kierkegaard argues, is simply to extend the causal logic of earthly possibility beyond the realm of the visible. There is nothing special about such paltry "faith," Kierkegaard thinks. What Kierkegaard understands as "faith" is the realization that, in *sacrificing* the temporal, one may then dwell—with presence, awareness, and gratitude— within it, that Abraham "had to draw the knife before [he] kept Isaac."[33] This accords with what Clare Carlisle calls "the logic of the gift": "Insofar as a gift is given to me it does become mine; but insofar as I continue to regard it as a gift, I continue to regard myself as someone who receives it—and receiving something is different from possessing it."[34] Kierkegaard's faith is a faith in *this* world, not some other; it is an intensive way of *occupying* the world, so as to fundamentally transform it, "to experience a crowded, hot, slow, consumer-hell-type situation as not only meaningful, but sacred, on fire with the same force that lit the stars—compassion, love, the subsurface unity of all things" (*TIW* 93). As David Wood writes, "There is no other realm, but there are radically different ways of inhabiting this one."[35]

Conclusion

Wallace's G.O.D. structurally mirrors Kierkegaard's understanding of God and the religious leap. In the world of *Broom*, the artifices and superficialities of the narrative—the banality and obvious pandering of Reverend Sykes's television program, Rick's obsession with the phallus, fraternity pranks, nursing home conspiracies, morally unhinged therapists, Rick's moral tales, the bizarre theatre of masks in the home of Lenore's sister (*BOS* 164–168, 169–170, 172–173), and so on—are elements that all hearken to Kierkegaard's aesthetic sphere, the sphere of immediacy, masks, and surfaces. The arc of Lenore's character, her pursuit of "three-dimensionality"—wherein she evolves from mere words on the page to an author in her own right, one who *chooses* to participate *in* the system by "*signing* the Other" (*BOS* 344), signifies her passage from the aesthetic to the ethical.

But the core of the novel lies in its empty center. Like Kierkegaard's God, G.O.D. is an outside—a "point of savage reference" (*BOS* 54)—at the heart of the inside. It is a harsh Other to the complacency of neoliberal modernity. It is a "wasteland," not merely in virtue of its barrenness and intolerability, but also in the sense of economic *waste* and inefficient expenditure required in order to bring it into being. As such, it in every way defies the logic and the ethos of modern America. G.O.D. deliberately disrupts the obsession with pleasure and comfort associated with the contemporary ideology of the "American dream," stripping away the layers of sedimentation associated with the societal strata and its materialistic and imperialistic endeavors. In addition, like Kierkegaard's God, G.O.D. is that which most fundamentally reveals the selfhood of the self. It is a "place to fear and love" (*BOS* 54), unifying the action of the novel, and revelatory in that it is the site in which Lenore comes into full possession of what she *can be*.

Nevertheless, despite their structural similarities, there is something fundamentally asymmetrical between Kierkegaard's God and G.O.D. Specifically, it is important to note that G.O.D. is a *human construction*, manufactured by way of tremendous *destruction* of forests, homes, and lives. It is also worth noting that of his two finished novels at the time of his death, *The Broom of the System* was the one from which Wallace later distanced himself, characterizing it as narcissistic, self-indulgent, and in many ways, a failure.[36] There is a word that most, particularly theistic, religions use to characterize a god that is *constructed* by human beings—that word is "idolatry." I cannot help but wonder if *The Broom of the System*'s central and constitutive act of idolatry is but one more symptom in Wallace's mind of the novel's ultimate failure, his unwillingness at this stage of his life to make the leap of faith. Given Wallace's remarks on worship in *This Is Water*, and on temples in *Infinite Jest*, I cannot help but wonder if G.O.D. in *Broom* is merely one more externalization of a shallow and inattentive selfhood, like Rick's projections of his own sexual inadequacies onto Lenore, or the line tunnels beneath the Bombardini building, heated to 98.6 degrees to accommodate Gramma Lenore. Perhaps the Great Ohio Desert is one more simulacrum in a book filled with them—a false God for a false sense of self. And perhaps this is why the penultimate section of the book focuses not on *Lenore*, but on the television program of Reverend Sykes, "*joined* here tonight, *together*," as he says, "in the electronic soil of *faith today*" (*BOS* 466). To quote Marilyn Manson, perhaps the novel's ultimate fear resides in the possibility that, for us today and perhaps for the foreseeable future, "God is in the TV."[37]

Notes

1. Marshall Boswell, *Understanding David Foster Wallace* (Columbia: The University of South Carolina Press, 2003), 34. To be clear, Boswell does not end his reading of G.O.D. at this point.

2. Kenōsis refers to the ancient Greek word κένωσις, best translated as "emptying." An existential ethics based upon the principle of kenōsis emphasizes the emptying or the renunciation of the self, typified in Christian theology by the death of Jesus. St. Paul refers to this in his letter to the church at Philippi, when he writes: "In your relationships with one another, have the same mindset as Christ Jesus: Who, being in very nature God, did not consider equality with God something to be used to his own advantage; rather, he made himself nothing (*ekénōsen*) by taking the very nature of a servant, being made in human likeness. And being found in appearance as a man, he humbled himself by becoming obedient to death—even death on a cross!" Phil. 2:5–8 (NIV). Kenotic Christianity had a profound impact on the work of Fyodor Dostoevsky who, as we also know, had a significant impact on Wallace. See David Foster Wallace, "Joseph Frank's Dostoevsky," in *CL*, 255–74.

3. David H. Evans, '"The Chains of Not Choosing": Free Will and Faith in William James and David Foster Wallace', in *A Companion to David Foster Wallace Studies*, ed. Marshall Boswell and Stephen J. Burn (New York: Palgrave Macmillan, 2013), 171–89; 183.

4. In a treatment of this length, such an explication, particularly where Kierkegaard is concerned, can only be cursory. There are excellent studies of the relations between Kierkegaard's notions of "God" and "self." See, for instance, Simon D. Podmore, *Kierkegaard and the Self Before God: Anatomy of the Abyss* (Bloomington: Indiana University Press, 2011); and Patrick Stokes, *The Naked Self: Kierkegaard and Personal Identity* (Oxford: Oxford University Press, 2015).

5. That is to say, to become more than just words on a page.

6. Boswell, *Understanding David Foster Wallace*, 34.

7. In my book, *Deleuze and Derrida: Difference and the Power of the Negative* (Edinburgh: Edinburgh University Press, 2018), I thematize this history as "the thought of the center."

8. "From the moment that there is meaning there is nothing but signs. We *think only in signs*. Which amounts to ruining the notion of the sign at the very moment when, as in Nietzsche, its exigency is recognized in the absoluteness of its right. One could call *play* the absence of the transcendental signified as limitlessness of play, that is to say as the destruction of ontotheology and the metaphysics of presence." Jacques Derrida, *De la Grammatologie* (Paris: Les Éditions de Minuit, 1967); Gayatri Spivak, trans. *Of Grammatology* (Baltimore: The Johns Hopkins University Press, 1974), 50.

9. "Logos" is a word with a rich philosophical and religious history. It can be translated as "structure," and has connotations connecting it with reason, and is the base of the word "logic," as well as sciences that end with the suffix

"-ology." The emphasis on structure thus also carries connotations associated with language. As such it is one of the prized concepts of the ancient Greek philosophers, among them Heraclitus, Plato, and Aristotle. But its linguistic connotations also convey the components of language, such as "word." As a result, the early Christian thinkers and authors employed the word "logos" to indicate the second person of the trinity, eternally "spoken" by God, as in The Gospel of St. John 1:1—"In the beginning was the Word, and the Word was with God, and the Word was God."

10 "I have identified logocentrism and the metaphysics of presence as the exigent, powerful, systematic, and irrepressible desire for such a [transcendental] signified." Derrida, *Of Grammatology*, 49.

11 Boswell, *Understanding David Foster Wallace*, 36.

12 See Ludwig Wittgenstein, *Philosophical Investigations*, 3rd ed. trans. G.E.M. Anscombe (Malden, MA: Blackwell, 1953).

13 "You're at once allowing the reader to sort of escape self by achieving some sort of identification with another human psyche—the writer's or some character's, etc.—and you're *also* trying to antagonize the reader's intuition that she is a self, that she is alone and going to die alone." Larry McCaffery, "An Expanded Interview with David Foster Wallace," in *CW*, 21–52; 32.

14 Allard den Dulk, *Existentialist Engagement in Wallace, Eggers, and Foer: A Philosophical Analysis of Contemporary American Literature* (New York: Bloomsbury Academic, 2015), 16. den Dulk also notes a letter that Wallace wrote to him, in which Wallace himself explicitly cites Kierkegaard. See p. 61.

15 See Søren Kierkegaard, *The Point of View*, ed. and trans. Howard V. Hong and Edna Hong, *Kierkegaard's Writings, Volume XXII* (Princeton: Princeton University Press, 1998).

16 One noteworthy exception is an essay by Michael J. O'Connell, who actually reads Wallace as a contemporary Christian existentialist, placing his work alongside figures such as Graham Greene, Muriel Spark, Flannery O'Connor, and Walker Percy. However, while O'Connell brings in the Christian and existentialist elements of Wallace's writing, Kierkegaard himself makes only one appearance in O'Connell's article. See Michael J. O'Connell, "'Your Temple is Self and Sentiment': David Foster Wallace's Diagnostic Novels," *Christianity and Literature* 64, no. 3 (2015): 266–92.

17 Allard den Dulk, *Existentialist Engagement in Wallace, Eggers, and Foer*, 198.

18 Boswell, *Understanding David Foster Wallace*, 145.

19 I realize this is a controversial claim. I am employing here a distinction between an "objective fideism" and a "subjective fideism," and while it makes perfect sense to refer to Kierkegaard by the latter designation, I do not think it makes sense to characterize him as an "objective fideist." By "objective fideism," I mean what is typically and traditionally referred to as a "blind faith" in specific interpretations of scriptural passages, as they pertain to an *objective* (i.e., external and communally shared) understanding of God and God's relation to the natural world. By "subjective fideism," I mean the view

that faith is a purely internal movement, *not* predicated upon the external evidence of science and reason. Rationality, however reliable it may be as far as logic and language (which are shared phenomena) are concerned, cannot, essentially, carry one to the point of faith—faith will always be an internal leap *beyond* the boundaries of reason, in the face of the absurd. As Kierkegaard's work tirelessly endeavors to demonstrate—one can push reason to its limit, and there will always be an aspect of human existence left unaddressed. My reason for steering clear, as a general rule, of the term "fideism" is that it is so easily and casually reduced to its objective form. I can think of no thinker who would have cared *less* about the debate over creation and evolution, or over the literal existence of Adam and Eve, than Søren Kierkegaard.

20 Søren Kierkegaard, *Either/Or Part I*, ed. and trans. Howard V. Hong and Edna Hong, *Kierkegaard's Writings, Volume III* (Princeton: Princeton University Press, 1987), 367.

21 Ibid., 381.

22 Søren Kierkegaard, *Fear and Trembling*, ed. C. Stephen Evans and Sylvia Walsh, trans. Sylvia Walsh (Cambridge: Cambridge University Press, 2006), 60.

23 Søren Kierkegaard, *The Sickness unto Death*, trans. Alastair Hannay (New York: Penguin Books, 1989), 79.

24 Kierkegaard, *Fear and Trembling*, 48.

25 Kierkegaard, *The Sickness unto Death*, 68.

26 Ibid., 112.

27 Kierkegaard, *Fear and Trembling*, 52.

28 Kierkegaard, *The Sickness unto Death*, 84.

29 See Kierkegaard, *Fear and Trembling*, 49.

30 Jacques Derrida, *The Gift of Death*, trans. David Wills (Chicago: The University of Chicago Press, 1995), 109.

31 Kierkegaard, *The Sickness unto Death*, 43.

32 Kierkegaard, *Fear and Trembling*, 17.

33 Kierkegaard, *Fear and Trembling*, 20.

34 Clare Carlisle, *Kierkegaard's* Fear and Trembling: *A Reader's Guide* (London: Continuum, 2010), 87.

35 David Wood, "Thinking God in the Wake of Kierkegaard," in *Kierkegaard: A Critical Reader*, ed. Jonathan Rée and Jane Chamberlain (Malden, MA: Blackwell Publishers, 1998), 53–74; 72.

36 "The popularity of *Broom* mystifies me. I can't say it's not nice to have people like it, but there's a lot of stuff in that novel I'd like to reel back in and do better. I was like twenty-two when I wrote the first draft of that thing. And I mean a *young* twenty-two" (CW 32).

37 Marilyn Manson, "Rock Is Dead," *Mechanical Animals*, Nothing/Interscope, 1998.

5

"Saying *God* with a Straight Face": Towards an Understanding of Christian Soteriology in *Infinite Jest*

Dave Laird

Since the death of David Foster Wallace in 2008, scholarship on his writing has centered heavily on the virtues of authenticity, sincerity, and post-ironic/post-secular belief that characterize his work. Wallace's 1996 encyclopedic opus *Infinite Jest* has garnered significant attention in its treatment of deeply felt human concerns, as it imagines a semi-distant future America where consumer capitalism has reached such an alarming point that year titles have been corporatized, environmental toxicity threatens regional livability,[1] entertainment has become fatally addictive, and substance abuse and various other addictions have reached a critical mass, threatening the fabric of responsible society. The novel presents a commercial dystopia in which the characters and society at large have generally embraced unfettered narcissism and addiction,[2] but in some cases struggle against these forces to achieve a semblance of community, compassion, and general restoration from the culture's pharmaceutical and spiritual toxicity.

It is here that the present analysis engages the spirituality discourse in Wallace scholarship, offering a deeper exploration of the theological tendencies and reflexes of the novel *Infinite Jest* in particular, which are substantial, and, I argue, inform the text at several foundational thematic levels.[3] I here offer that the novel's universe is one that exhibits significant elements of the biblical metanarrative, in soteriological terms, namely those of a specifically New Testament, Pauline derivation, as mediated through a Protestant lens, exhibiting elements of the Christian worldview as integral to notions of human worth, moral values, the fallen human condition, and most significantly, to salvation and redemption.

While other religious traditions—especially within monotheistic belief systems—incorporate many similar ideas to Christianity about the value of human life, the objectivity of ethical responsibilities, and prescriptions for salvation, I argue that *Infinite Jest* intersects perhaps most closely with a New Testament paradigm through its form and characters, exhibiting Pauline notions of worth, depravity, and grace-based redemption that are unique among the world's religious traditions.[4] These three categories—referred to more technically in Christian theological discourse as axiology (the study of value, worth), hamartiology (the study of sin), and soteriology (the study of redemption, salvation), respectively—function in the present argument most significantly in relation to the characters Don Gately and Mario Incandenza, and their relationships to these branches of theology, informing what I argue here is a theological map of Pauline Christianity throughout *Infinite Jest*. While others before me have commented on the theological proclivities of Wallace's fiction, I offer another way in which *Infinite Jest* may be read, one which pays close attention to the way salvation is articulated in the novel in relation to central tenets of historic Christianity, to the end that the novel resists the ironic gaze of literary postmodernism, and subconsciously demonstrates a reconsideration of traditional faith in relation to human recovery.

"There but for the grace of God Goeth D.W. Gately" (*IJ* 196)

While *Infinite Jest* essentially offers two primary protagonists in Hal Incandenza and Don Gately, the former of which generally demonstrates an unredeemed state of fallenness, anhedonia, and spiritual ennui, in which he is ultimately found to be isolated from himself and others, it offers a more hopeful portrayal of salvific grace in Don Gately. Gately's beginnings are sordid and mired in addiction, stemming from an unimaginable childhood steeped in parental alcoholism and the ongoing physical abuse of his mother at the hands of her boyfriend. While Gately's backstory comprises some of the most alarming scenes of depravity in the novel, he ultimately transforms into a character that typifies sobriety, community engagement, and self-sacrifice. Gately is thus set up to be a quintessential sinner from the novel's outset, a low-life drug addict and burglar, and is, therefore, a perfect candidate for a Christian notion of conversion or salvation, a passing from figurative spiritual death to newness of life. It is worth noting, however, that "sobriety doesn't exactly mean instant sainthood" (*IJ* 137). As this quotation implies, Gately's transition is more complicated and nuanced than a simple formulation of sobriety instantly translating to piety. But as a figure of redemption, Gately marks an attempt by Wallace to think through what salvation entails in the hyper-capitalist age of *Infinite Jest*, in which entertainment and consumption are high societal values, as well as what the limitations of such redemption might look like in this highly commercial setting.

New Testament theology affirms the inherent fallenness of humankind since the advent of original sin (Romans 5.12),[5] but offers a system of salvation from this condition by grace through faith (Eph. 2.8–9), predicated on the atoning work of Christ's self-sacrificial crucifixion and subsequent resurrection, rather than on one's own acts of righteousness and observance of divine law (Galatians 2.21). Through the spiritual progression of Don Gately's character, *Infinite Jest* relates significantly to many elements of the salvation prescription outlined above, such as grace and faith, though other ingredients beyond this understanding are involved as well, such as the reliance on human community as a support structure for sobriety, and not exclusively on a personal relationship with the divine. Gately's redemption is evidenced by the fallenness of his life in drug addiction and crime, his advancement to sobriety through Ennet House and its associated spiritual programs, the indication of his personal reformation through acts of penance and humility, and ultimately by his own Christological self-sacrifice in the defense of arguably the novel's most morally destitute character, Randy Lenz. In this way, Gately comes to resemble an unlikely saint in his imitation of Christ (Ephesians 5.1–2), most notably through his act of graceful intervention on behalf of the undeserving Lenz. Through this progression from sinner to saint, Don Gately illustrates core tenets of the Christian soteriology model, and represents a wide range of the salvation spectrum seen throughout *Infinite Jest*.

The nadirs of Gately's fallenness[6] are manifested in his accidental suffocation of A.F.R. organizer Guillaume DuPlessis and his "disastrous two nights of Dilaudid" (*IJ* 886) with Gene Fackelmann. This flashback binge sequence that finishes the novel sees Fackelmann with his eyes sewn open before his death at the hands of Whitey Sorkin's vindictive henchmen (*IJ* 979), and Gately being spared, coming to alone on the ocean shore, "flat on his back on the beach in the freezing sand … raining out of a low sky, and the tide … way out" (*IJ* 981). This final line possibly marks Gately's "rock bottom" moment, and presumably the beginning of his transition into recovery at Ennet House.[7] The implication of Gately's beach scene is of course that he has been spared death by Sorkin's underlings and deposited in a remote location, having been given a second undeserved chance at life,[8] with the beach serving as a kind of liminal space between his addicted life and the possibility of a fresh start, the latter of which he chooses. Gately's reawakening out of water in this last sentence, "And when he came back to" (*IJ* 981), invokes the Christian imagery of the sacrament of baptism, a symbol of spiritual rebirth through water, a passing from death into new life, as in Paul's characterization of it in Romans 6.4. From this point, Gately obtains something akin to the "newness of life" spoken of here by Paul, as "about four months into his Ennet House residency, the agonizing desire to ingest synthetic narcotics had been mysteriously magically removed from Don Gately," even despite his not having any previous "God or J.C.-background" (*IJ* 466). As with the Christian doctrine of Sanctification,[9] Gately's baptismal awakening on the beach is a beginning point for his transition into sobriety, which is long and arduous, but ultimately fruitful given his aspired-to list of virtues that are interestingly couched in relation to Gately's personal challenges with Randy Lenz, "Patience, tolerance, compassion, self-discipline, restraint" (*IJ* 279), resembling the qualities endorsed by Twelve-step programs such as Alcoholics Anonymous (AA), and foreshadowing the significance of Gately's later act of self-sacrifice to save Lenz's life. These also closely parallel what St. Paul calls "the fruit of the Spirit ... love, joy, peace, patience, kindness, goodness, faithfulness, gentleness, self-control" (Galatians 5.22–23), marking another clear association with Pauline notions of salvation and sanctification.

While Gately's recovery is not an explicitly orthodox Christian conversion *per se* in that he does not specifically name the name of Christ—nor does it need to be, since the important link to my argument here is that Wallace values this tradition and reinvigorates what redemption looks like and signifies in a postmodern context—Gately's personal reformation is demonstrated through his acts of penance and humble service, in line with Christ's encouragement to "bear fruit in keeping with repentance" (Matthew 3.8). In a passage that catalogues Gately's prison tattoos, one of which—perhaps proleptically—is a "sloppy cross on the inside of his mammoth left forearm" (*IJ* 210), Wallace notes that "these irrevocable emblems of jail are minor Rung Bells compared to some of the fucked-up and *really* irrevocable impulsive mistakes Gately'd made as an active drug addict and burglar, not to mention their consequences, the mistakes', which Gately's trying to accept he'll be paying off for a real long time" (*IJ* 211). Part of the penance of Ennet House and AA's programs is its advocacy of menial physical labour, and part of being "*Active*" in Boston AA includes "sweeping the footprinty floor after the Lord's Prayer and making coffee and emptying ashtrays of gasper-butts and ghastly spit-wet cigar ends" (*IJ* 354). Similarly, Gately "has become, in sobriety, a janitor" (*IJ* 434), at the Shattuck Shelter For Homeless Males, an establishment that includes some of the basest and most grotesque descriptions in *Infinite Jest*, with the clients of the shelter suffering from "every kind of physical and psychological and addictive and spiritual difficulty you could ever think of, specializing in ones that are repulsive" (*IJ* 434–5). Gately's primary job here is to clean floors, toilets, and showers, in which there is "human waste ... on a daily fucking basis"

(*IJ* 434). In sobriety, Gately thus comes to serve a very marginalized subset of the population, who might be called "the least of these my brothers" (Matthew 25.40), which psychologically tormented and destitute men could be included with St. James's call for believers to tend to other neglected and marginalized groups in society (James 1.27).

In the process of Gately's salvific transformation, he goes from deeply fallen sinner to the novel's "hero," according to Bell and Dowling, "doing his best to aid other battered souls in their struggle with their own demons."[10] The pinnacle of Gately's transformation in this context begins in the climactic scene involving Randy Lenz, who is chased by the irate Canadian "Nucks" to Ennet House as a result of his throat-slitting of their dog (*IJ* 587). Lenz, a "small-time organic-coke dealer" (*IJ* 276) and secret cocaine user throughout his time in rehab (*IJ* 543), embarks on the disturbing torture and mutilation of domestic animals on his walks back to Ennet house from sobriety meetings in what is described as his "own dark way to deal with the well-known Rage and Powerlessness issues that beset the drug addict in his first few months of abstinence" (*IJ* 538). Descriptions of Lenz's dark behaviors of cruelty, among creepy physical descriptions of him as moving vampirically with a "melting and wraithlike quality in the different shades of shadow" (*IJ* 587), mark him as one of the novel's most disturbing characters, and it is thus significant in the context of theological grace that Gately steps in to defend him in the altercation with the enraged Canadians.

Christian understandings of grace typically define it as entailing undeserved or unmerited favor, bestowed on humans by God through no goodness or righteousness of their own, as outlined in Protestant and Catholic Catechisms. In this mode, Don Gately performs a self-sacrificial act in defending Lenz—an impartation of grace—who is clearly guilty of awful crimes, and does not deserve sanctuary from the consequences of his actions in any lawful sense. "There But For the Grace of God Goeth D.W. Gately" (*IJ* 196) gets turned neatly around in the action sequence involving the Canadians, as Lenz becomes the vicarious recipient of grace through the actions of Gately, who takes a literal bullet on Lenz's behalf, becoming a surrogate of the punishment due to Lenz. Gately's defence of Lenz and the rest of "the herd" (*IJ* 605) evokes the biblical allusion of his last name, in the context of his being a good shepherd of the sheep, and of his willingness to "lay down his life for the sheep" (John 10.11). His being pierced is also symbolic of the Old Testament notion that the Messiah would be "pierced" in an act of vicarious self-sacrifice, as in Isaiah 53.5 and Zechariah 12.10, with these finding purchase in the Gospel records, with the piercing of Christ's wrists, feet, and side (John 19.34). In this sequence, Gately transitions from the recipient of grace seen in his redemption story to the one bestowing grace upon an undeserving Randy Lenz in a Christ-like act of self-sacrifice, evidence of Gately's own sanctification. This act marks an expression of his role as a "kinsman redeemer," someone in Mosaic Law who acts vicariously on the behalf of someone—usually a relative—in significant distress or need.[11] In New Testament theology, Christ is considered the superlative kinsman redeemer, and Gately's graceful action on behalf of Lenz that results in his own near-death mark a point of dialogue between *Infinite Jest*'s vision of salvation and that of Pauline doctrine, in the sense that Lenz's life is undeservedly preserved through Gately's act of grace, despite the consequences for sin being death that should otherwise result for Lenz.[12]

In response to the curious claims in Hubert Dreyfus and Sean Dorrance Kelly's *All Things Shining*, that "one finds in Wallace no hope for salvation by God" and "Wallace's vision is a Nietzschean one ....God casts no shadow at all in the world of *Infinite Jest*,"[13] I have undertaken to demonstrate here that Don Gately's redemption narrative is a significant counter-point to such assertions. While their claim may find greater purchase in the storyline and conclusion of Hal Incandenza's unredemptive narrative,[14] I believe that Gately provides significant refutation of such a notion that *Jest*'s is a nihilistic universe. Since Gately's "spiritual journey" follows a redemptive progression, Dreyfus and Kelly's further assessment that Wallace's is a "godless world" that requires "an escape ... by constructing a happier meaning for it out of nothing, literally ex nihilo as God himself once had done"[15] is also puzzling in light of the theistic implications of Gately's story, as well as in Mario's Christologically figurative narrative explored next.

"Mario floats" (*IJ* 316)

In the previous section, I analyzed *Infinite Jest*'s display of salvation predicated on divine grace and the means of salvation, namely through community, service, and sacrifice, with the discovery that the novel envisions a new mode of conceiving of redemption in a post-Christian, hyper-capitalist society that reinvigorates orthodox ways of thinking about the personal salvation process. Having looked at the novel's preoccupation with the salvation state of Don Gately as a redeemed addict-turned-kinsman redeemer—which are leveraged toward demonstrating a tension in the Christian soteriological ethos—I now turn to the culmination of *Infinite Jest*'s doctrinal engagement with Christian soteriology in the character of Mario Incandenza, who, in several significant ways, bears a figurative imitation of Christ, in terms of his physical disabilities—which, I argue, have theological resonances—and his role as redeemer. This is not to say that I am suggesting Mario is to be conceived of as a supernatural being by any means, or that the surrounding details of his life are even largely analogous to Christ's,[16] but instead that there are elements of Mario's role in the novel that strongly suggest his character, actions, and spiritual disposition situate him as having a special role in the redemption picture the novel presents.

As theologian Karl Barth conceives of human identity not in terms of nature, but through a Christological framework "based in a grace-filled *disruption of* nature,"[17] Mario's role is similarly disruptive in *Infinite Jest*, providing a counterexample to the decadent, addicted world in which most of the novel's characters find themselves enmeshed. His character is thus unique and unparalleled in the novel's cast of messy and deeply addicted characters, having a purity so refined it is almost as if he appears to have no need of salvation himself, and pointing the way for others toward a more rich way of being alive and human. He rather demonstrates the ability to convey a disruptive sense of grace to others, evoking a figurative rendering of redemptive power according to Pauline and Apostolic expressions throughout the New Testament. Mario thus fulfills the soteriological spectrum, serving as the pinnacle example of the salvation states demonstrated in the world of *Infinite Jest*, as one who, at times, bears an almost allegorical likeness to the Messianic figure in Judeo-Christianity.

Physically, Mario is described throughout the novel as profoundly deformed, and challenged by a range of medical issues that accompany his physical complications. Krzysztof Piekarski notes that the extensive, encyclopedic list describing his disabilities serves to underscore the fact that Wallace desires for Mario to be "a symbol that is trans-human," wanting us to "conceive of Mario as somehow 'Other' and metaphorically inhuman,"[18] having "a kind of presence that merely resides in a human body for the narrative purposes of cohabiting with other humans and acting as a foil."[19] Mario's trans-humanity thus marks a patent site of confluence with the doctrine of hypostatic union[20] in Christianity, which holds that Christ, while fully God, was also fully human, or "God-human."[21] Through the incarnation, Christ is viewed in New Testament theology to be essentially a God-human "cohabiting with other humans"[22]—and as Wallace says to Larry McCaffery about the role of fiction—Christ fully "illuminate[s] the possibilities for being alive and human" in the world (*CW* 26). In this way, the incorporeal Word and the written word of literature intersect in the character of Mario, who demonstrates sincerity, authenticity, and human empathy like no other character in the novel, evoking den Dulk's sentiment that "Mario is good faith"—as in the very embodiment of it—and "the paragon of what it means to be human,"[23] which has a very Christological resonance indeed.

While descriptions of Christ's form in the New Testament nowhere approach the level of Mario's disabled body,[24] there is a curious confluence in the way Mario's bodily characteristics function amidst a whole community of other perfected, hyper-developed bodies. This similarity bears a significant theological resonance, namely that in New Testament doctrine, the resurrected bodies of saints are held to be glorious and perfect, without pain or disability,[25] while the Gospels make it clear that Christ bears the marks of his crucifixion *after His resurrection*, serving as an eternal reminder of His salvific act. In the famous "Doubting Thomas" passage of John 20,

Thomas denies the first resurrection appearance to the disciples, from which he was absent. At a later appearance, Christ addresses Thomas's skepticism, offering an empirical demonstration of his corporeality after death: "Put your finger here, and see my hands; and put out your hand, and place it in My side. Do not disbelieve, but believe," to which Thomas responds, "My Lord and my God!" (John 20.27–28). Reflecting on the Passion wounds of Christ revealed to Thomas, theologian Hans Urs Von Balthasar notes that "these wounds indicate the presence of Christ's past in eternity not just as a memory but as a present reality ... since they exist now in the resurrected, victorious Christ."[26] The post-resurrection scarring/disability of Christ thus illustrates the wounds to be carried forward into eternity.

The feature of wounds on the risen body of Christ thus makes His the only disabled body in the Christian conception of the afterlife, and a distinct point of comparison with Mario's disabled body amidst the array of hyper-perfected athletic bodies at E.T.A. This analogy secures an important site of discussion for my reading of Mario's elevation, in that his character is much more than an appeal to sympathy, but that his disabilities are, in part, what makes his character's figurative comparison to Christ's act of grace tenable. The novel evokes this specifically Christological imagery in its treatment of Mario to the effect that it establishes a pinnacle for its intersection with soteriology, and to reinforce its preoccupation with the concepts of grace and salvation.

Mario's redemptive role is most significantly realized in his life-affirming interactions with E.T.A. trainer Barry Loach, a marked social pariah during his tenure living on the Boston streets. The chronicle of Loach showcases the effects of Mario's redemptive character, as is foreshadowed early in the novel: "Trainer Barry Loach all but kisses the kid's ring,"[27] since it is Mario who through coincidence saved him from the rank panhandling underbelly of Boston Common's netherworld and more or less got him his job" (*IJ* 316). This story is not told in full until the last chapter of the novel, just prior to the presentation of Don Gately's backstory, and has a mythic reputation on the Enfield campus: "One E.T.A. tradition consists of Big Buddies recounting to new or very young Little Buddies the saga of Loach and how he ended up as an elite Head Trainer" (*IJ* 967). As previously noted, Barry Loach takes to the streets in a social experiment about the goodness of humanity in a wager with his seminary-dropout brother, who:

> Suffered at age twenty-five a sudden and dire spiritual decline in which his basic faith in the innate indwelling goodness of men like spontaneously combusted and disappeared—and for no apparent or dramatic reason; it just seemed as if the brother had suddenly contracted a black misanthropic spiritual outlook ... a kind of Lou Gehrig's Disease of the spirit—and his interest in serving man and God-in-man and nurturing the indwelling Christ in people through Jesuitical pursuits underwent an understandable nosedive. (*IJ* 967–8)

Seeking to restore his brother's faith in a meaningful Christian universe, and being "understandably way out his depth on the theological turf of like Apologia and the redeemability of man" (*IJ* 968), Barry Loach becomes homeless to demonstrate "that the basic human character wasn't as unempathetic and necrotic as the brother's present depressed condition was leading him to think" (*IJ* 969), with the simple goal of "instead of stemming change simply ask passersby to touch him. Just to touch him. Viz. extend some basic human warmth and contact" (*IJ* 969). After almost ten months of unsuccessful experimentation, "Loach's own soul began to sprout little fungal patches of necrotic rot, and his upbeat view of the so-called normal and respectable human race began to undergo dark revision" and his near "disappearing forever into the fringes and dregs of metro Boston street life and spending his whole adult life homeless and louse-ridden and stemming in the Boston Common and drinking out of brown paper bags" (*IJ* 970) is interrupted by the intervention of Mario Incandenza. In a humanity-affirming act, Mario "extended his clawlike hand and touched and heartily shaken Loach's own fuliginous hand, which led through a convoluted but kind of heartwarming and faith-reaffirming series of circumstances to B. Loach, even w/o an official B.A., being given an Asst. Trainer's job at E.T.A.," from which he is promptly promoted to Head Trainer (*IJ* 971). Mario's exchange with Loach here, and the subsequent redemption that results, is perhaps the highest representation of disruptive grace and recovery in *Infinite Jest*, and a distinct moment highlighting Mario's Christological resonance, extending him into the realm of allegorical savior.

The redeeming handshake in the Barry Loach street sequence unwaveringly evokes the account of Jesus and the leper, which is recorded in all three Synoptic Gospels: "While He was in one of the cities, there came a man full of leprosy. And when he saw Jesus, he fell on his face and begged Him, 'Lord, if you will, you can make me clean.' And Jesus stretched out his hand and touched him, saying, 'I will; be clean.' And immediately the leprosy left him" (Luke 5.12–13). While Barry Loach is not afflicted physically with such an infirmity, Loach's "necrotic rot" is essentially a leprosy of the soul, and Mario's willingness to physically touch him causes Loach's socio-emotional and existential healing, restoring his faith in basic human goodness. Mario—as figurative Christ—thus performs the crucial action in Loach's redemption, through an extension of grace that re-affirms his human value, saving him from a future of literal and spiritual homelessness and social exile.

Beyond Mario's character, disabilities, and his role as redeemer, the statement "Hal's next-oldest brother Mario doesn't seem to resemble much of anyone they know" (*IJ* 101) can be read as more than a physical description, signifying Mario's divine symbolism and Christological significance. Bolstering this Messianic connection further, "Hal almost idealizes Mario, secretly. God-type issues aside, Mario is a (semi-) walking miracle, Hal believes. People who're somehow burned at birth, withered or ablated way past anything like what might be fair, they either curl up in their fire, or else they rise ... Mario floats, for Hal" (*IJ* 316), and like Christ in biblical theology, Mario rises.[28] The point may be raised about whether Hal's elevated view of Mario is distinct from that of the novel or narrator's view, but given the ways in which Mario is treated and revered by most of the E.T.A. characters and is frequently discussed in the context of empathy, sincerity, and authenticity, I hold that Hal's high view of Mario is synonymous with the rest of the novel's. In the salvific trajectory of Gately and Mario, Mario thus fulfills an elevated, symbolic Christological role in *Infinite Jest*, thus rounding out the novel's dialogue with Christian theology's soteriological concerns. Mario is thus a disruptive force, representing the possibility of change, which is difficult to contemplate for so many characters in the novel. His importance may not be as a literal savior of the citizens of O.N.A.N. and beyond, but rather as a representation of a better way to be more completely human, leading others by the example of his benevolent existence, and serving to pose the question of what redemption means and how it is most fully expressed. Reading Mario this way enables us to appreciate Wallace's retelling of the Biblical salvation narrative, as understood by historic Christian doctrine and thought, and secures a full picture of the salvation spectrum expressed throughout the range of characters in *Infinite Jest*.

Conclusion

In my analysis of *Infinite Jest*'s dialogic engagement with Christian soteriology, we have seen an exchange of ideas between some of the novel's recovery-oriented thematic concerns and Pauline theology that establishes the significance of creation, humanity's deep fallenness, and its options for recovery and redemption. In the guru character Lyle's estimation that "the truth will set you free. But not until it is finished with you" (*IJ* 389), the novel offers no tidy answers about how deeply addicted humans can achieve freedom from their narcotized temples of worship and the entertainment that so thoroughly enslaves them. Instead, the novel presents a messy, chaotic world whose parody of the cultural, political, and environmental landscapes of North America comes much closer to the present moment's situation than might be desirable, in an oddly prophetic forecast, that over twenty years after its publication, rings more true than ever, given the rise of Netflix, Skype, Facebook, virtual reality, and the presidency of Donald Trump, whose policies bear a staggering resemblance to those of *Infinite Jest*'s fictional president, Johnny Gentle.

The novel's disjointed and challenging organizational form thematically adds to the ways in which it envisions its characters navigating the tensions of what it means to be "alive and human" in this world (CW 26), contributing to the messiness of its portrayal of the human condition. As Krzysztof Piekarski says, *Infinite Jest* is "an encyclopedia of suffering,"[29] and its characters are clearly bound in the world of pain in which they must seek to escape their various torments. Lyle's adage rings true in that some characters do approach a semblance of freedom by the novel's end, but only through great physical and psychological hardship and tough personal choices, with no truly clear sense of finality. Through a long trajectory of despair, Gately finally appears to be on his way toward personal reclamation by the novel's end, and Mario seems to have known it all along, offering a spectrum of conditions of salvation that explore the range of human decision and experience in a theological context. The novel thus provides fertile ground for thinking about what redemption is, how it is meaningful and urgent, and through what means it is acquired or achieved.

This articulation of a redemptive schema is primarily done through *Infinite Jest*'s tripartite fascination with three core tenets of the orthodox Christian metanarrative:

1 Humanity is infused with innate, sacred, and infinite value, and thus has purpose being created in the *Imago Dei* (image of God). Furthermore, this created value implies that moral imperatives are binding, that human beings have specific responsibilities toward each other and their Creator.

2 Despite this value and purpose, humanity has fallen from its original, created intention through the exercise of free will, which has created a departure from the way the world was intended to be. Regardless of this condition, humanity still maintains its sacred value, and each person is deserving of respect, love, and compassion. This point of fallenness or ontological poverty—generally articulated through the ubiquitous addictions, afflictions, and criminal behaviors of the novel's characters—is perhaps *Infinite Jest*'s greatest territory of theological exploration in terms of sheer page-space granted to the topic, as well as those of Wallace's other works. Yet despite such a lamentable condition—indeed, *because* of it—the novel's narrative voice maintains compassion and empathy for its characters, as they are reflective of humanity's condition *en masse*.

3 Humanity's significance and fallenness are married through a redemptive, self-sacrificial schema predicated on the concept of grace that provides a semblance of renewal to its original, created intent. While only a few of *Infinite Jest*'s characters are redeemed in a palpable way within the given pages, there are numerous poignant

moments of restoration that furnish the reclamation of human value, most notably seen in and through the characters Don Gately and Barry Loach, with Mario Incandenza playing a specifically Christological role in the text. As a result of Don Gately's conversion narrative, many of his specific actions embody a self-sacrificial, New Testament ethos.

As such, *Infinite Jest* presents a universe infused with theistic meaning, where the characters are deeply significant—not just as conduits of narrative plot but as representational human beings—while simultaneously being extremely messy and fallen, mired in addiction and narcissism, who ultimately benefit from a redemptive model typified by grace—or undeserved favor—that provides an escape from their purgatorial hopelessness. These resonances in *Infinite Jest* are thus best described as Pauline, primarily due to the nature of a redemptive schema based on grace that is unique to Christianity. While the other major monotheistic religions of Judaism and Islam also contain notions of creation, value, and human fallenness, Christianity contains the distinctive notion of redemptive grace, in salvific relation to human value and fallenness, which *Infinite Jest* bears a marked preoccupation with. My close look at salvation states in the novel—most particularly through the characters of Don Gately and Mario Incandenza—reveals that *Infinite Jest* is a soteriological novel, preoccupied with the question of human redemption, and as such, engages the biblical metanarrative which is consumed with the same concerns.

Wallace thus shows that redemption can speak to the strange present and to a fictional conception of the world in ways that not only affirm existing moral prescriptions, but also identify the possibility of creating new ones that relate to the technological developments so culturally prevalent in the world he writes. Such a progression does not invalidate a strict orthodox understanding of biblical redemption, but instead ratifies its importance and courageously develops what it can mean for the present, echoing Mario's experience at Ennet House: "once he heard somebody say *God* with a straight face" (*IJ* 591). Wallace similarly envisions good art as that which "locates and applies CPR to those elements of what's human and magical that still live and glow despite the times' darkness" (*CW* 26), a sentiment which I have shown to have been successfully achieved through the soteriological elements of *Infinite Jest*. Since this kind of identification with regeneration is at the heart of Wallace's project, it makes sense to consider his work in theological terms, as empathy is also the cornerstone of the Christian metanarrative's conception of the Incarnation of God in Christ, in which God comes to fully identify with creation, knowing firsthand what it is like to be human and to suffer, to live in the tension of a fallen world with the hope of redemption for all.

Notes

1. With a contained nuclear waste site called the Great Concavity having taken over four northeastern U.S. states, with giant fans that blow toxic fumes up into Quebec and the Maritimes, giving the novel an apocalyptic sensibility.
2. Which novelist Don DeLillo describes as a "dead serious frolic of addicted humanity." See Don DeLillo, "Informal Remarks from the David Foster Wallace Memorial Service in New York on October 23, 2008," in *The Legacy of David Foster Wallace*, ed. Samuel Cohen and Lee Konstantinou (Iowa City: University of Iowa Press, 2012), 23–4; 23.
3. Wallace's own personal interest in theology and Christian writing, and his near-conversion to the Catholic Church in the early 1990s lends credibility to the idea of his intentional inclusion of theological themes in *Infinite Jest*, but is by no means essential to my argument.
4. Particularly the idea of salvation by grace through faith.
5. *The English Standard Version Bible: Containing the Old and New Testaments* (Oxford: Oxford University Press, 2009). All Bible quotations are taken from this version and subsequent quotes in this chapter will be cited parenthetically in the text.
6. Indeed, Alcoholics Anonymous founder Bill W. uses the phrase "nadir of ... despair" to describe the rock-bottom type ennui that accompanies substance dependency (169), demonstrating that the novel engages several different theologically-based redemptive threads profoundly influenced by a Pauline foundation. See *Alcoholics Anonymous: The Story of How Many Thousands of Men and Women Have Recovered from Alcoholism*, 4th ed. (New York: Alcoholics Anonymous World Services, 2001).
7. Although this is not entirely clear or settled, as Rob Short notes in his dissertation: "Wallace chooses to leave out the particulars of Hal and Gately hitting bottom from the narrative. They exist just outside the bounds of the text, but because we see Hal and Gately both before and after their epiphanic experiences, we are faced with the simple truth that they have changed—just not how." "Big Books: Addiction and Recovery in the Novels of David Foster Wallace," Ph.D. Diss. (University of Florida, 2017).
8. Which, given the fraudulent situation Gately had been involved in with the Dilaudid, seems like a form of grace considering the brutal methods of Sorkin's ultraviolent and sadistic employees. As indicated in the final pages, "C told Gately quietly how Whitey said to say he knew Donnie wasn't part of Fackelmann's score to fuck Sorkin ... That he didn't need to do anything except kick back and enjoy the party and let Fackelmann face his own music and to not let any like nineteenth-century notions of defending the weak and pathetic drag Gately into this ....That he hoped Gately wouldn't hold it against him ... and wanted no beef, later" (*IJ* 977–8).
9. Sanctification being the idea that the Christian believer is made progressively more into the image of Christ, shedding their former slavishness to sin in a gradual trajectory toward holiness. St. Paul's classification of the Christian

believer as a "new creation" (2 Corinthians 5.17), while true at the moment of conversion, implies the coming process of sanctification as defined by Rowan Williams as "the model of Christian growth and struggle." See M.J. Knight, "Christ Existing in Ordinary: Dietrich Bonhoeffer and Sanctification," *International Journal of Systematic Theology* 16, no. 4 (2014): 414–35; 415.

10 Robert H. Bell and William Dowling, *A Reader's Companion to Infinite Jest* (Bloomington: Xlibris, 2005), 95–6.

11 Walter A. Elwell, ed., *Evangelical Dictionary of Biblical Theology* (Grand Rapids: Baker Books, 1996), 456.

12 As in Romans 6:23, "for the wages of sin is death."

13 Hubert L. Dreyfus and Sean D. Kelly, "David Foster Wallace's Nihilism," in *All Things Shining: Reading the Western Classics to Find Meaning in a Secular Age* (New York: Free Press, 2011), 22–57; 46.

14 But even despite Hal's unredeemed state, he is still treated with dignity and great care, both as a human being and as an addict actively seeking respite from his narcotic dependency.

15 Dreyfus and Kelly, "David Foster Wallace's Nihilism," 46.

16 That is, virgin birth, twelve disciples, betrayal for thirty pieces of silver, crucifixion and resurrection, etc. Indeed, many elements of Mario's situation directly contradict such an analogy, such as his absent, suicided father-figure who is referred to as "Himself" by many of the novel's characters (a god-like title), and who has created a killer video capable of eradicating humanity. It might be conceivable, however, to think of the parodic play between James and Mario in dichotomous Old Testament judge/destroyer versus New Testament rescuer/redeemer roles, respectively.

17 Brandy Daniels, "Grace Beyond Nature? Beyond Embodiment as Essentialism: A Christological Critique," *Feminist Theology* 24, no. 3 (2016): 245–59; 253.

18 Krzysztof Piekarski, "Buddhist Philosophy in the Work of David Foster Wallace," Ph.D. Diss. (University of Texas at Austin, 2013), 156.

19 Piekarski, "Buddhist Philosophy," 160.

20 Also known as "the Incarnation." See John 1.1 and 1.14 for primary foundation for this doctrine.

21 Christopher R.J. Holmes, "The Aseity of God as a Material Evangelical Concern," *Journal of Reformed Theology* 8, no. 1 (2014): 61–78; 63.

22 As in John 1.14, "And the Word became flesh and dwelt among us."

23 Allard den Dulk, "Good Faith and Sincerity: Sartrean Virtues of Self-Becoming in David Foster Wallace's Infinite Jest," in *Gesturing toward Reality: David Foster Wallace and Philosophy*, ed. Robert Bolger and Scott Korb (New York: Bloomsbury Academic, 2014), 199–220; 213.

24 Though there is a prophecy in Isaiah 53.2 concerning the Messiah that "he had no form or majesty that we should look at him, and no beauty that we should desire him."

25 As Paul writes in 1 Corinthians 15.40–4: "There are heavenly bodies and earthly bodies, but the glory of the heavenly is of one kind, and the glory of the earthly is of another. There is one glory of the sun, and another glory of the moon, and another glory of the stars; for star differs from star in glory. So is it with the resurrection of the dead. What is sown is perishable; what is raised is imperishable. It is sown in dishonor; it is raised in glory. It is sown in weakness; it is raised in power. It is sown a natural body; it is raised a spiritual body. If there is a natural body, there is also a spiritual body."

26 Quoted in Gerard F. O'Hanlon, *The Immutability of God in the Theology of Hans Urs Von Balthasar* (Cambridge [England]; New York: Cambridge University Press, 1990), 100.

27 A papal reference that signals Loach's Catholic background.

28 Figuratively speaking, of course.

29 Krzysztof Piekarski, "Buddhist Philosophy in the Work of David Foster Wallace," Ph.D. Diss. (University of Texas at Austin, 2013), 153.

6

Infinite Jest, C.S. Lewis's *Tao*, and Religious Community

Peter Spaulding

Although the name "New Sincerity" has always seemed a little odd to me—how is the sincerity of these artists any different than the sincerity of earlier writers?—it turns out to be quite helpful for this project because it strikes a break between contemporary writers like Zadie Smith, Jonathan Franzen, and Wallace, and the postmodernists of a generation before such as Thomas Pynchon, William Gaddis, and early Don DeLillo, whose primary literary mode was what Wallace called "hip irony" in his famous "E Unibus Pluram" essay. If New Sincerity defies the hip irony of its previous generation's lauded postmodern cynics, is it also in part reaching back in solidarity to the generation the postmodern ironists ironized and rebelled against? Well, of course, yes and no. These generational categories can quite easily fall apart when given any portion of serious attention. But C.S. Lewis, writing primarily in the 1940s and 1950s, certainly felt an oncoming tide of irony in the forthcoming generation of writers and philosophers and feared it long before Wallace rebelled against it. Although for most of Lewis's writing, his main stake in public discourse was a defense of the Christian worldview, *The Abolition of Man*, a work primarily concerned with education, approaches its topic on purely philosophical grounds, addressing a latent aloofness, very similar to that of the American postmodern novelists, encouraged in his time by textbook writers and the intelligentsia. Wallace finds in Lewis a partisanship to sincerity uncommon both in Lewis's time and in the later writers of postmodern philosophy and literature that Wallace took intentional steps away from in his work after *Girl with Curious Hair*. Most explicitly in his essays, but even through certain characters' voices in his fiction, Wallace tries to produce positive assertions of goodness, putting forward potential answers to life's most pressing existential questions. His work tries to avoid aloof superiority, while simultaneously seeking real solutions to human problems, risking sentimentalism to try to achieve genuinely moral fiction and prose. Here I hope to (1) establish a precedent for reading Lewis as influential to Wallace, (2) explore their attitudes toward authority in their works *Infinite Jest* and *The Abolition of Man*, and (3) show how Wallace's attitude toward religion informs his literary project.

Central to Lewis's argument in *The Abolition of Man* is his borrowed term, the "Tao." He defines this as synonymous with the Natural Law, a set of universal, principle values that unite all cultures. But Lewis also explains his use of this term as deriving from Chinese Taoism:

> The Chinese also speak of a great thing (the greatest thing) called the *Tao*. It is the reality beyond all predicates, the abyss that was before the Creator Himself. It is Nature, it is the Way, the Road. It is the Way in which the universe goes on, the Way in which things everlastingly emerge, stilly and tranquilly, into space and time. It is also the Way which every man should tread in imitation of that cosmic and supercosmic progression, conforming all activities to that great exemplar.[1]

He further defines it as "the doctrine of objective value, the belief that certain attitudes are really true and others really false."[2] Although Lewis certainly appropriates the term from the Taoism of the Lao-tzu (sixth century BCE), Lewis regards his "Tao" as not entirely separate from Taoist thought—and cites Lao-tzu's texts extensively in *The Abolition of Man*—but considers his Tao an umbrella term for the pan-cultural understanding of Natural Law. Lewis uses this term and not "Natural Law" most probably for inculcating in his English readers the true universality of it, its cultural transcendence, and to divorce it from purely Western metaphysics.

The connection between Wallace and Lewis has on occasion been recognized, but it usually surprises lay readers because of their vastly different subjects. As a professor, Wallace used *The Lion, the Witch, and the Wardrobe* as a required text for his class on literary analysis in the fall of 1994,[3] and Wallace highlighted observations about Lewis in books that can be found in his personal library.[4] Moreover, as noted by J. Peder Zane's *The Top Ten*,[5] Wallace picked Lewis's *The Screwtape Letters* as his favorite book, which came as a surprise to many. Jonathan Franzen, in his heartfelt essay, "Farther Away," not only confirms Wallace's obsession with *Screwtape*, but also implicates it in Wallace's suicide, imagining a Screwtapean logic infesting the interior life of Wallace's final days.[6] Oddly enough, Wallace and Lewis expressed similar sentiments of dissatisfaction after their respective completions of their books. In a 1960 preface to the new edition of *The Screwtape Letters*, Lewis described a rather unsatisfying and painful experience: "Though I had never written anything more easily, I never wrote with less enjoyment ... though it was easy to twist one's mind into the diabolical attitude, it was not fun, or not for long. The strain produced a sort of spiritual cramp ... It almost smothered me before I was done."[7] Don DeLillo, in a BBC Radio documentary on Wallace said he "received a letter from [Wallace] shortly after he finished writing *Infinite Jest*. And in it [Wallace] said that this was the most serious work he'd ever done, and he thought the best work he'd ever done. However, he was upset over the fact he did not feel the pleasure he ordinarily [felt] in writing fiction."[8] The presence of evil in *Infinite Jest*, particularly the nightmarish "face in the floor" (*IJ* 62), certainly feels of the same energy as *Screwtape*.

David Lipsky also documents Wallace's interest in *The Screwtape Letters* in *Although of Course You End Up Becoming Yourself*. Wallace recommends the book to Lipsky for its honesty and rhetoric, that it's "honest with a motive."[9] Wallace says that "it's a very childlike, simple book. But Lewis is incredibly smart."[10] He admires that Lewis's rhetoric is subjected to a cause, something that he can believe in, that he's smart, but that he does not need to appear very smart in his fiction. Wallace says that he is himself interested in writing something that, like *The Screwtape Letters*, "feel[s] true ... taste[s] true."[11] Wallace finds in Lewis a fresh mode of writing that directly prescribes or argues on behalf of something for the purpose of building it up in the minds of its readers and convincing them of its veracity. It becomes very important to Wallace to be read more as someone who is honest than as someone who is merely smart.

Stephen J. Burn's work on Wallace's fiction sees Lewis as a positive influence on Wallace's work and "conception of the value of literature."[12] Burn points out that for both *The Pale King* and Lewis's *An Experiment in Criticism*, attentiveness is of utmost importance: in *The Pale King*, paying attention to others; in *An Experiment in Criticism*, paying attention to written language, written others. Burn writes, "underpinning attentive reading is a solution to the metaphysical loneliness we suffer within the prison of ourselves."[13] Wallace and Lewis both believe in literature's power to embattle existential loneliness by drawing the reader's attention into the mind of another. *The Abolition of Man* puts forward a similar argument but with education rather than literature as its subject, asking us to consider the loneliness of an education that insists on epistemological phenomenology. Burn identifies exactly the most important similarity between these two writers: their understanding of isolation as a danger with real consequences for the individual and society.

D.T. Max identifies three main threads or styles in *Infinite Jest*, each corresponding to a period in Wallace's life,

> beginning with the playful, comic voice of his Amherst years, passing through his infatuation with postmodernism at Arizona, and ending with

the conversion to single-entendre principles of his days in Boston. These three approaches correspond roughly to the three main plot strands of the book: the first, the portrait of the witty, dysfunctional Incandenza family; the second, the near-future dystopian backdrop of the book ... the third, the passion of Don Gately, set in the thinly fictionalized version of Granada House.[14]

Max can't help but describe the Gately narrative using implicitly religious terms like "conversion" and "passion." Max implies both that Wallace's fiction is not entirely given to the Alcoholics Anonymous (AA) thread, nor the postmodern play of the Incandenzas. No one can really identify the connection Gately and Hal end up having in the time between Gately's horrific hospital scenes at the novel's close and the Year of Glad section at its beginning. Whatever connection Gately and Hal have—either via the wraith or via some external adventure to Jim's grave (as is implied by the pregnant burst of plot on pages 16–7)—remains largely unexplored by most of the book and left to the imagination of readers. The atmospheres of Ennet House, Enfield Tennis Academy, and the political world of Marathe, Steeply, and Johnny Gentle are starkly different from each other, and they only cross over each other a few times in the novel's action. And, further to our purposes here, the pat and aggressively simple lessons Gately learns in AA are not necessarily applicable or communicable to Hal, Orin, and Jim. Whereas most of Gately's story seems to be a bold-faced endorsement of AA, the main theme of Hal's story seems to be a sort of failure of language akin to *The Broom of the System*'s main themes (heavily influenced by Pynchon's *The Crying of Lot 49*). Not only do these fragments have separate themes, their messages—inasmuch as they each have one—contradict each other. Gately finds meaning, purpose, and recovery in a community, while Hal becomes increasingly cut off from everyone as he tries to recover from his marijuana addiction.

Lewis's influence is therefore most relevant with Gately and the AA thread of the novel and becomes complicated when applied to the Incandenza thread. Although Lewis's Tao is not wholly irrelevant to the Incandenzas (especially Mario and his longing for connection with Madame Psychosis), the Gately/AA bits of *Infinite Jest* make the strongest break from the Pynchonian tradition Wallace was flirting with in college. Whereas *Gravity's Rainbow* constantly evokes the parabolic shape of the rainbow (i.e. the missile's trajectory), the Incandenza's thread of *Infinite Jest* constantly evokes the circle: the chapter headings' symbol is itself a circle; the "cardiod" (*IJ* 983) shape of Enfield is also circular and reminiscent of the chapter headings' symbol. The praxis of AA, however, is linear: from addiction to sobriety. The novel itself becomes a medium for people suffering with addiction to feel a community-like sense of solidarity with Wallace. The Incandenzas are Ovid's *The Metamorphoses*; Gately is Virgil's Aeneas. Yet these are held taught against one another, balanced together, and left irresolute. The book is not linear, but not entirely un-linear either. The end of Gately's story can be read as both one of relapse and recovery, though neither is fully satisfied nor embraced. Submission to an established authority is fine for drug addicts, but it takes a slightly darker turn when manifested politically.

Given all these complexities, I have chosen here to privilege the Gately/AA portion of the book—while also making comment on Lyle, Marathe, and Schtitt—to delimit the breadth of Lewis's influence and to address the explicitly religious components of the book. When read through the lens of his Kenyon College commencement address, the Gately portion seems most important, most indicative of what is to come ideologically for Wallace. It may be that *Infinite Jest* is the cusp from which Wallace turns from postmodern play to sincerity, from the fun absurdity of characters like "the Antichrist" in *Broom*, to the austere importance of the IRS in *The Pale King*: "Gentlemen, you are called to account" (*PK* 235).

For *Infinite Jest*'s characters who reach "Rock Bottom," submission of the individual will to a larger body becomes the only viable escape from solipsistic enslavement to fleeting, individual desires. Both *Infinite Jest* and *The Abolition of Man* are alike in their near-apocalyptic anxieties regarding solipsistic pleasure seeking. Both writers go to lengths to present religious community as the solution to this problem—for Lewis, the *Tao*; for Wallace, AA. An element in *Infinite Jest* looks forward to Wallace's later defense of religion's usefulness in warding off despair communicated in *This Is Water*. Lewis's *The Abolition of Man*, though not explicitly religious, puts forward an argument for the necessity of objective reality in a functional society. The alternative to this is Lewis's hell in *The Great Divorce*: an infinitely expanding exurb of people so constantly irritated with one another they must be always moving further out and away from each other.

The Abolition of Man was occasioned by what he renames for anonymity's sake "the Green Book," a classroom text that Lewis saw as encouraging what we would now call solipsism. Instead of describing a waterfall as sublime, students are encouraged to think that in identifying a waterfall as sublime they are only recognizing their own sublime feelings for the waterfall.[15] To Lewis, this goes far beyond the territory of the composition classroom and well into something like the field of epistemology. He also faults the authors of the book for their insistence on teaching students to "debunk" poor writing without ever prompting them to wonder what good writing looks like. Lewis's solution is to teach students how to write well by putting poor writing up against good writing, "debunking" the appeal of the former. The Green Book educators teach students how to be snobs without ever teaching them the importance of responding in earnest to social and individual problems: with hateful feelings toward things that are hateful, and with loving feelings toward things that are lovely.

Enfield Tennis Academy's unofficial guru, Lyle, has an odd preoccupation with objects. Throughout many of his encounters with students, Lyle repeatedly advises them not to underestimate the value of objects, that proper attention to objects reveals whole secret worlds of potential. When Ortho Stice goes to Lyle to get some answers regarding the recent, inexplicable movement of his bed while he sleeps on it, Lyle tells a story of a man he once knew who could pull himself up off the ground by the back of a chair he was standing on just because "he had not underestimated" it (395). This of course does Stice no good, or so he thinks, but it communicates Lyle's belief in objects' essential potential, that a true appreciation of objects themselves yields supernatural results. Lewis's conviction regarding objects is that "until quite modern times all teachers ... believed ... that objects did not merely receive, but could *merit*, our approval or disapproval,"[16] implying that we have forgotten how to teach students the importance of paying objects our attention for their own sake. Lewis's whole complaint with the Green Book's insistence about the waterfall is that it tries to erase the waterfall, to make it only a perception of the viewer, making any consequent praise the observer gives to the waterfall only self-praise. Lewis's philosophy of education is that, in observation, students should subject themselves to their respective objects of study. Later on, Lewis elaborates that stripping objects of their "qualitative properties"[17] is to see them as Stice does, in less than their full reality and potential. Lyle, however, seems to exist in a spiritual reality beyond the limits of the world Stice has been told to believe is all that exists. Lyle subsists solely on caffeine-free Diet Coke and students' sweat, but his spirituality brings him to a greater understanding of materiality, albeit as bizarre as it appears in *Infinite Jest*.

The Green Book's insistence on the importance of "debunking" bad writing resembles *Infinite Jest*'s Geoffrey Day as he tries to avoid assimilation into the Ennet House community. Central to AA's praxis is the belief that the intellect is a common inhibitor to substance abuse recovery. When Day joins Ennet House, his mind immediately sets about the process of deconstructing or "seeing through" some of AA's ideological tenets, complaining that he now "lives by the macramé samplers ordered from the back-page ad of an old *Reader's Digest*" and has to think in monosyllables (271). Like the authors of the Green Book, Day focuses on advertising and its inadequacies. He is the product of the kind of education whose main goal is to make its adherents fear the ridicule of peers, to be above the simple rhetoric of advertisement and politics. Rather than pairing AA's praxis with a separate, better way of life to examine their qualitative differences—as Lewis recommends—Day contents himself with "scanning the room for somebody else to ... piss off so he can prove to himself that he doesn't fit in" (*IJ* 274). Gately's mentor, Gene M., believes that newcomers to AA "with some education ... are the worst ... They identify their whole selves with their head, and the Disease makes its command headquarters in the head" (*IJ* 272). Lewis's opponents, or those who stand outside of the *Tao*, "must regard all sentiments as equally non-rational, as mere mists between [them] and the real objects."[18] What we see in Day is a manifestation of Lewis's depiction of those without the *Tao*: he is immune to sentiment, above the rote clichés of AA, because he has seen through the propaganda and deemed it to be "good old Norman Rockwell-Paul Harvey wisdom" (*IJ* 271). Day has seen through it all and consequently lost sight entirely. In Wallace's biography, D.T. Max argues that Day's presence in Ennet House came in part from Wallace's own experiences at Granada House:

> No one really cared for [Wallace's] cleverness. He was to them a type they'd seen before, someone who, like the character Geoffrey Day in *Infinite Jest*, tries to 'erect Denial-type fortifications with some kind of intellectualish showing-off' ... 'My best thinking got me here' was a recovery adage that hit home, or, as he translated it in *Infinite Jest*, 'logical validity is not a guarantee of truth.'[19]

Although intellectualism itself was not the problem, Wallace's immodest sense of self-importance was. Appearing smarter than others was just something that he cared about more than getting clean at the time, a kind of spirit he had to exorcise.

Lewis's claim that the *Tao* requires admittance and adherence to its values before they can be truly understood, that it is essentially an exclusive group that requires a leap of faith, further resembles *Infinite Jest*'s portrayal of AA. After the ex-stripper's disturbing recounting of how her adoptive family life had been so revolting that she was pressured, by circumstance, to "flee and strip and swan-dive into the dark spiritual anesthesia of active drug addiction" (*IJ* 372), the narrator explains an important quality of AA life:

> The Boston AA 'In Here' that protects against a return to 'Out There' is not about explaining what caused your Disease. It's about a goofily simple practical recipe for how to remember you've got the Disease day by day and how to treat the Disease day by day ... In other words check your head at the door. (*IJ* 374)

The narrator proceeds to identify AA's structure as "almost classically authoritarian" and "proto-Fascist." Drug addicts have to surrender their previous mindset in order to truly move beyond their addictions. They must become a part of the exclusive "In Here" in the same way Lewis believes students must be inducted into the *Tao*: "In the *Tao* itself, as long as we remain within it, we find the concrete reality in which to participate is to be truly human: the real common will and common reason of humanity, alive, and growing like a tree, and branching out, as the situation varies, into ever new beauties and dignities of application."[20] For Lewis, inclusion inside of the *Tao*, though incredibly restrictive, is central to full living. That the *Tao* is an authority matters in the same way that AA as an authority matters: because the untethered will tends toward despair. Into what *Infinite*

Jest's addicts prefer to think of as free human living, AA imposes the rather terrifying binary that life without authority is lonely and solipsistic. Although AA seems to be the pinnacle of the novel's "sincerity," its honesty reveals a dogmatism (as told by an engraving in a bathroom at Ennet House) that resembles early-twentieth-century fascism more than anything else: "Do not ask WHY/If you don't want to DIE/Do like your TOLD/If you want to get OLD" (*IJ* 375). Lewis believes that it is only the "well-nurtured man, the *cuor gentil*, and he alone, who can recognize Reason when it comes."[21] What began as an indictment of educational snobbery becomes suddenly almost anti-intellectual, a tautology; only those who participate can know the goodness of the thing that they are participating in. Both require a leap of faith, and both *Infinite Jest* and *The Abolition of Man* admit that it is children who do this most unconsciously and willingly.

But the promise of both Wallace's AA and Lewis's *Tao* is that submission to them results, paradoxically, in freedom from oppression. The political future in *Infinite Jest*'s North America verges on fascism. Canada and Mexico are annexed more or less without their given consent, and the consequent environmental and social harms, though peripheral, still echo throughout the novel. AA exists in the same world where President Johnny Gentle's regime and Jim Incandenza's inventions have caused many environmental problems. AA's "fascism" is set apart from the sociopolitical chaos elsewhere in the novel because its ideal result is an internal freedom that can contend with external oppression and restriction. The program's goal is the production of people capable of putting limitations on their own consumption of substances (illicit or otherwise) and encouraging others to achieve the same. There is nothing invasive about AA because it is entirely self-driven, almost to a fault: "If you don't obey, nobody will kick you out. They won't have to. You'll end up kicking *yourself* out, if you steer by your own sick will" (*IJ* 357, emphasis Wallace's). What the Tao and AA offer their participants is the ability to choose to not have to choose for themselves any longer, resulting in the type of citizens who would be less likely to pollute the environment with the dross of their consumption. Although the Crocodiles at first seem to be pulling the strings of the organization, they have nothing to gain from their authority in the program and are only given authority by the newcomers who choose to view them as authorities. AA requires a leap of faith before it works, just as Lewis's *Tao*, but neither ultimately accepts human authority. Alternatively, they prefer the authority of a communal body, relieving the self from the oppression of itself by choosing community. Whereas other O.N.A.N.ites like Randy Lenz are busy engaging in masturbatory self-consumption, Gately becomes one of the few characters in the book (apart from Mario) who constantly behaves selflessly. At first seeming like a group interested only in its own survival, Boston AA becomes quite the opposite and the only entity in *Infinite Jest* that is noncompetitive and whose goal is essentially to be no longer needed.

Lewis's concerns for the future of English education are also present in Remy Marathe's anxieties over what happens to the United States in *Infinite Jest's* near future. He fears that young Americans are not taught to conform to what is real or good, but to conform the real or good to themselves: "Who teaches your U.S.A. children how to choose their temple? What to love enough not to think two times?" (*IJ* 107). Lewis contends that a student "must be trained to feel pleasure, liking, disgust, and hatred at those things which really are pleasant, likeable, disgusting and hateful."[22] Although Lewis argues for the existence of Natural Law and particular commonalities across all cultures, he does not argue that education is therefore unnecessary or useless. Marathe believes that Americans will be unable to reject the *samizdat* even if given foreknowledge of its effect on its viewers. In fact, he argues, foreknowledge of the fatality of watching it will only make watching it all the more appealing to O.N.A.N.ites. He laments that someone "who had authority, or should have had authority" failed to teach young Americans that choosing is "the only thing of importance" (*IJ* 319). In the same way that Lewis fears posterity will not be trained to know sentiment, Marathe notices that young Americans are incapable of rejecting suicide when wrapped in pleasure. Both Marathe and Lewis blame educators, not students, for this phenomenon. Marathe claims that "if there is no loving-filled father to guide," there can be only "a child's greedy choices" (*IJ* 320). This correlates as well with Marathe's Kierkegaardian concern that Americans only long to be free from authorities and not free-to duties or responsibilities: "How is there freedom to choose if one does not learn how to choose?" (*IJ* 320). And Lewis claims that all of history's great educators knew that the "right defense against false sentiments is to inculcate just sentiments."[23] The similarity between Lewis's and Marathe's concerns about education helps us understand Wallace's intervention into American fiction writing. His concern moves beyond the mere debunking or ironizing of his predecessors and tries to put forward a solution for the future of American living. Wallace suggests that American kids need more to worship than drugs or other material distractions from immaterial anxieties and existential questions. He prefers religion to material solutions in *This Is Water* because of their willingness to give questions of existence the attention he believes they deserve.

Schtitt and other authorities at Enfield also share this concern for the future of American kids, though his approach is far more didactic than AA's. He addresses a group of the junior tennis players by saying, in his broken English, that for the privileged boys and girls of the tennis academy, there is "always something that is *too*" (*IJ* 458, emphasis Wallace's). He elaborates how, when they play outside, it is always too cold, but playing inside means having ceilings that are too low, that the lighting is bad, but that outside there is crabgrass that grows in the cracks of the court, and "Who could give the total, with crabgrass?" (*IJ* 459). Schtitt tries to teach the students to "like and dislike what [they] ought," Lewis's "aim of education."[24] Schtitt's concern that the players are always living in a world of idealized comfort, that they always long for something better, coincides with Lewis's ideal for education: that the pupil will be bent toward a new way of liking and disliking, what Schtitt calls: a "New type citizen" (*IJ* 459) because of his implicit nationalism. Both authors approach a kids-these-days type of rhetoric almost lost on readers because of its didacticism. But Wallace's choice of a German nationalism for Schtitt and his constant references to his latent Nazism beg the question of the sociopolitical consequences of not just religion, but a kind of religion in which group acceptance is so central. Whereas Schtitt's most immediate analogy for teaching self-transcendence is political, Lewis sticks with education for teaching self-transcendence, though there may be political undertones. This is also key in terms of developmental timing for both Lewis and Schtitt's/Enfield's philosophies of indoctrination. Hal reflects on how people of his age and demographic seem to all be "dying to give [their] lives away to something," and that they get "started ... so young" at Enfield so that they will give themselves away to tennis "before the age when the questions *why* and *to what* grow real beaks and claws" (*IJ* 900, emphasis Wallace's). Lewis quotes the *Republic*, saying that before the pupil is "'of an age to reason,'" he must "'see most clearly whatever [is] amiss in ill-made works of man or ill-grown works of nature ... so that when Reason ... comes to him ... he will hold out his hands in welcome.'"[25] Indoctrination requires the weak mind of the pupil. Otherwise—for Plato and, by extension, Lewis—the pupil runs the risk of rejecting Reason when she or he comes of age. Although many of the students at Enfield appear not to be indoctrinated—or at least not as noticeably as characters in other more dystopian works would—Schtitt's approach nonetheless includes indoctrination and manipulation of younger minds in preparation for their New citizenry. This philosophy of Lewis's comes across as less Christian than simply authoritarian: much more like the values typical of "most Europeans" in Schtitt's (and Lewis's) generation: "with a whiff of proto-fascist potential about them" (*IJ* 82).

Schtitt represents Wallace's concern and fear of fascism and his knowledge of its appeal to religious people. Although Schtitt as a character remains mostly comical and even inspiring to players like Stice, Schtitt shows Wallace's knowledge that the AA praxis is just a defanged and depoliticized fascism. Though Wallace's attitude toward AA's rigidity is positive, he expresses in Schtitt, in the novel's geopolitical dystopia, and in the character of Johnny Gentle that this kind of rigidity does not work under autocratic authority. Authority is essential and inevitable and not entirely unappealing to people generally, as Marathe argues, but the authority must be a group or a "higher being," a Way, not an individual or new political scheme. Perhaps Wallace's message is not so straightforward; perhaps Wallace is ultimately arguing that the presence of authoritarianism in AA problematically directs people to real, nationalistic fascism. But the presence of self-forgetfulness in *Infinite Jest* overwhelmingly favors the recovered addicts than the consumptive O.N.A.N.ites. The fascism of self, rather than geopolitical fascism, is the central problem for most of the novel's characters. *Infinite Jest* rejects the connection between recovered addicts and political authoritarianism in any way. If anything, recovered addicts are less prone to giving themselves over wholeheartedly to political saviors.

Especially when read through *This Is Water*, AA in *Infinite Jest* appears to be one of the many legitimate escapes from self-worship. The novel attempts many different answers to the question of how to live in an other-centered and nonsolipsistic way, namely by giving yourself in service to athletic achievement (Schtitt), a nation (Marathe), or a religious group (AA/Gately). *Infinite Jest*, never fully endorsing any particular one of these solutions to solipsism, leads scholars to believe that Wallace's fiction is putting forward "a worldview that values the possibility of transcendence and universal meaning"[26] or "something that shifts the solitary perspective beyond the self-absorbed concerns of the contemporary individual."[27] But the novel begs readers to ask whether the solutions for solipsism presented in *Infinite Jest* are valid or not. Gately's new life of recovery is fairly miserable: his job is grisly, he has to put up with some of Boston's least pleasant inhabitants, and he ends up being hospitalized without anesthetic because of Randy Lenz's selfish and senseless consumptive habits. But his future is still far more hopeful than Lenz's, even though Gately only receives what he does not want and Lenz what he does. The religious mode encouraged by the novel is the kind of meditative devotion Gately shows to AA in spite of all earthly discomfort and suffering.

Wallace's primary worry about postmodern American fiction in "E Unibus Pluram" is that, "irony, poker-faced silence, and fear of ridicule are distinctive of those features of contemporary U.S. culture (of which cutting-edge fiction is a part) that enjoy any significant relation to the television whose weird pretty hand has my generation by the throat" (*SFT* 49). Later he elaborates, "an ironist is *impossible to pin down*" (*SFT* 67, emphasis Wallace's). Although *Infinite Jest* defies categorization on nearly all fronts, at least Gately's portion of the book is an attempt to embattle the disinterested ironist. Educators of Lewis's era, according to Lewis, were mostly concerned with making young boys into "knowing fellow[s] who can't be bubbled out of [their] cash."[28] It is particularly the distanced, disinterested attitude they want to foster. For Lewis, there is an external, knowable world beyond the individual that is singular and the creation of God. He is an apologist and argues for the existence of objective, external reality. Although there are elements of a kind of objectivity that float to the fore of much of Wallace's writing, he never accedes a singular, objective reality beyond the mind. Choice, however, becomes much more important for his characters and his nonfiction. For Lewis, the problem is subjectivity; for Wallace, solipsism;

but their common denominator is the importance that communities play in the life of the individual. Lewis's philosophical frameworks are rhetorically fascinating to Wallace, but they are also an example of the sort of work Wallace sees as productive in a world of increasing consumption. There is also an inherently anti-übermencshean attitude in both Wallace's AA and Lewis's *Tao* that almost encourages their adherents to be taken advantage of and trodden upon. Although their adherents never end up as mere puppets of the state, they do end up servants of "a higher being." Rather than making their adherents vulnerable to political authorities, these groups reject the uniquely American notion that to be ruled by anything is a moral failure. In other words, those within the *Tao* and Wallace's AA are aware of their addictions and self-involvement, and choose to resist them.

It is important to note, however, that Wallace never fully endorsed a particular religion, though D.T. Max suggests[29] Russian Orthodoxy would have been appropriate for him, and I think, along with Piekarski,[30] the Buddhist elements in Wallace's fiction have the most potential for scholarly attention. We are constantly tempted to read religion into Wallace's work because the religious mode is so central to so many of his characters. But it is ultimately a kind of communalism that Wallace was really singing out: anything that allowed one to avoid the solipsistic superiority of the pure social critic, pure intellectual *übermensch*, rising above the masses. Instead, Lewis and Wallace prescribe the attitude of an everyman, one careful of overconsumption and in service to a Higher Being. Wallace "treasured" his "regular-guyness,"[31] even if he could not always make others believe it. Whereas Lewis sought after the *Tao* and found an Anglican faith, Wallace looked all over and was never fully satisfied by the many voices that claimed to connect him to it.[32] But his fiction never surrenders to the despair that would seem to flow naturally from that failure.[33] What makes *Infinite Jest* feel so honest to its readers is that it tries to put forward an answer to the loneliness of modern living even in spite of its author's own loneliness. "It's all search with him," says Max.[34] Yet because *Infinite Jest* does not only try to posture itself as disinterestedly above its readers' habits, but also prescribes a possible solution, it should be understood as moving past the postmodernists toward something like sincerity.

Notes

1   C.S. Lewis, "The Abolition of Man," in *The Complete C.S. Lewis Signature Classics* (New York: HarperOne, 2002), 689–738; 701.
2   Ibid.
3   David Foster Wallace, "Syllabus for David Foster Wallace's class 'English 102-Literary Analysis: Prose Fiction'," typescript, Box 32.6. David Foster

Wallace Papers. Harry Ransom Humanities Research Center, Austin, TX. Available online: http://www.hrc.utexas.edu/press/releases/2010/dfw/teaching/.

4   In Anthony de Mello's *Awareness*, Wallace underlines the following passages that described Lewis's diary, e.g., "Lewis ... said in his diary that we cannot know anything about God and even our questions about God are absurd. Why? It's as though a person born blind asks you, 'The color green, is it hot or cold? *Neti, neti,* not that ... '."

5   J. Peder Zane, ed., *The Top Ten: Writers Pick Their Favorite Books* (New York: W.W. Norton & Company, 2010).

6   Jonathan Franzen, "Farther Away: 'Robinson Crusoe', David Foster Wallace, and the island of solitude," *The New Yorker*, April 18, 2011. Available online: https://www.newyorker.com/magazine/2011/04/18/farther-away-jonathan-franzen.

7   C.S. Lewis, *The Screwtape Letters* (New York: Macmillan Publishing Company, 1982), xiii–xiv.

8   "Endnotes: David Foster Wallace." Interview with Geoff Ward. BBC Radio 3, February 12, 2012. https://www.bbc.co.uk/programmes/b00y6ggl.

9   David Lipsky, *Although of Course You End Up Becoming Yourself: A Road Trip with David Foster Wallace* (New York: Broadway Books, 2010), 215.

10 Ibid.

11 Ibid., 216.

12 Stephen J. Burn, "A Paradigm for the Life of Consciousness: Closing Time in *The Pale King*," *Studies in the Novel* 44, no. 4 (2012): 371–88; 379.

13 Ibid.

14 D.T. Max, *Every Love Story Is a Ghost Story: A Life of David Foster Wallace* (New York: Penguin, 2013), 159.

15 Lewis, "The Abolition ...," 693–4.

16 Ibid., 699, italics original.

17 Ibid., 726.

18 Ibid., 702.

19 Max, *Every Love Story*, 139.

20 Lewis, "The Abolition ..., " 727.

21 Ibid., 716.

22 Ibid., 700.

23 Ibid., 699.

24 Ibid., 700.

25 Ibid.

26 Michael J. O'Connell, "'Your Temple Is Self and Sentiment': David Foster Wallace's Diagnostic Novels," *Christianity & Literature* 64, no. 3 (2015): 266–92.

27 Timothy Jacobs, "The Brothers Incandenza: Translating Ideology in Fyodor Dostoevsky's The Brothers Karamazov and David Foster Wallace's Infinite Jest," *Texas Studies in Literature and Language* 49, no. 3 (2007): 265–92.

28 Lewis, "The Abolition …," 697.
29 D.T. Max, "DT Max and James Wood on David Foster Wallace," YouTube video, 1:56:34, December 13, 2012. https://www.youtube.com/watch?v=QsbKT50ud04. See around 1:37:08 in interview.
30 See Piekarski's Chapter 12 in this collection: "Zen Buddhist Philosophy Lurking in the Work of David Foster Wallace."
31 Lipsky, *Becoming Yourself,* 42.
32 Max, *Every Love Story,* 166 and 251.
33 As, for example, a nihilist would. See Chapter 3 in this collection: "'Not Another Word': Nietzsche, Wallace, and the Death of God" by Michael McGowan.
34 Max, "D.T. Max and James Wood on David Foster Wallace," YouTube video, 1:56:34, December 13, 2012. https://www.youtube.com/watch?v=QsbKT50ud04. See around 1:37:08 in interview.

7

"Somewhat Lost and Desolate Inside": Overcoming Acedia in *The Pale King*

Michael O'Connell

At the time that he was finishing work on *Infinite Jest*, David Foster Wallace wrote,

> To me, religion is incredibly fascinating as a general abstract object of thought—it might be the most interesting thing there is. But when it gets to the point of trying to communicate specific or persuasive stuff about religion, I find I always get frustrated and bored. I think this is because the stuff that's truly interesting about religion is inarticulable.[1]

Although he might have been frustrated by his inability to fully articulate his thoughts about religious faith and doubt, throughout his oeuvre we can see him wrestle with this question of how to make belief both coherent and interesting, and I contend that his attempts get more successful as his career progresses. As a result, *The Pale King*, although unfinished, is one of the great spiritual novels of the twenty-first century.

Infinite Jest, for all of its "elegant complexity" (to borrow Gregory Carlisle's term[2]), contains a theological vision that is, in some ways, relatively simple: we

---

This chapter has been adapted from a longer essay on Wallace and Christianity, "'Your Temple is Self and Sentiment': David Foster Wallace's Diagnostic Novels," originally published in *Christianity and Literature* 64, no. 3 (2015): 266–92. I am grateful to the editors for permission to republish a revised portion of the essay here.

are a fallen people, and the only thing that can help us in our fallen condition is surrendering to a God that surpasses all understanding (with the added dimension that we need community to help us make this surrender work). In *The Pale King*, Wallace's treatment of faith is both more complicated and more central to the work's overall thematic concerns. Unlike *Infinite Jest*, which focuses on the dramatic and extreme symptoms of disease and dis-ease that permeate the modern world, *The Pale King* focuses on a more mundane, but equally pernicious, symptom: the restlessness at the heart of American cultural life. In the novel, boredom is not simply a widespread societal problem that needs to be overcome; it is a symptom of a deeper crisis in the culture.

Although the problem of boredom appears in a number of forms in the novel, we can view Lane Dean Jr.'s struggle with the debilitating monotony of his job at the IRS as a focal point for Wallace's exploration of the issue. Dean, who is Wallace's most explicitly Christian character and one whose story is central to the theological insights of the novel, is a relatively inexperienced auditor suffering "boredom beyond any boredom he'd ever felt" (*PK* 377), which is so extreme that he begins to contemplate all manner of suicide (including "ways to kill himself with Jell-O" (*PK* 380)). In the midst of this existential crisis he is visited by one of the "two actual, non-hallucinatory ghosts haunting Post 047's wiggle room [where the auditors work]" (*PK* 315), who begins to explain the etymology of the word boredom. The ghost introduces the concept of "*accidia*" which, he explains, was "made so much of by monks under Benedict. ... Also the hermits of third-century Egypt, the so-called *daemon meridianus*, when their prayers were stultified by pointlessness and tedium and a longing for violent death" (*PK* 383). Since Dean, the committed Christian, was himself just longing for a violent death, and since debilitating boredom is one of the key themes of the novel, it is worth pursuing this concept of acedia in greater detail.

Acedia, as the ghost tells Dean, has a long history in Christian monastic tradition. Evagrius Ponticus (345–99), one of the early Christian monks and ascetics known as the Desert Fathers, described it thus:

> The demon of acedia—also called the noonday demon—is the one that causes the most serious trouble of all. He presses his attack upon the monk about the fourth hour and besieges the soul until the eighth hour. First of all he makes it seem that the sun barely moves, if at all, and that the day is fifty hours long. Then he constrains the monk to look constantly out the windows, to walk outside the cell, to gaze carefully at the sun to determine how far it stands from the ninth hour, to look now this way and now that to see if perhaps [one of the brethren appears from his cell]. Then too he instills in the heart of the monk a hatred for the place, a hatred for his very life itself, a hatred for manual labor. He leads him to reflect that charity has departed from among the brethren, that there is no one to give encouragement. ... He depicts life stretching out

for a long period of time, and brings before the mind's eye the toil of the ascetic struggle and, as the saying has it, leaves no leaf unturned to induce the monk to forsake his cell and drop out of the fight.[3]

The popular spiritual writer and poet Kathleen Norris's *Acedia and Me: A Marriage, Monks, and a Writer's Life* (2008) explores the history of acedia, as well as its present-day manifestations. In a diagnosis of modern society that reads like a précis of the thematic concerns of both *Infinite Jest* and *The Pale King*, Norris claims, "much of the restless boredom, frantic escapism, commitment phobia, and enervating despair that plagues us today is the ancient demon of acedia in modern dress."[4] The great twentieth-century spiritual writer Thomas Merton arrived at a similar conclusion, describing acedia as "an interior and spiritual sloth that seems, at times, to shirk the obligation of living. ... [It is] a paralysis of the spirit combined with restlessness and indecision. Acedia is in fact one of the great spiritual diseases of our time. ... Acedia is the disease which afflicts the whole world, especially the unbelieving world."[5]

It is unclear how well-versed Wallace was in the literature of the Desert Fathers, or if he had encountered any of the more contemporary literature that explored the phenomena of acedia, but *The Pale King* reads, in many instances, like a fictionalized dramatization of this condition as it is described by these theologians and spiritual masters. Indeed, it is evident that Wallace does not view acedia as a symptom of our current age, but rather as the primary pathologic condition. The symptoms originally described by the Desert Fathers, and reinterpreted to the present day—listlessness; obsession with passive entertainment; the inability to focus or sit still; mindless eating, sleeping, or visiting with acquaintances; "chronic withdrawal from reality"—are the symptoms that permeate Wallace's diagnostic novels.[6]

It is even possible that the phantom who introduces the concept into *The Pale King* is supposed to be a literal figuration of the noonday demon.[7] He appears less than a page after a discussion of the movie *The Exorcist*, which alerts the reader to the concept of demons and possession. And although the phantom for the most part appears harmless and disinterested in human affairs, he reveals a different aspect when Dean's coworker apprehends his presence. The ghost responds by making "his hands into claws and [holding] them out ... like a demon or someone possessed. The whole thing happened too fast to almost be real to Lane Dean" (385). After revealing its true nature, the phantom/demon then immediately returns to his disquisition on boredom, describing it as "*soul murdering*" (PK 385, emphasis original). Dean, as a devout Christian, responds as one of the Desert Fathers might have counseled: Wallace writes, "It occurred to Lane Dean that he might pray" (PK 385). Directly on the heels of this invocation of prayer, the phantom leaves and Dean "let himself look up and [he] saw that no time had passed at all" (PK 385).

For Wallace, the way to overcome the problem of "soul murdering" boredom is not to hide from it, although as *Infinite Jest* demonstrates, many people do just this; rather, *The Pale King* at least hints at a solution found in the embrace of suffering, which is, of course, a very Christian solution to the problem. John Cassian, another Desert Father, writes:

> When I was beginning my stay in the desert, and had said to Abbot Moses, the chief of all the saints, that I had been terribly troubled yesterday by an attack of accidie, and that I could only be freed from it by running at once to Abbot Paul, he said, 'You have not freed yourself from it, but rather have given yourself up to it as its slave and subject. For the enemy will henceforth attack you more strongly as a deserter and runaway, since it has seen that you fled at once when overcome in the conflict: unless on a second occasion when you join battle with it you make up your mind not to dispel its attacks and heats for the moment by deserting your cell, or by the inactivity of sleep, but rather learn to triumph over it by endurance and conflict.' Whence it is proved by experience that a fit of accidie should not be evaded by running away from it, but overcome by resisting it.[8]

In the appendix of notes that concludes the novel, Wallace writes what might be a contemporary gloss on this passage:

> It turns out that bliss—a second-by-second joy + gratitude at the gift of being alive, conscious—lies on the other side of crushing, crushing boredom. Pay close attention to the most tedious thing you can find (tax returns, televised golf), and, in waves, a boredom like you've never known will wash over you and just about kill you. Ride these out, and it's like stepping from black and white into color. Like water after days in the desert. Constant bliss in every atom. (*PK* 546)

Once again, Wallace's description is strikingly similar to that of the Desert Fathers. Evagrius wrote that after the monk overcomes the noonday demon, "No other demon follows close upon the heels of this one (when he is defeated) but only a state of deep peace and inexpressible joy arise out of this struggle."[9] Wallace, like the Desert Fathers before him, contends that if we can overcome acedia then we will come out the other side into a moment of transcendence. It is a beautiful vision, and it clearly seems that he is drawing on the traditions of Christian mysticism as a solution to what he viewed one of the central problems of our age.

The novel in fact points the reader toward this mystical tradition. Besides referencing early Christian monastic tradition, *The Pale King* includes a lengthy description of various Christian mystics. Chapter 36, which focuses on a young boy who seeks the ability "to press his lips to every square inch of his own body" (*PK* 394), also includes a description of five reputed stigmatics. Wallace begins this section thus: "Facts: Italian stigmatist Padre Pio carried wounds which penetrated the left hand and both feet medially throughout his lifetime. The Umbrian St. Veronica Guiliani presented with wounds in one hand as well as in her side, which wounds were observed to open and close on command" (*PK* 398–9). He continues in the same clinical style, describing the wounds of Giovanna Solimani and St. Francis of Assisi (and, a few pages later, Therese Neumann), before concluding: "And yet (fact): Hands lack the anatomical mass required to support the weight of an adult human. ... Hence the, quote, 'necessarily simultaneous *truth* and *falsity* of the stigmata' that existential theologian E. M. Cioran explicates in his 1937 *Lacrimi si sfinti*, the same monograph in which he refers to the human heart as 'God's open wound'" (*PK* 399). Wallace foregrounds the myriad tensions inherent in the stigmata: it is demonstrably real, and yet the wounds cannot literally match Christ's, since "classical crucifixion required nails to be driven through the subject's wrists, not his hands" (*PK* 399). Wallace is demonstrating that there are elements of even formal organized religion that, like the alcoholic's surrender to the Higher Power in Alcoholics Anonymous in *Infinite Jest*, defy rational explanation, and yet are still (in the words of his Kenyon Commencement address) "capital-T true" (*TIW* 94).

One of the difficulties in writing about an unfinished work is that we do not know how Wallace envisioned all of the parts coming together, or even if all of these sections would have made the final cut. Although the chapter that includes the sections on the stigmatics does not seem to directly connect to the plot elements in the rest of the work—the identity of the boy at the center of the chapter remains unclear in relation to other named characters in the book—there is a strong connection between these Christian mystics, who defy rationality not simply through their faith but in their very bodies, and the overall themes of the novel. The boy, in his single-minded desire to master his own body, demonstrates that such self-mastery is possible, although it would be a mistake to align his actions too closely to those of the stigmatics themselves. The boy explicitly "had no conscious wish to 'transcend' anything" (*PK* 400), whereas stigmatics like Padre Pio and St. Francis receive the stigmata in connection to a life lived in service to God, and the wounds become a manifestation of a supernatural, transcendent reality.

The Pale King demonstrates that Wallace is not solely interested in the mystical elements of Christianity, though; he also explores the impact of a transcendent, and explicitly Christian, worldview on everyday life. He shows that such a belief structure can help overcome the paralysis, listlessness, and fear of commitment that afflict modernity. We see how a transcendent worldview affects day-to-day decision making in Chapter 6.[10] The main character of the story is none other than Lane Dean, Jr., the same man who will eventually be so beset by acedia that he contemplates suicide. This story takes place a few years before he joins the IRS, and details his internal thought process as he and his girlfriend Sheri wordlessly contemplate aborting their accidental pregnancy. Both Lane and Sheri are evangelical Christians, the type of people who reference scripture in regular conversation and unapologetically talk about "turn[ing] a matter over to Jesus Christ in prayer" (*PK* 37). Despite his religious scruples, Dean's initial desire is to ask Sheri to get an abortion. This desire, though, renders him unable to act. He is emotionally, spiritually, even physically frozen by this unforeseen challenge; throughout the story, Dean is "very still and immobile" (*PK* 36). There is almost no physical movement in the story, which reflects his internal paralysis. This crisis brings about an extreme form of the symptoms of acedia. The Cistercian monk Michael Casey links acedia to "the vice of noninvolvement" which he describes as "endemic in the Western world."[11] He describes the acediac as "a person without commitment, who lives in a world characterized by ... the effective denial of the validity of any external claim."[12] Dean struggles with just this inability to form a personal commitment, and his desire to deny the validity of Sheri's claim on him leaves him feeling like he is "freezing more and more solid" (*PK* 38). Although Dean "knew something was required of him and knew it was not this terrible frozen care and caution," he cannot bring himself to act (*PK* 37–8). Like the acediac, he cannot communicate with his God: he "tried to pray but could not" (*PK* 38).

The story turns, though, as Dean experiences what he calls a "*moment of grace*" (*PK* 42, emphasis in original), in which he is able to actually get inside his girlfriend's head for a moment and see their predicament from her eyes. This leads him to a true insight into love:

> Why is one kind of love any different? What if he has no earthly idea what love is? What would even Jesus do? ... What if he was just afraid, if the truth is no more than this, and if what to pray for is not even love but simple courage, to meet both her eyes ... and trust his heart. (*PK* 43)

What Wallace dramatizes here is that a worldview informed by Christianity is capable of getting the isolated individual out of his own head, enabling him to reach out and feel someone else's pain and anxiety; it helps him break through his emotional and spiritual paralysis. For Wallace, who repeatedly dramatizes that one of the great failures of our modern age is the inability to get outside of the self long enough to act meaningfully in the world, it is significant that it is Christian character who is able to make this leap, and show this empathy in action.[13]

Lane Dean, Jr., though, is not the only character in *The Pale King* able to actively transcend his own ego in service to another. In the last major set piece before the conclusion of the novel, Shane Drinion is shown to be the embodiment of empathy. As he listens to his coworker Meredith Rand relate her life story, he is so totally engrossed in actively listening to her and attempting to fully understand what she is telling him that he begins to levitate off of his chair. Wallace offers no explanation for Drinion's levitation, the narrator simply states, "Drinion is actually levitating slightly, which is what happens when he is completed immersed" (*PK* 485). By the end of Rand's story, Drinion is "1.75 inches off the chair seat" (*PK* 497–8). In a novel that has already referenced the supernatural capacities of the mystics, Drinion's quasi-mystical ability to levitate connects him with the metaphysical abilities of the saints. Wallace is drawing a direct connection between the ability to remain focused despite the myriad distractions of life (Drinion's most remarkable quality is the ability to give "whoever's speaking his complete attention" (*PK* 448)), and a horizon of transcendence. It is a somewhat curious connection to make, unless one is willing to grant that Wallace's diagnosis of the modern condition is correct—that our inability to overcome, or even countenance, acedia is undermining our very cultural life. If this is the case, then Drinion's capacity to focus really is akin to the mystics' ability to transcend empirical understanding; it points us toward a whole new horizon of understanding.

Unfortunately, but perhaps not surprisingly, Drinion is the novel's least interesting character. Unlike the other characters who struggle with their faith and beliefs, or even those who lack faith altogether and are somewhat adrift, Drinion is static, and thus there is no way for the reader to enter into his experience. Wallace wants to hold Drinion up as an example for the modern age—in the notes at the end of the novel we read Wallace's description of the character: "Drinion is *happy*" (*PK* 546, emphasis in original), which is a stark contrast to Wallace's other characters. But it is impossible for the reader to fully identify with Drinion because he lacks an interior life. All of his comments are directed back to Meredith Rand, reframing her thoughts and statements so as to clarify what she is thinking; Drinion's careful attention helps make Rand, in Jonathan Raban's words, "the single most interesting person in the book."[14] While I disagree with this characterization of Rand, I do think Drinion's focused attention helps make her more interesting and dynamic. At the same time, it makes Drinion himself less relatable, and thus less interesting.

Drinion's character demonstrates a conundrum of the diagnostic novel: the characters who have managed to overcome the disease, or to not get sick in the first place, are the ones we least want to read about. What is of interest to readers is both the sickness itself (because we can identify with this) and the process of overcoming the dis-ease (because this gives us a model for how healing is possible). Fortunately, *The Pale King* does contain a powerful depiction of this process of overcoming dis-ease, and it is the most memorable scene in the novel.

Wallace is interested in the phenomenology behind the process of coming to live a life in service to a transcendent reality,[15] and he addresses this directly in Chapter 22, which is the emotional center of the novel. This chapter is a long (ninety-eight pages) monologue by Chris Fogle, a young man who describes his younger self as, "the worst kind of nihilist—the kind who isn't even aware that he's a nihilist. ... My essential response to everything was 'Whatever'" (*PK* 154). Although he does not use the word, Fogle clearly was in the grip of acedia; he spends his days passively watching (significantly) *As the World Turns*, "being feckless [and] a wastoid," and working only at affecting a pose of "directionless drifting and laziness" (*PK* 222–3). Fogle claims, "I was, in a way, too free ... I was free to choose 'whatever' because it didn't really matter. But that this, too, was because of something I chose—I had somehow chosen to have nothing matter" (*PK* 223). This awareness corresponds to the Christian position on freedom, which is that true freedom is not the ability to choose just anything, but rather the ability to choose for the good.[16] Fogle comes to see that he has structured his life such that there is no real possibility to choose anything good, because his worldview does not allow for anything to have any inherent value. He concludes, "If I wanted to matter—even just to myself—I would have to be less free, by deciding to choose in some kind of definite way" (*PK* 224). He realizes that he needs to actively resist the grip of acedia. The rest of the chapter details how, exactly, he is able to actually accomplish this.

One thing that makes Fogle's narrative so compelling is the style Wallace uses to relate it to the reader. Fogle acknowledges, "the conscious intention of confronting major questions like '*Am I currently happy?*' or '*What, ultimately, do I really care about and believe in?*'" is usually a fruitless exercise, because "the questions often end up not answered but more like beaten to death, so attacked from every angle and each angle's different objections and complications that they end up ever more abstract and ultimately meaningless than when you first started" (*PK* 191). But if Fogle (and by extension, Wallace) is right that we cannot address such questions directly, then how do we answer them? Fogle says he answered them "by accident," when he wandered into the wrong classroom by mistake and ended up listening to a Jesuit priest deliver a life changing lecture, or sermon, about (of all things) accounting, but, significantly, his account of this accidental encounter is preceded by a conversion narrative given by a born-again Christian, who gives Fogle her testimony "of how she was 'saved' or 'born again' and became a Christian" (*PK* 211). Wallace has Fogle recount both the girl's conversion and his own reaction to it, and although Fogle dismisses her account it leaves him feeling "somewhat lost and desolate inside" (*PK* 214).

Fogle comes to recognize that even though he finds the girl's conversion narrative "stupid and dishonest," this "doesn't mean the experience she had in the church that day didn't happen, or that its effects on her weren't real" (*PK* 214). Once again, Wallace circles around to the questions of "capital-T

Truth," reality, and faith. Just because the girl's story sounds overly familiar[17] does not mean that it is untrue; conversion stories are, for the most part, only radical and innovative to the ones who are experiencing them. Having Fogle acknowledge this fact preempts the reader's own dismissal of such conversion narratives, which (perhaps) allows the reader to hear and respond to Fogle's own account with less cynicism. This is important because Chapter 22 is, essentially, Fogle's own conversion narrative (although, to be clear, his is not a conversion to Christianity, it is a conversion to an account of human experience and meaning that transcends biological determinism). The careful reader notes a number of parallels between the Christian girl's story and Fogle's own. Fogle contends that, "sudden, dramatic, unexpected, life-changing experiences are not translatable or explainable to anyone else" (*PK* 214), but Wallace surely places the Christian girl's account before Fogle's own to establish a parallel between Fogle hearing her account and the reader hearing Fogle's. We, as the audience, might dismiss any connections between these stories and our own experiences, just as Fogle does, but that does not mean such connections are not there.

While life-changing conversion moments are undeniably idiosyncratic and personal, they do rely on, in Fogle's words, "everything in your previous life-experience which has led up to it and made you exactly who and what you are when the experience hits you" (*PK* 214), which, for Fogle, although he does not acknowledge it, clearly includes his having heard the Christian girl's witness. By extension, our having heard both the girl's story and Fogle's own account means that we have now become, in Fogle's words, "primed"— just as Fogle was. Perhaps we, as readers, recognize parts of ourselves in Fogle's account of his aimless youth (just as Fogle identified with aspects of the girl's story), and perhaps we will find his account of discovering meaning and value in some system beyond his own personal wants and desires to be compelling. If this is the case, then we have come around to an indirect consideration of the "big questions" that Fogle says are the most important ones, but also the ones that cannot be tackled head on. Wallace's techniques of narrative digression and self-reflexive awareness, particularly his drawing attention to the inherent falseness of some aspects of these conversion accounts, work to prepare the reader to actually hear and respond to them in a way they might not be otherwise able to do. In this sense, *The Pale King* is not only a diagnostic novel, it is also an attempt at a cure.

While *The Pale King* is clearly an unfinished work, it does contain a complete diagnosis of the modern condition (acedia), a description of how to overcome this condition that also doubles as an attempt at a cure enacted on the reader (Fogle's conversion story), and a depiction of what life looks like for those able to transcend the condition (in the stories of young Lane Dean, Jr. and Drinion). What is remarkable about *The Pale King* is the strongly Christian element in both diagnosis and cure. While Christian themes were evident in Wallace's earlier work, they are much more overt in this, his last novel. As Wallace continued to hone his ability to, in Percy's words, "render the unspeakable speakable," and thus help his readers to face the "entrapment and loneliness and death" that they would rather not acknowledge (*CW* 32), he apparently found the transcendent worldview of Christianity to be one, although surely not the only, effective counter to the dis-ease of the culture. Thus, while Wallace was not an orthodox Christian believer, his work does manifest a sensibility profoundly influenced by his engagement with the Christian tradition. As such, his fiction stands as one of our most powerful testaments to the tensions and anxieties, but also the hopes, of the religious imagination in contemporary America.

Notes

1. David Foster Wallace, "Quo Vadis—Introduction," *Review of Contemporary Fiction* 16, no. 1 (1996): 7–8.
2. Gregory Carlisle, *Elegant Complexity: A Study of David Foster Wallace's Infinite Jest* (Los Angeles: Sideshow Media Group, 2007).
3. Evagrius Ponticus, *The Praktikos and Chapters on Prayer*, trans. John Eudes Bamberger (Kalamazoo, MI: Cistercian, 1981), 18–19.
4. Kathleen Norris, *Acedia and Me: A Marriage, Monks, and a Writer's Life* (New York: Riverhead, 2008), 3.
5. Thomas Merton, *Cassian and the Fathers: Initiation into the Monastic Life*, ed. Patrick F. O'Connell (Kalamazoo, MI: Cistercian Publications, 2005), 185.
6. My use of the term diagnostic novel derives from the Catholic novelist Walker Percy, who explains the concept in his essay "Diagnosing the Modern Malaise": "To the degree that a society has been overtaken by a sense of malaise rather than exuberance, by fragmentation rather than wholeness, the vocation of the artist … can perhaps be said to come that much closer to that of the diagnostician rather than the artist's celebration of life in a triumphant age. Something is indeed wrong, and one of the tasks of the serious novelist is, if not to isolate the bacillus under the microscope, at least to give the sickness a name, to render the unspeakable speakable." Walker Percy, *Signposts in a Strange Land* (New York: Picador, 1991), 206.
7. In Chapter 26 Wallace provides background on the department's two ghosts. Based on the description of his rhythmic upper body movement and odd headlamp, the ghost who visits Dean is almost surely Garrity, who had "evidently been a line inspector for Mid West Mirror Works in the mid-twentieth century" (315). Unlike the other ghost who "died at his desk unnoticed" and continues to companionably show up for work, Garrity embodies the endpoint for the misery of rote work: "In 1964 or 1965 he had apparently hanged himself from a steam pipe in what is now the north hallway off the REC Annex's wiggle room" (*PK* 316). That he is given an identity does not necessarily preclude the possibility that he is also an instantiation of the demon.

8 John Cassian, "Book X: Of the Spirit of Accidie," in *The Institutes of John Cassian*, trans. Edgar C. S. Gibson. archive.osb.org.

9 Evagrius Ponticus, *The Praktikos and Chapters on Prayer*, 19.

10 Originally published as "Good People," *The New Yorker* on February 5, 2007.

11 Michael Casey, *Fully Human, Fully Divine: An Interactive Christology* (Liguori, MO: Liguori Publications, 2004), 57.

12 Ibid.

13 Of course, as his later encounter with the phantom demonstrates, this Christian perspective is no protection against acedia, the spirit of the age, but the Desert Fathers were far more committed Christians than Lane Dean (or most other people) and they were particularly beset. I do think, though, that Wallace has Lane in particular struggle so mightily in order to demonstrate that Christianity in and of itself is not some sort of magical protection against a problem that Wallace saw as endemic.

14 See Jonathan Raban, "Divine Drudgery," *The New York Review of Books*. May 12, 2011, https://www.nybooks.com/articles/2011/05/12/divine-drudgery/.

15 Wallace also addressed the phenomenology of belief in the short story "All That," published in *The New Yorker*, December 14, 2009, which was part of the manuscripts for *The Pale King* but ultimately not included in the published version of the novel. The story is a beautiful evocation of childhood belief in supernatural reality, which the adult narrator connects to the "religious feeling that has informed most of [his] adult life." As in the other treatments of religion found in *The Pale King*, the story foregrounds the tension between belief in the supernatural and a commitment to "reason, skepticism, intellect, empirical proof, human autonomy, and self-determination"; and, as in the rest of the novel, Wallace leaves this tension unresolved, but the narrator's own account points toward a transcendent reality.

16 See *The Catechism of the Catholic Church*, Part 3, Section 1, Chapter 1, Article 3: "Man's Freedom": "The more one does what is good, the freer one becomes. There is no true freedom except in the service of what is good and just."

17 Wallace could not have written a more conventional conversion narrative: the young woman, feeling "totally desolate and lost and nearly at the end of her rope" somewhat miraculously finds herself in "the parking lot of what turned out to be an evangelical Christian church, which by coincidence happened to be right in the middle of holding an evangelical service" (PK 211–12). The girl enters the church and the pastor announces, "'There is someone out there with us in the congregation today that is feeling lost and hopeless and at the end of their rope and needs to know that Jesus loves them very, very much'" (PK 212). This moment of identification—of someone recognizing exactly what she is feeling, and giving it a name—makes her feel "completely reassured and unconditionally known and loved," and gives her life "meaning and direction" such that "she had not had a down or empty moment since" (PK 212). Of course, it is just this sort of identification of alienation that Wallace's own work seeks to enact.

8

"The Moral Equivalent of War": Fungible Transcendentals in *The Pale King*

Robert Hamilton

Roughly midway through the text of *The Pale King*, Chris Fogle, one of the novel's principal characters, describes in detail a life-changing Advanced Tax course into which he stumbled by accident (*PK* 215–16). He notices a transparency projected "onto the A/V screen without comment" and records it; this transparency turns out to consist of a (slightly misquoted) passage from William James: as the text has it, "'What we now need to discover in the social realm is the moral equivalent of war'" (*PK* 219–20). It is a small passage in a large novel, but it provides a vital key for understanding a text that can appear diffuse or lacking in unity, and better still, it situates *The Pale King* directly into a philosophical landscape that preoccupied David Foster Wallace throughout the majority of his career: that of spiritual fungibility, of understanding religious truth from a subjective and empirical vantage point.

William James, certainly the most eminent exponent of this tradition, urged pacifists to find a way to inculcate military discipline and valor even in a world devoid of war; Wallace goes a step further by not merely urging to seek, nor seeking himself, but actually *finding* a "moral equivalent" of war, tribulation, and all the difficulties that are traditionally believed to bear fruit in a spiritual tradition. The quality that Wallace finds is, of course, boredom. In *The Pale King*, boredom is the Vale of Tears, it is *dukkha*, it is quite manifestly the greatest challenge to be overcome in contemporary American culture; it is also—or more appropriately, the various paths by which it is endured are—the cure to this malaise. Wallace is by no means unique among his contemporaries in positing a type of pragmatic, ecumenical solution to the question of faith. Nevertheless, Wallace is arguably the most frank and the most scrupulously tautological of all the big-tent believers of the postmodern era. I argue, therefore, that *The Pale King* is the crown jewel in an accretive argument that Wallace built in essays, fiction, and letters across his career; that this argument is, in short, that belief without reference to content is a struggle and that life is imbued with meaning only by means of this struggle; and finally, that Wallace asserts this paradoxical faith-without-faith to bridge the ironic distance that he himself so obviously felt between a native *milieu* of ironic distance and his own preferred stance of unironic sincerity. This process, culminating in *The Pale King*, makes Wallace perhaps one of the most interesting religious pragmatists of the turn of the century.

David Foster Wallace and religious doubt/pragmatism: Background

The evidence that David Foster Wallace was drawn to religious pragmatism is strong, and much of the interest appears to derive from his own experiences. In his biography of Wallace, *Every Love Story Is a Ghost Story*, D.T. Max highlights a relatively early episode from the young Wallace's struggle with addiction and stint in an Alcoholics Anonymous (AA) group:

> The simple aphorisms of [AA] seemed ridiculous to him [...] He was astonished to find people talking about 'a higher power' without any evidence beyond their wish that there were one. They got down on their knees and said the Thankfulness prayer. Wallace tried once [...] but it felt hypocritical.[1]

It is impossible to stress enough how much this episode alone explains the older Wallace's religious orientation. So much is there: the "astonishment" at the lack of evidence for a higher power, the "hypocritical" feeling of attempting to pray without actually believing in a deity to whom one might pray, and the attempt nevertheless to exist in this uncomfortable nexus of outward form and inward doubt. This episode from Wallace's life appears to have been sublimated almost directly into *Infinite Jest*, where recovering addict Don Gately struggles mightily with the "clichéd directives" he is offered (*IJ* 273), chafes at the idea of recognizing a "Higher Power," and when given the chance to design his own object of worship, settles on "not nothing but *Nothing*, an edgeless blankness that somehow feels worse than the sort of unconsidered atheism he Came In With" (*IJ* 273, 366, 443).

The doubt did not vanish with time. Max later notes that when Wallace was hoping to marry poet and memoirist Mary Karr, he "was trying to pray, because, even though he did not necessarily believe in God, it seemed like a good thing to do. Karr had become attracted to Catholicism—for her baptism would be a key moment in her recovery from alcohol."[2] Note, again, the emphasis on effects: prayer "seemed like a good thing" in the context of a relationship with a religious woman. And why? Not because of metaphysical truth, but because Karr's own conversion had borne fruit in her life. The lack of metaphysical certainty was obvious to those around Wallace, because as Max notes, "Ultimately the priest told him he had too many questions to be a believer, and he let the issue drop."[3] The process appears to have been repeated later in Wallace's life as well; Max records a stint of religious initiation with the Cursillo Movement where again the end of the program, the unambiguous commitment to a faith tradition, gave Wallace trouble: "At the final ceremony," Max writes, "when the participants were meant to attest their belief in God, Wallace expressed his doubts instead. Faith was something he could admire in others but never quite countenance for himself."[4] Wallace summed it up best himself in an interview he gave to Patrick Arden: "I enjoy church and I enjoy being part of a larger thing. I think it's just not in my destiny to be part of an institutional religion, because it's not in my nature to take certain things on faith" (CW 99).[5]

Indeed, Wallace appears to have avoided "institutional religion," which is far from unique in its own right. Most original is the precise nature of the "larger thing" that Wallace found, or developed, or accommodated himself to, in lieu of a formal church. There are a few pieces of evidence from Wallace's life that point to the fluid nature of the "larger thing": for example, in letters to Jonathan Franzen, Wallace offers subtly shifting thoughts on religion. "If words are all we have as world and god," he writes, "we must treat them with care and rigor: we must worship."[6] Art-as-religion is, again, a time-worn idea that, while arguably meritorious, would not distinguish Wallace as an innovator. More telling is another letter: "Fiction," Wallace wrote, "for me is a conversation for me [sic] between me and something that May Not Be Named—God, the Cosmos, the Unified Field, my own psychoanalytic cathexes, Roqoq'oqu, whomever."[7]

This quotation provides a strong hint at the nature of Wallace's "larger thing": namely, that it has no nature except as a "larger thing." Naming it is both forbidden and apparently otiose; the symbols that stand for the concept do not matter and one can be substituted for another in a sort of transcendent fungibility, ranging from the utterly traditional ("God") to the narcissistic and solipsistic: "[Wallace's] own psychoanalytic cathexes" and what appears to be a nonce word, "Roqoq'oqu," conjured off-hand merely for this private observation and never used again. The tension between whatever "May Not Be Named" on the one hand, and a profusion of names for it on the other, hints at the mainspring of Wallace's spiritual philosophy: the nameless and unutterable is approximated by not just one cultic name, but a concatenation of names, not identical but fungible. The fullness of truth is approximated by the as-if, and since the truth is unutterable, the as-if must become all of the truth that exists, phenomenally, for us.

Arguably, Wallace's most crystallized expression of this spiritual pragmatism comes in his Kenyon College commencement address, published as *This Is Water*. Offering the next generation his spiritual advice, he stresses that he is not out to convince them "that that mystical stuff's necessarily true. The only thing that's capital-T True is that you get to decide how you're going to try to see it. This, I submit, is the freedom of a real education [...] you get to consciously decide what has meaning and what doesn't. You get to decide what to worship" (*TIW* 94–6). This is almost exactly the offer Don Gately receives in AA; he summarizes his sponsor's line of thinking thus: "It's supposed to be one of AA's major selling points that you get to choose your own God" (*IJ* 443). This only goes to show how inextricable Wallace's spirituality was from the sense of struggle: life-long struggle against nearly overwhelming odds (addiction, for one, but also boredom and late-capitalist malaise, the principal antagonist in *The Pale King*). In *This Is Water*, Wallace defends the practice of choosing a name for the nameless:

> [A]n outstanding reason for choosing some sort of god or spiritual-type thing to worship—be it J.C. or Allah, be it Yahweh or the Wiccan mother-goddess or the Four Noble Truths or some infrangible set of ethical principles—is that pretty much anything else you worship will eat you alive. (*TIW* 102)

These words are both striking and terrifying. Wallace is issuing something tantamount to a threat: not the "eat or be eaten" of cliché, but either worship a worthwhile object or perforce end up with a Moloch that will lead to your utter destruction. Also unsettling is the implication that human beings cannot *not* worship; in the case of Gately, who brought his "unconsidered atheism" to AA, one can only conclude that Wallace saw him as a worshipper of the ecstatic experience offered (at the cost of destruction) by opioids. In other words, atheism is only conceivable as the worship of a reified Nothing, and not as merely "worshipping nothing," i.e., not worshipping at all.

William James, religious pragmatism, and the contemporary novel

Wallace's discussion of worship in *This Is Water* is also rooted in the pragmatic tradition best exemplified by William James, because it judges the value of worship solely by its effects; that which destroys you should be avoided, that which heals you should be worshipped, and asking about the noumenal truth of the thing is impossible, impolite, or unnecessary. It is curious, then, that *The Pale King*, the final statement by an author whose religious experiences and novelistic expressions are so clearly haunted by the pragmatic spirituality described in James's *The Varieties of Religious Experience*, quotes not that work but the little-known and brief essay "The Moral Equivalent of War." This allusion makes perfect sense in context, and we will soon return to it. However, the overall pragmatist-Jamesian outlook of Wallace must be established first, in order to understand most fully the spirituality that reaches its fullest expression in *The Pale King*.

The Varieties of Religious Experience offers a distinct vision of religion entirely through the effects it produces in its adherents, while remaining entirely agnostic as to the truth of the various matters asserted by religious sects. For example, James is quite explicit when discussing what he calls the "Mind-Cure Movement" and contrasting it with the more overtly truth-seeking school of scientific positivism:

> But here we have mind-cure, with her diametrically opposite philosophy, setting up an exactly identical claim [to that of scientific positivism]. Live as if I were true, she says, and every day will practically prove you right [...] And that experience does largely verify these primeval religious ideas is proved by the fact that the mid-cure movement spreads as it does, not by proclamation and assertion simply, but by palpable experiential results.[8]

Whatever the *Ding an sich* (thing in itself) might or might not be, James and Wallace reason that casting oneself upon *something* for help will result in an improved situation, at least psychologically; whether that help is actually divine or merely a placebo effect is immaterial, or put another way, the latter is indistinguishable from the former.

Interestingly, both James and Wallace seem willing to risk blasphemy by clinging fast to these pragmatic views. In another crucial passage, James insists that

> Our spiritual judgment [...] must be decided on empirical grounds exclusively. If the *fruits for life* of the state of conversion are good, we ought to idealize and venerate it, even though it be a piece of natural psychology; if not, we ought to make short work with it, no matter what supernatural being may have infused it.[9]

That supernatural being James wishes to "make short work of" should be analogized to the objects of worship that Wallace insists, in *This Is Water*, can "eat you alive" (*TIW* 102). Does it matter? Should practitioners of "empirical" spiritual judgments worry about, for example, getting this wrong and risking judgment? Apparently not; judgment is precisely following, opening oneself to, or surrendering to these "gods" that devour their adherents, to the conversion experiences that do not produce good "fruits for life." A nonpragmatic understanding of religion might hold that "there is" a divine being or pantheon, that one either "gets it right" and worships said god or pantheon, or "gets it wrong" and suffers some kind of damnation. The implication of James's philosophy, incarnated and made more explicit in Wallace's fiction, offers the reverse: damnation is not the punishment inflicted by a spurned deity, but the negative result of choosing poorly among the deities on offer.

Boredom and pragmatic religion: *The Pale King*

Unfortunately for us, choosing correctly is not necessarily simple, and the difficulty of attaching oneself to the right sort of higher power is what necessitates the bellicose imagery of "The Moral Equivalent of War" and the rigors that *The Pale King*'s characters undergo in their battle to the death with boredom. It is worthwhile to document exactly how William James is conjured in this text: as mentioned above, Chris Fogle, confused and enduring a lecture he is not signed up for, sees a transparency bearing the nonquote "What we now need to discover in the social realm is the moral equivalent of war"; Fogle notes that "the only written attribution at the end [was] 'James', which, at the time, I believed referred to the biblical apostle James, for obvious reasons"—those reasons presumably being that the lecturer is a Jesuit (*PK* 220). The confusion is humorous, of course, but it is also telling: given how "Jamesian" the ensuing passage is, and how preoccupied *The Pale King* is with Jamesian pragmatism, William James occupies a genuinely apostolic office in this text.[10]

What Fogle does is draw a connection between his experiences in the Advanced Tax course and his memory of an Evangelical roommate, a person he liked "to mock and bait and judge," and the roommate's girlfriend, who recounts a conversion experience (*PK* 211–14). In brief, the girlfriend pulls over and enters a church while "feeling totally desolate and lost and nearly at the end of her rope" and feels as if "the preacher or father or whatever they called them" had "somehow address[ed] himself directly to the girlfriend and her circumstances at just that moment of deep spiritual need" (*PK* 211–12). William James, writing of the "sick soul," evokes this feeling: "here is the real core of the religious problem: Help! Help!"[11] Fogle, no Jamesian yet, goads her by comparing her story to "those *Sun-Times* horoscopes that are specially designed to be so universally obvious that they always give their horoscope readers [...] that special eerie feeling of particularity and insight" (*PK* 213). Fogle's conclusion, judging by what D.T. Max has recorded about Wallace's own back-and-forth flirtation with various religious traditions, must be more or less tantamount to Wallace's own: "It's true," he recalls in hindsight, "that her story was stupid and dishonest, but that doesn't mean the experience she had in the church that day didn't happen, or that its effects on her weren't real" (*PK* 214). This might as well be William James speaking; as he notes in *Varieties*, "Mystical states [...] are, and have the right to be, absolutely authoritative over the individuals to whom they come."[12] The very next line injects another, deeper, and also Jamesian dubiety into the text: "I'm not putting it very well, but I was both right and wrong about her little story. I think the truth is probably that enormous, sudden, dramatic, unexpected, life-changing experiences are not translatable or explainable to anyone else" (*PK* 214). James concurs: "Mystics have no right to claim that we ought to accept the deliverance of their peculiar experiences, if we are ourselves outsiders and feel no private call thereto."[13]

This is an important passage, even though it shifts like quicksand and its importance and subtlety are not easy to grasp. The doubt itself ("I'm not putting it very well," "probably") is not the caustic skepticism that Fogle had heaped upon the Evangelical girlfriend at the time, but an eloquent expression of the difficult world of the both-and and the as-if—essential ingredients of a pragmatic spirituality. An experience judged by its fruits, after all, can be *both* "stupid and dishonest" *and* "dramatic" or "life-changing." One sees the stupidity and dishonesty—this is part of the essential experience of the Fogles and Wallaces of the world, after all—and treats it *as if* it were cogent and honest, and one can do this because the conversion *behaves like* an honest, authentic event. Is it in absolute, unequivocal truth? It simply does not matter. Fogle, naturally, fails to understand this until he himself, somewhat to his embarrassment, also receives a seemingly personalized call: "it," he writes of the experience in the Advanced Tax course, "was ultimately much more like the evangelist girlfriend with the boots' own experience than I could have ever admitted at the time [...] much of what the Catholic father (I thought) said or projected seemed aimed directly at me" (*PK* 220). This narrative could hardly be structured to more persuasively signify a Jamesian equivalency: the outward manifestations of the perceived "call" are completely different—a sermon and an accounting class—and neither is contrived to seem particularly spectacular *per se*. Both, however, can be judged by their "fruits for life" to have been positive: uplifting, conferring a sense of purpose, and aiding the Christian girlfriend and Fogle alike to contend with human existence. They are, in short, fungible: one can be exchanged for the other, transformed into the other, without serious effect. From a third-person perspective, though, the experiences are of the *both-and* sort: both meaningless and meaningful simultaneously.

It is precisely a process of warlike struggle for which these characters must arm themselves with their vague senses of "calling." The "Jesuit" professor makes this clear, and his ensuing speech is one in which Wallace fictively incarnates the threat of being "eaten alive" invoked in *This Is Water* (102). The accountant's life, as depicted by the "Jesuit," is fearful indeed: "the accounting profession to which you aspire is, in fact, heroic," he says;

it is also "Exacting," "Prosaic," "Banausic to the point of drudgery," and "Often tedious" (*PK* 228–9). The connection is simple: "Enduring tedium over real time in a confined space is what real courage is [...] True heroism is you, alone, in a designated work space" (*PK* 229–30). And finally, "Routine, repetition, tedium, monotony, ephemeracy, inconsequence, abstraction, disorder, boredom, angst, ennui—these are the true hero's enemies, and make no mistake, they are fearsome indeed. For they are real" (*PK* 231). During this lecture, Fogle thinks again of the phrase "the moral equivalent of war," again putting the spotlight on James's essay (*PK* 229). At this point, it becomes clear why Wallace has Fogle mention "The Moral Equivalent of War": the drudgery of life itself, against which Fogle and his IRS compeers must wage their heroic struggle, is already a kind of battlefield. The "moral equivalent" of war has, the novel implies, been found already; it is the moral equivalent of warriors, of heroes, who must be found through the infinitely productive, always fungible process of pragmatic religion.

James's argument in the essay is fairly simple; he lends enthusiastic support to the cause of pacifism, but warns pacifists that abolishing war is neither simple nor without consequence. "[T]he military feelings," he writes, "are too deeply grounded to abdicate their place among our ideals until better substitutes are offered than the glory and shame that come to nations as well as to individuals from the ups and downs of politics and the vicissitudes of trade."[14] The idea of the "substitute" is, of course, deeply pragmatic; if what matters is simply the effect of warfare, there is no sense in preserving warfare *provided that* the positive results of warfare (e.g., valor, discipline, equanimity in the face of death) are not abolished together with it. Where Wallace, I think, goes beyond James is that Wallace does not see a need to search for the moral equivalent of war: it has been found, and it is (among other things) boredom. We do not need to take the word of the "Jesuit" alone; as I have argued elsewhere, Fogle, Shane Drinion (who is "incredibly boring" and manages to physically levitate as a result), and the young boy of Chapter 36 "who (quite tediously) attempts to touch his lips to every inch of his body" all lead "tremendously insignificant" lives while still being "described in terms that are either explicitly religious, or highly reminiscent of religious discourse."[15] Boredom, in other words, suffuses the novel and also provides just those opportunities for "heroism" that the "Jesuit" describes; it is homeopathic, a *pharmakon*, both disease and cure in the contemporary, late-capitalist landscape.

Boredom: Plague and cure

In *This Is Water*, Wallace singles out "boredom, routine, and petty frustration" (*TIW* 65) as significant scourges of the contemporary world, and there is no doubt that in *The Pale King*, he was developing this idea to its limit. If entertainment and addiction were the twin, inextricable plagues of *Infinite Jest*, the absence of entertainment typifies the wasteland in the last novel. But Wallace remained consistently convinced that these problems were not unconquerable; he could be dire, but he was no nihilist. In *This Is Water*, he argued:

> If you've really learned how to think, how to pay attention, then you will know you have other options. It will actually be within your power to experience, a crowded, hot, slow, consumer-hell-type situation as not only meaningful, but sacred, on fire with the same force that lit the stars—compassion, love, the subsurface unity of all things. (*TIW* 92–3)

In other words, the *Ding an sich* (thing in itself) is once again hidden. The core of Wallace's spirituality, we have seen, is the *deus absconditus* who is hailed by an endless chain of individually tailored names and whose essence matters little in comparison with the effects produced by belief therein. Here, in *This Is Water* and *The Pale King*, we find something like *acedia abscondita*: there is no "essence" to boredom, only the active, participatory response to life, whereby attitude rescinds or confers significance. As Max notes, speaking of the manuscript of *The Pale King*, "dullness, in Wallace's conceit, was what ultimately set [the IRS characters] free. The lack of stimulation gave them a chance to open themselves up to experience in the largest sense of the word. The idea connected to Buddhism."[16]

It connects to mysticism in general, in fact, something that Wallace spells out in vivid detail in the thirty-sixth chapter of *The Pale King*. This chapter, which stands alone like a short story but is thematically near the text's core, concerns a "particular boy [whose] goal was to be able to press his lips to every square inch of his own body" (*PK* 394). The story is facially absurd, of course; the narrator has "little to say about the original animus or 'motive cause' of the boy's desire," and yet documents the quest in enormous detail across thirteen pages. This quest introduces the unnamed child "to the adult idea of quiet daily discipline and progress toward a long-term goal"; the project "was going to require maximum effort, discipline, and [...] commitment" (*PK* 396), something that unites him to the very adult and likewise banal-yet-committed IRS agents like Fogle. How does this perfectly absurd, absolutely vacant activity affect the boy—put another way, what are its "fruits for life"? The narrator ends up comparing him to the following saints and mystics: Padre Pio, St. Veronica Giuliani, St. Francis of Assisi (Wallace quotes E.M. Cioran as having spoken of the "necessarily simultaneous *truth* and *falsity* of the stigmata" Francis is said to have received) (*PK* 399, emphasis original), Therese Neumann, and the Bengali Prahansatha the Second, whose "eyes exited their sockets and ascended to float above his head" during meditation—this levitation being a favorite trope of Wallace's, a sort of mandorla or halo with which he adorns certain admirable or pathologically focused characters (*PK* 398–402). The child, at the end of the chapter, "did not yet know how, but [...] believed, as he approached pubescence, that his head would be his" (*PK* 407). One more absurd *credo* that is presented in double focus: *both* foolish *and* arriving at the very acme of the mystical.

It is important, I think, that this boy be in utterly different circumstances from Fogle and his IRS coworkers. Wallace surely would have woven the story into his text in a different way had he lived to complete *The Pale King*, but the fact remains that he needs both, because this cannot be a text about the IRS alone (nor, for that matter, about self-osculation): the point is that life is suffused with the soporific and the insignificant; this is nearly, or perhaps truly, all that there is, and not only in certain select zones of experience. The attention and praxis that elevates characters out of the abyss are, like all spiritual truths in Wallace's *œuvre*, fungible and available in a profusion of forms. Most of these forms are, taken *per se*, not much to look at: they are risible, foolish, dishonest, pathetic. Wallace's point is that this does not matter, because each one is the "moral equivalent" of the others.[17] The ultimate expression of this point that Wallace found (and I mean "ultimate" in the sense of "last" and also "highest") is appended to the text of *The Pale King*, as it was never worked into the text and functions more like a note: "pay close attention to the most tedious thing you can find," Wallace enjoins, and

> [I]n waves, a boredom like you've never known will wash over you and just about kill you. Ride these out, and it's like stepping from black and white into color. Like water after days in the desert. Constant bliss in every atom. (*PK* 546)

Conclusion

The gulf separating "the most tedious thing" from "[c]onstant bliss in every atom" is absolutely enormous, and one can be forgiven for sensing that it may be unbridgeable, or at least that *The Pale King* does not manage to bridge it. There is no doubt that the text will remain forever haunted and ironized by the truth that its author committed suicide before finishing it. While comprehending the factors that lead to a suicide is difficult if not impossible, one cannot escape the impression that Wallace's fascinating and original advice was insufficient to keep him alive, to enable him to tolerate the pain and boredom that, for him, inhered in every moment. Is there, then, value in *The Pale King*'s spirituality, or does the text merely document a fascinating but failed experiment?

In the novel's own spirit, I would answer *both-and*. The novel, and much of the rest of Wallace's work, is characterized by active tension, productive dissonance; we see people who are both dishonest and true, actions that are both stupidly absurd and heroically mystical, wars that are not wars, gods who are not gods. This tension pervaded Wallace's career, for instance, in his simultaneous identification by critics as an exponent of "postmodern maximalism"[18] and desire to see American writers "eschew self-consciousness" and "instantiate single-entendre principles" (*SFT* 81). After all, are not characters like Fogle, his roommate's Christian girlfriend, the "Jesuit" tax instructor, and the young boy working on touching his lips to every part of his body "Too sincere," "Clearly repressed," "Backward, quaint, naïve, anachronistic" (*SFT* 81)? In 1993, when "E Unibus Pluram" was published, Wallace felt that he was in "residency inside" the "aura" of postmodern "hip fatigue" and believed a new generation would have to rebel against his own (*SFT* 81). While I do not believe his major works show him as entrenched in this *milieu* as he claims to have been, there is no doubt a progression from more irony to less across this career, and whether or not Wallace was able to heed his own advice in flesh and blood, *The Pale King* resolves this tension by means of a spirituality of the fungible. Sincerity and irony are not really separate options, just as worship and nonworship are not serious options: the one is the other, transformed through intense praxis, and judged pragmatically. Sincerity is the religious transcendence of irony, accomplished by declaring that the stupid is also the profound. Worship is the willful choice of the absurd in the wild hope that it will transform consumer hell into mystical heaven.

Notes

1 D.T. Max, *Every Love Story Is a Ghost Story: A Life of David Foster Wallace* (New York: Viking, 2012), 140.

2 Ibid., 166.

3 Ibid.

4 Ibid., 251.

5 Charles Harris, Wallace's department chair and close friend at Illinois State University, confirmed to the editors of this book what Max mentions in *Every Love Story*, 263, that most often when Wallace said "church" he actually meant AA.

6 Max, *Every Love Story,* 166.

7 Ibid., 145.

8 William James, *The Varieties of Religious Experience*, ed. Martin E. Marty (New York: Penguin Books, 1982), 120.

9 Ibid., 237.

10   It is worth noting, also, that the "biblical apostle James" is one of the most overt pragmatists in the New Testament, insisting that "faith, if it hath not works, is dead, being alone" and challenging those who value theory over practice thus: "Yea, a man may say, Thou hast faith, and I have works: shew me thy faith without the works, and I will shew thee my faith by my works" (James, 2:17–18). In short, how does one judge the veracity of faith? Only by, as the later James puts it, their "fruits for life."

11   James, *The Varieties of Religious Experience*, 162.

12   Ibid., 422.

13   Ibid., 424.

14   William James, *The Moral Equivalent of War and Other Essays*, ed. John K. Roth (New York: Harper Torchbooks, 1971), 3.

15   Robert Hamilton, "'Constant Bliss in Every Atom': Tedium and Transcendence in David Foster Wallace's *The Pale King*," *Arizona Quarterly* 70, no. 4 (Winter 2014): 170–1.

16   Max, *Every Love Story*, 257.

17   Fascinatingly enough, at least one empirical study puts Wallace on steady footing. Bernardi et al. found that both "the Ave Maria in Latin" and the typical yoga mantra "om-mani-padme-om" confer "a feeling of well-being, and perhaps an increased responsiveness to the religious message"; both last about the same time and seem keyed to typical human breath patterns. Classic prayers, it seems, may be no stranger to fungibility. Luciano Bernardi et al., "Effect of Rosary Prayer and Yoga Mantras on Autonomic Cardiovascular Rhythms: Comparative Study," *BMJ: British Medical Journal* 323, no. 7327 (December 2001): 1447.

18   Marshall Boswell, *Understanding David Foster Wallace* (Columbia: University of South Carolina Press, 2009), 117.

9

A Spoon, Some Eskimos, and the Wise Old Fish: Religion and the Evolution of Wallace's Kenyon Commencement Address

Matt Bucher and Martin Brick

About halfway through the movie *The Matrix,* a little boy holds up a spoon and effortlessly bends it using his mind. Neo, the protagonist played by Keanu Reeves, takes the spoon but the boy tells him, "Do not try and bend the spoon. That's impossible. Instead only try to realize the truth."

"What truth?" Neo asks.

"There is no spoon," the boy imparts. "Then you'll see it is not the spoon that bends. It is only yourself."[1]

In the first few drafts of his now-famous commencement address, David Foster Wallace admits that he was tempted to walk up to the podium and say, "There is no spoon," and quickly sit down. Part of that temptation surely lies in the brevity, but in this joke Wallace reveals his reluctance to impart traditional commencement wisdom and his unease in the role of secular high priest.

Wallace left readers few truly first-person narratives. One might argue that he penned three collections worth of essays—*A Supposedly Fun Thing, Consider the Lobster,* and *Both Flesh and Not,* anthologized posthumously—and each of those books contains essays reflecting his own personal life's experiences. In that sense, he left a strong impression of his voice and disposition. But in reality, the essays are most often rather constructed facades: take, for example, the fact that Mrs. Bracero's "useless and irritating son, Duane" from "The View from Mrs. Thompson's" appears as "Eddie" in early drafts of the essay, and details about his clothing, such as his SLIPKNOT hat, change through the drafts.² Or on a more personal level, he identifies his childhood home as Philo, IL in "Derivative Sport in Tornado Alley," a detail Charles Harris sets straight in a short article in *Critique*.³ These changes reveal Wallace's tendency to shape characters, not to be disingenuous but rather to forge an emotional stamp on his works. Another example, and more closely connected to religion, Mrs. Thompson is not, after all, a "longtime member and leader in the congregation" of his church (*CL* 135), but rather the mother of a fellow Alcoholics Anonymous member, identified in the essay as "my very best friend here, F—" (*CL* 135), actually Francis B. These alterations suggest that while Wallace was uncomfortable revealing his own personal background, he enjoyed creating a moral and ethical persona that was not overtly pedantic, but neither was the persona entirely disinterested or relativistic.

This Is Water may then become one of the most crucial works in Wallace's oeuvre if it functions as a portal to his personal approach to life and God. True, much of his fiction and nonfiction offers windows as well, but the Kenyon address is likely the most transparent, tinted the least by literary conventions such as character and symbolism. Scholars, biographers, and other commentators have been split when it comes to interpreting Wallace's spiritual agenda. In an April 2012 symposium at the Harry Ransom Center at University of Texas Austin, the moderator, Douglas Brinkley, notes that Wallace "would go to church constantly throughout his life," and asks panelists D. T. Max and Seth Coulter Walls for thoughts on the source and motivation for this practice.⁴ Brinkley stages this question awkwardly, stemming from an observation of Wallace's love for dogs and the belief that people who suffer depression often find comfort in animals, hence implying that Wallace's religious practice might have been merely therapeutic. Both panelists honestly, and accurately, admit that the archive does not offer much evidence of Wallace's spiritual life. Max admits he is reluctant to "tightly lace something to a cause," and never directly addresses the question of religion.⁵ However, in a March 2009 forum published on the *New Yorker*'s website, readers posed questions to Max. In response to queries about Wallace's religion, Max notes that the author once told Jonathan Franzen that his own thoughts on religion were "banal," and Max goes on to speculate that Wallace's interest in religion arose as a result of addiction recovery, or perhaps as a maneuver to construe himself as "a middle-class Midwesterner."⁶ Max admits that he does not know "whether Wallace believed that God perched on his shoulder and advised him on every move or whether he/she was a generalized concept inherent in every heart," but the insinuation that religion functioned as a coping mechanism permeates Max's assessment.⁷

Since *This Is Water* directly addresses questions of belief, but as a publicly delivered speech contains rhetorical tactics, an exploration of the drafts of the Kenyon Commencement address, including consideration of Wallace's inspirations and sources, allows us to more definitively understand what made the man tick and how he approached questions of faith. *This Is Water* is overtly religious, though certainly not narrow or pedantic. The primary message that emerges, from the earliest drafts on through to the final delivery, is that an individual ought to be spiritual, though the form of that belief can easily vary. Wallace asserts, "In the day-to-day trenches of adult life, there is actually no such thing as atheism ... Everybody worships. The only choice we get is *what* to worship" (*TIW* 98–101, emphasis Wallace). Wallace goes on to allow a wide berth for belief, from the traditional Christian, Islamic, and Buddhist practices, to worshiping "the Wiccan Mother Goddess" (*TIW* 102). However, he warns against worshiping material objects or abstract ideas such as beauty, power, or intellect. These forms of worship will leave you unsatisfied, will "eat you alive" (*TIW* 102).

It is easy to view such sentiments—delivered in a commencement speech that, even given Wallace's eccentric style, remains a venue for truisms—as examples of pop psychology or spiritual relativism. And in this light, it becomes easy to dismiss the depth of Wallace's thoughts on religion. An examination of Wallace's drafts for this address, however, reveals a line of thinking that more closely echoes traditional Christian beliefs than the delivered speech might indicate. If nothing else, the language he uses in the drafts points toward something not merely "spiritual," but "religious," something drawing on tradition and a set of collective beliefs. Words such as "faith" appear, which are absent from his presented version (and its published form, *This Is Water*). Following his above-mentioned statement on atheism and worship, Wallace, in the draft, advises that overcoming the wrong, solipsistic kind of worship requires "wisdom, which is really a sexed-up word for humanity, the kind that's required for faith, the kind that can be supplied only by the spirit."[8] The article "the" before "spirit" is particularly telling. While readings such as "human spirit" are feasible, the Holy Spirit appears to be the most readily available interpretation.

When Wallace agreed to give the commencement address to Kenyon's 2005 graduating class, he had several stated reservations. For one, he had never before ventured into the special oratorical genre of the commencement address before and, more worrisome, he knew nothing about the conventions of the genre. He asked the student organizers to send him a copy of previous Kenyon commencement addresses for reference. They sent him only one: critic George Steiner's 1996 address titled "The Crucible for a Fundamental Question."

Steiner is an interesting choice for a commencement speaker: author, critic, essayist, sometimes called a polymath. It might be fair to call him the wise old fish, a role that Wallace flatly denounced.[9] The speech Steiner delivered surely sounded erudite to him, but it is not clear that he read it aloud before he delivered it. Consider this excerpt:

> "Become what you are not," urges Hegel. On one level, this mandate can be understood as a lapidary expression of enlightened morality. Purge yourself, deploy resources which have only been latent, educate yourself in new possibilities. But Hegel's intent is more complicated. He would have us think and feel against the grain of our "natural," lazy, static self. He would have subvert the unexamined conventions of personal "pre-packaging." We are to enter into a dialectical, dynamic exercise of self-negation. A successful schooling and higher education will more or less deliberately demolish the fabric of your preceding unawareness.[10]

In many ways, Steiner's mostly forgotten speech is the antithesis, the negative blueprint for Wallace's. Although they end up making many of the same points and touch upon many of the same commencement-speech clichés, Steiner's style presents itself as very much lecturing the young graduates rather than appealing to a personal, shared sense of empathy with them.

The "fundamental question" for Steiner is whether or not there can be serious literacy, whether there can be "an adult entry into your lives and of the mind of society without a complete grounding in the exact and applied sciences."[11] Steiner argues that, at this point in history, it is the hard sciences that enlist the "upper end of the curve of talent and intellect."[12] In fifteenth-century Florence we would want to meet the painters, but such as it is today, we would clamor to meet with top scientists. The vector of the sciences is that of futurity whereas the humanist is practically a "custodian of the past."[13]

Steiner then questions how the humanities can lead us to be more empathetic, and also how "major literature can applaud and ornament despotism or racial hatred."[14] Ultimately, he blames the "abdication of the clerics in the face—at once risible and barbaric—of 'political correctness.'"[15] This sets the foundation for the imperative question Steiner wants his audience to ask themselves: "Can we have a liberal program in the humanities—a program with tremendous place in human enrichment, to moral evolution, to your becoming ever more richly humane—can we have such a program that does not at least face the question of a theological foundation?"[16]

To answer this question, Steiner acknowledges that "To most educated men and women, notably in the technocratic, mass-media communities of the West, the question itself has become inert and more or less fatuous."[17]

Wallace picks up on this particular aspect of Steiner's speech. In notes he made on early drafts of his speech, it is clear that he envisioned the thrust of his address to be advice on overcoming solipsism. Among these notes he observes, "This stuff is primarily religious (Atheism vs. flabby agnosticism in Steiner)."[18] A photocopy of Steiner's speech, as printed in the *Kenyon Alumni Bulletin*, with Wallace's annotations, accompanies early speech drafts in the Ransom Center archives. Following Steiner's inquiry of a theological foundation to education he goes on to note that art or literature that offers a "rigorous denial of God's existence" at least challenges our intellectual facilities. By contrast, he believes that contemporary culture's inclusiveness refuses to take a stance on God's existence, that this "technocratic, mass-media" society considers the question of God's existence "fatuous."[19] Steiner's thoughts appear to have resonated with Wallace, hence his note regarding "flabby agnosticism" and his early inclusion of "the spirit" and "faith." A reader or listener not privy to this archival information may be tempted to read Wallace's casual reference to Jesus Christ as "JC," and his inclusion of Allah, the Four Noble Truths, and the Wiccan Mother Goddess in the same breath, as evidence of an anything-goes fatuousness. However, Wallace, like Steiner, calls for a rigorous awareness that acknowledges something larger than one's own thoughts and feelings. While Steiner dismally predicts, "The teaching of the humanities without a metaphysical basis [...] will continue in its current mood of compromise and decline,"[20] Wallace's speech also points directly toward this need for metaphysical contemplation, though without the bleakness. In a passage that was struck out, he writes, "it's a simple matter of being awake to the truth or not" and proceeds to set up a parable that illustrates the "difference between my mind and my spirit."[21] Here follows an old Chinese proverb, often called "Good luck, bad luck. Who knows?," which is explored later in this chapter.

From what Box 28 of the Wallace Papers at the Ransom Center reveals, Steiner's was the only speech Wallace read in preparation to deliver his own commencement address. The following section explores the drafts, particularly focusing on the parables and anecdotes Wallace used, displaying how he directly responds to Steiner's speech and challenges the underlying assumptions Steiner presents in his advice and arguments and also challenges the format and style of the commencement address genre itself.

Draft history

There are at least eight separate drafts of the commencement address in the Ransom Center archives. In three drafts, Wallace begins the speech with a tale about his temptation to walk up to the podium and simply says, "There is no spoon." He then carries this spoon metaphor throughout the speech, weaving into a few other parables and anecdotes before ending with "Bon appetit."[22] It is not until the fourth draft that he shifts his approach and brings in the parable of the two fish swimming, though in the second paragraph, not as the opening hook. The obviously strained transition from this spoon joke to *"This Is Water"* likely led Wallace to remove the *Matrix* anecdote, and with this edit the spiritual center of the speech begins to congeal.

The structure of the speech evolves throughout the drafts, but Wallace included "didactic little parablish stories" (*TIW* 5) in each one. Which parables made the cut determined the structure of the speech. Only two parables—the fish and an Alaskan atheist saved by Eskimos—made the final cut, but there were five or six other contenders that easily could have been slotted into the same spaces. When the speech was built around "There is no spoon," several drafts included another spoon-based parable in the closing. This parable, sometimes called the "Allegory of the Long Spoons," explains the difference between heaven and hell. In hell there is an exquisite banquet laid out on tables but the only spoons available are five feet long, meaning that no one is able to bring food to their mouths and thus they starve for all eternity. Heaven provides exactly the same arrangement, with the banquet and long spoons, except in Heaven the people decide to use the spoons to feed each other. This parable is sometimes attributed to the Hasidic Jewish teacher, Rebbe Haim of Romshishok, Lithuania, but has widespread variations—Hindu, Buddhist, Christian, as well the Japanese and Chinese folk tradition.[23] In a handwritten draft, Wallace calls it "a story they tell ten-year olds in Sunday school that's either a trendy, cloying bromide or a world-shattering profundity, depending how you see it."[24] Wallace emphasizes the point of the story again by saying, "the neighbor you feed is the neighbor you need. That service and survival are one—as are we."[25] The moral behind this parable bears considerable similarity to another cloying bromide Wallace offers in *Infinite Jest*: a church announcement-board reads, "LIFE IS LIKE TENNIS THOSE WHO SERVE BEST USUALLY WIN" (*IJ* 952).

Another anecdote that appears in one draft is about Mandrake the Magician, a comic strip character from the 1930s who was known for his ability to gesture hypnotically. Wallace had planned to tell a story about a Mandrake comic in which a client visits the magician and asks to be hypnotized only to discover that they were already hypnotized and actually needed to be deprogrammed instead. This reference allowed Wallace to contemplate whether a liberal arts degree acts as a solution to or a source of human's lack of awareness—the hypnosis—the so many people live with.[26] Another draft of the speech included an alternate *Matrix* anecdote about Morpheus asking Neo whether he thinks that is real air he is breathing right now. The common thread through these stories is the recalibration of one's assumptions regarding reality and one's interaction with it; however, Wallace ultimately decided not to include pop culture references like Mandrake and *The Matrix* (and a mention of an iPod), which is part of what prevents the speech from sounding too dated. More significantly, the remaining anecdotes all bear a similar feeling of traditional, folksy wisdom.

As Wallace neared a final version of the address the drafts are typed, and in two separate documents titled "My Commencement Speech" he wrote that the "overlong speech's conventional climax" was a "parable-ish illustration of the difference between my mind and my spirit."[27] This observation introduced a narrative he called the best church story he ever heard. "In many ways," he wrote, "it's the story of my life, of all my friends' lives, and probably you guys's upcoming lives, too."[28] The story he then conveys is a famous Zen parable about a Chinese farmer, sometimes summarized as "Good luck, bad luck. Who knows?"[29] Wallace tried to make it sound more relatable by splicing in lines like, "I actually heard this story one year at a Seder, which is why this old Chinese man sounds kind of Yiddish."[30] One could argue that the very contemporary anecdote that Wallace does include—that of working a long day, battling through traffic, and the irritating experience at the grocery store—serves the same purpose. Both stories promote living in the present, reserving judgment, and persevering through setbacks or trials. Both contain very universal lessons that are readily transferable to nearly any religious tradition.

Both Wallace and Steiner make moral arguments, though Steiner excludes the individual in his critique of the broader atheistic liberalism of "anything goes" whereas Wallace focuses almost exclusively on the personal. Wallace grapples with his own moralizing by insisting in draft after draft that "this is not about morality or being a good person as our culture has defined good. And it's not about spirituality in the sense of organized religion or metaphysical drama or life after death."[31] The point that Wallace emphasizes continuously is one of intellectual, but more importantly transcendent, awareness; as he states in the final version,

> I have come gradually to understand that the liberal arts cliché about teaching you how to think is actually shorthand for a much deeper, more serious idea: learning how to think really means learning how to exercise some control over how and what you think. It means being conscious and aware enough to choose what you pay attention to and to choose how you construct meaning from experience. (*TIW* 52–3)

It is clear, however, that Steiner's speech appealed to Wallace because it was overtly religious, because it was daring enough to ask a group of privileged liberal arts students if they believed in God or not. No doubt Steiner's bluntness on this topic helped Wallace frame his own approach to addressing Kenyon graduates.

Christian inspiration

While Wallace avoided explicitly calling for a Christian approach to the problems outlined in his address, the archive provides evidence to suggest that his own approach did call upon this religious tradition and the thoughts of Christian theologians. Several books in Wallace's personal library reflect

Wallace's study of religion in general.[32] One religious book stands out, strongly resonating the same spiritual philosophy that Wallace espoused in the Kenyon speech: Richard Rohr's *Everything Belongs: The Gift of Contemplative Prayer*. This book, which also echoes the themes present in *The Pale King*, teaches that the death of the ego leads to true seeing, that one should value attention and awareness as the path to understanding God and enlightenment.[33] One passage that Wallace underlined reads, "All spiritual disciplines have one purpose: to get rid of illusions so we can be present. These disciplines exist so that we can see what is, see who we are, and see what is happening. On the contrary, our mass cultural trance is like scales over our eyes. We only see with the material eye."[34]

Rohr perceives reality to be something experiential, something felt that functions as a "revelatory place for God."[35] His advice calls for is an outlook that involves a paradox of self-awareness. This quasi-mystical paradox resembles the Freudian concept of the Unheimlich—that of familiarity and foreignness in one—and asks the individual to overcome awareness of the self as an object in the world, while becoming aware of the self's experience as part of the world. This paradox becomes an increasingly prominent theme in Wallace's fiction, as recognized by Michael Silverblatt, who in an interview suggested to Wallace that *Infinite Jest* was a book that "needs to be made strange before it becomes familiar ... which contains both the banality and extraordinariness of various kinds of experience."[36] In Wallace's fiction, reality is something that needs to be both recognized and escaped.

Similarly, Rohr explores human anxiousness and uncertainty, something evident in the above-cited examples regarding materialism and the need to achieve. Wallace marked other passages in which Rohr comments on human fear. This arises as the individual's awareness of the world increases; Wallace underlined Rohr's observation that, "Living and accepting our own reality will not feel very spiritual. It will feel like we are on the edges rather than dealing with the essence."[37] This point clearly aligns with Wallace's observations about human "default settings." Regarding his grocery shopping scenario he writes, "I'm gonna be pissed and miserable every time I have to food-shop, because my natural default setting is that situations like this are really all about me" (*TIW* 77). He challenges the Kenyon graduates to use their liberal arts education to choose to focus on other individuals in these scenarios as human, but such an outlook will not in-and-of-itself feel spiritual. It will at best feel like the edges of a spiritual existence, not the center. But Wallace stresses the importance, because failing to recognize other individuals as humans with legitimate experiences of their own is the reflex of individuals who feel threatened and compensate with distance. Rohr's individuals on the edges "run toward more esoteric and dramatic postures instead of *bearing the mystery of God's suffering and joy inside themselves.*"[38] Wallace's take on "dramatic postures" is to see the self as victimized by every external event.

We can feel fairly certain that Wallace believed such sentiments, that he was not simply offering what he considered the requisite advice expected of a commencement address, in part due to his notes in Rohr's book. The copy of *Everything Belongs* in the Ransom Center is heavily annotated with initials in the margins. This is a practice carried over from self-help books read as a young adult. In books such as *The Drama of the Gifted Child* he scribbled notes like "Mom fostered this illusion," and in R. D. Laing's *The Divided Self* we find "DFW Summer 1985" and "DFW—anxiety phase 79–83."[39] With the notes in Rohr his attention seems much more individual; his mother and environmental conditions give way to more concerted self-analysis. "DW" appears next to this marked passage: "God is patient ..., gives us little plateaus ..., where we unfortunately get ensconced again ... We need failure and quiet time to recognize this pattern."[40] Wallace clearly used such books, both self-help and spiritual guides, to assess his own life, not simply to gather material for this speech or for his fictional characters.

In turn, this self-referentiality appears in the Kenyon drafts. At times Wallace addresses the speech to himself. He frames one whole draft of the speech as a conversation between himself at forty and himself at twenty, all interspersed with "Daves" and "listen, Dave." One line reads, "Consider that the world may not be what it looks like from your tiny Dave-centered perspective" and "here's why it has to be a choice, Dave." The presence of a self-dialogue in both his reading annotations and a speech draft may lead us to read *This Is Water* as not simply a public oratory, but rather as an argument to himself. Indeed, when examined in aggregate, the parables and anecdotes from the drafts and final version all share a common theme of doubt. The nature of his doubt covers a spectrum. The *Matrix* spoon and the fish tend toward the existential inability to fully grasp our reality. The "good luck, bad luck" parable does not deny our ignorance but rather promotes a Zen-like acceptance of the unknowable. The Eskimo joke might be said to endorse doubt in a *via negativa* manner, criticizing the smug assurance of the lost atheist. Perhaps, then, Wallace included the Eskimos in the final draft to add a vaguely uplifting balance to the panicked uncertainty of the fish. The long spoons fable is the only truly positive story in the mix, but likely felt too directly religious.

One ought to keep in mind as well the suicide references which serve as a dark echo to the existential doubt present in the stories. At the end of the speech, when he makes the point about feeling like you had and lost some infinite thing, Wallace struggles with the language of how to communicate his radical openness. He writes "Because I feel weirdly naked and uncool talking about it so directly," and then he changes that to "Because I'm embarrassed talking about this stuff so bluntly to people I don't know."[41] There are many cut lines about suicide and the fight to stay alive, and one remains in the final draft: "It is not the least bit coincidental that adults who commit suicide with firearms almost always shoot themselves in the head"

(*TIW* 58). This line comes as a macabre joke of sorts to illustrate the mind being a terrible master. But Wallace also tells us, "the two greatest vectors of meaning in daily life are jokes and clichés."[42] The Alcoholics Anonymous (AA) meetings of *Infinite Jest* also tell us that so many of the most difficult things to discuss can only be couched in jokes, humor, and parables, so it is not too surprising that the fish joke makes an appearance there as well.[43]

It is fair, then, to argue that Wallace took this assignment seriously enough to actually try to make himself vulnerable and distill what served as his day-to-day moral and religious beliefs into sincere advice for college graduates. This distillation process took many drafts and the overhauling of entire sections. Since Wallace never wrote a memoir or any essay more personal than this speech, it is understandable that we might search it and its many drafts for clues to what the author truly believed.

Notes

1. *The Matrix*, Film. Directed by Lana Wachowski and Lilly Wachowski (Burbank, CA: Warner Bros. Pictures, 1999).
2. CL 137–8. Draft material: David Foster Wallace, "The View from Mrs. Thompson's" handwritten and typescript drafts, Box 30.11. David Foster Wallace Papers. Harry Ransom Humanities Research Center, Austin, TX.
3. "David Foster Wallace's Hometown: A Correction," *Critique* 51, no. 3 (2010): 185–6. According to Harris's conversation with Wallace's father, James, the operative word in his creative nonfiction was creative, and "David was after a better truth."
4. "A Life through the Archive." YouTube Video, 1:23:42. Posted by Harry Ransom Center at The University of Texas at Austin. April 6, 2012. Available online: https://www.youtube.com/watch?v=ikkbXkVjMq0.
5. Ibid.
6. D.T. Max, "Questions for D. T. Max," *The New Yorker*, February 27, 2009. Available online: https://www.newyorker.com/books/ask-the-author/questions-for-d-t-max.
7. Ibid.
8. Wallace, "My Commencement Speech," handwritten and typescript drafts, Box 28.10–11. David Foster Wallace Papers. Harry Ransom Humanities Research Center, Austin, TX.
9. " ... but if you're worried that I plan to present myself here as the wise old fish explaining what water is to you younger fish, please don't be." (*TIW* 6).
10. Steiner, "The Crucible for a Fundamental Question," *Kenyon College Alumni Bulletin* 19, no. 1 (Summer 1996), 15.
11. Ibid., 12.

12 Ibid.
13 Ibid.
14 Ibid., 13.
15 Ibid.
16 Ibid.
17 Ibid.
18 Wallace, "My Commencement Speech."
19 Steiner, The Crucible for a Fundamental Question, 13.
20 Ibid.
21 Wallace, "My Commencement Speech."
22 Ibid.
23 Rabbi Marc Gellman believes it likely predates Haim. See Marc Gellman. "GOD SQUAD: A Religious Parable with Universal Appeal," *Newsday*, August 25, 2012. Available online: https://search-proquest-com.worthingtonlibraries.idm.oclc.org/docview/1034912621?accountid=57459.
24 Wallace, "My Commencement Speech."
25 Ibid.
26 The word "hypnotized" does survive to the final draft: "[I]t is extremely difficult to stay alert and attentive instead of getting hypnotized by the constant monologue inside your head" (*TIW* 50).
27 Wallace, "My Commencement Speech."
28 Ibid.
29 Briefly, the story involves a Chinese farmer who has a son and a horse. The horse runs away, which prompts neighbors to note his bad luck. He replies, "Good luck, bad luck. Who knows?" The horse returns and brings wild horses along. Neighbors regard this as good luck, but he repeats his mantra. The son breaks his leg trying to tame the horses, but then avoids being drafted into the emperor's army. Whatever happens, the farmer reserves judgment and lives in the moment. The moral's similarity to Alcoholics Anonymous's "Serenity Prayer"—"God grant me the serenity to accept the things I cannot change; courage to change the things I can; and wisdom to know the difference."—was surely not lost on Wallace.
30 Wallace, "My Commencement Speech." The final draft contains a similar line: "None of this is about morality, or religion, or dogma, or big fancy questions of life after death" (*TIW* 128).
31 Ibid.
32 Many of the books in Wallace's personal library were on religion and spirituality. For a detailed discussion of the archive, see the Conclusion to this collection.
33 Not surprisingly, such an outlook also resonates with Buddhism, and likely inspired Christopher Hamacher to initiate a correspondence about Buddhism after he read a transcript of the address online. See Max, *Every Love Story*, 291.

34 Rohr, *Everything Belongs*, 31.
35 Ibid., 16.
36 David Foster Wallace. Interview with Michael Silverblatt. *Bookworm*. KCRW. April 11, 1996. Available online: https://www.kcrw.com/news-culture/shows/bookworm/david-foster-wallace-infinite-jest.
37 Rohr, *Everything Belongs*, 18.
38 Ibid., emphasis in original.
39 Some of these books have been removed from the personal library at Wallace's family's request, but others, like Laing, remain. For a good overview of Wallace's reading of self-help books, see Maria Bustillos, "Inside David Foster Wallace's Self-Help Library," *The Awl*, April 5, 2011. Available online: https://www.theawl.com/2011/04/inside-david-foster-wallaces-private-self-help-library/.
40 Rohr, *Everything Belongs*, 53.
41 Wallace, "My Commencement Speech."
42 Ibid.
43 Essentially the same joke is told to Don Gately by a biker named Bob Death after an AA meeting (*IJ* 445).

10

David Foster Wallace and Postsecularism

Ryan Lackey

In the introduction to the twentieth anniversary edition of *Infinite Jest*, Tom Bissell suggests that "it is a mistake to view [Wallace] as anything other than a religious writer."[1] Similar, if less polemic, gestures to spiritual practice and religious belief appear throughout Wallace scholarship. Lee Konstantinou, for example, suggests that Wallace adopts "a kind of religious vocabulary (God, prayer, etc.) emptied out of a specific content."[2] Likewise, David Evans identifies a spirituality in *Infinite Jest* concerned with "practical consequences,"[3] and Allard den Dulk has linked Wallace with the spiritually inflected philosophy of Soren Kierkegaard.[4] Outside of the academy, a different sort of spiritual reading of Wallace's work manifests in the popular enthusiasm for the image of Wallace as sagacious monk, tortured but enlightened. This hagiography tends to draw from *This Is Water* and its fashionableness as pop-psych self-help; together, the cultural meme of Wallace as writer of difficult books and the fact of his suicide have helped reinforce this version of Wallace as "benignant and morally clairvoyant artist/saint," to borrow Jonathan Franzen's terms.[5]

Though religious readings of Wallace's work continue to proliferate, the application of a theoretical framework can help us more accurately describe his work's religious impulse, which is less straightforward than it may seem. As Bissell writes in his introduction, he has "never been able to get a handle on Wallace's notion of spirituality."[6] After all, while Wallace's work deploys language and social structures we can recognize as religiously influenced, it does not advocate a simple return to established forms of religion. His characters who move, or try to move, from solipsistic modes of being toward vulnerability and community do not follow straightforwardly prodigal paths, and they demonstrate attitudes toward traditional religious activity—prayer, offering, worship—that include apathy, confusion, and hostility. At times Wallace interrogates the very nature and purpose of religion, its power to effect personal change or establish social justice.

Given the complex sense of religion in his work, we can term Wallace's religious mode fundamentally postsecular. By reading Wallace through a postsecular paradigm, directing our attention toward religious ambiguities, tensions, and contradictions, we might better understand how religious concerns inform his work. At the same time, this rigorous reading might help combat the tendency toward hagiography that reduces Wallace and his texts into a monolithic cultural icon, eliminating the possibility of nuanced reading and encouraging the dismissal of problematic or offensive facets of his texts and his biography.

The postsecular turn

Broadly put, postsecularism names the critical response across multiple academic disciplines—philosophy, sociology, political theory, religious studies, literary criticism—to the "secularization thesis." According to the secularization thesis, religious and spiritual ways of understanding the world have, since the Enlightenment, gradually ceded authority in western culture to secular modes: rationalism, materialism, empiricism, and realism. As Jose Casanova explains, this model of secularization so dominates our notion of western history that it becomes the unconsidered assumption, the "unremarkable fact," from which we all begin.[7]

Early postsecular studies drew inspiration from scholars like Charles Taylor (especially his study *A Secular Age*), Jurgen Habermas, Talal Asad, Mark C. Taylor, and Saba Mahmood. Together, they form what we might call "first-wave" postsecularism. Drawing from previous work by poststructuralists like Jacques Derrida and postcolonial theorists like Homi Bhabha, the first wave responds to the secularization thesis by pointing out not only the resurgence of religious belief in the West but also that religion was never really on the wane at all. At the same time, it recognizes the eurocentrism of the secularization thesis, which denies the heterogeneity of western culture and the importance of nonwestern influences. In his essay, "Secularism's Crisis of Faith," Habermas identifies the global presence of western missionaries, radical fundamentalism, and the potential political cooption of supposedly "innate" religious violence as evidence of religion's ongoing relevance.[8]

Building on these foundations, more recent postsecular thought rethinks what terms like "religious" and "secular" actually mean. As Michael

Kaufmann explains, postsecularism calls into question the stability of, and the distinction between, those very terms.[9] Understood as historically relative, the secular and religious no longer exist in a zero-sum relationship that demands one diminish as the other expands. Instead, the secular and religious are cooperatively defined and change over time. As Kaufmann explains, "[s]ince the secular and religious depend on *each other* for meaning, they must always be present at the same time ... each concept is meaningless in isolation."[10] What we term conclusively secular might in another moment or another context suddenly appear religiously significant. In other words, our sense of religion is an adjustable frame. Hence Gregor McLennan's opinion that the postsecular turn brings about a weakening, not an outright rejection, of the secularization thesis; while we need not assign religious ways of understanding the world a *superior* access to truth, they must "be reconsidered, to say the least, *non-reductively*."[11] As Judith Butler writes in a recent essay, "the language of religion is part of what we live even if we think we are now perfectly secular, for the fragments of the unthought weigh on the living."[12]

Postsecularism and literary studies

In literary studies, postsecularism describes both a set of texts and a method of reading. That is, there are postsecular texts and postsecular ways to read texts. Magdelena Mączyńska makes a comparison between postsecularism and feminism, which seeks to both identify feminist texts and read all varieties of texts through feminist lenses. In Mączyńska's words, both postsecular and feminist criticism can refer "either to a theoretical approach or a textual canon."[13] Though Kaufmann contends that no established definition of postsecularism exists in literary studies, he cites central characteristics that enjoy "broad general agreement," including efforts to "unmoor certitudes" and disassemble "simple binary oppositions."[14] In the same spirit, Mączyńska suggests that postsecular texts might "be defined as narratives that openly question or destabilize the religious/secular dichotomy," and that postsecular reading "would entail examining works of any period with an eye to uncovering what postsecular writing announces overtly."[15]

Within the discipline of literary studies, postsecularism's most famous exponent is John McClure, whose early essays from the 1990s and his book *Partial Faiths: Postsecular Fiction in the Age of Pynchon and Morrison* are frequently cited. Other important texts include Amy Hungerford's *Postmodern Belief* and a 2009 *Religion & Literature* forum on postsecularism that attempts to sketch its definition and methodology. McClure reads a fragmentary and uncertain religious return in postmodern literature—hence the title of *Partial Faiths*—whose characters practice doubt as much as faith and avoid wholesale subscriptions to rigid or dogmatic religious structures. Even as these characters explore religious cosmologies as viable alternatives, thereby enacting "a religiously inflected disruption of secular constructions of the real," the religious inclinations (if any) that result emerge "dramatically 'weakened'" and always alongside "secular, progressive values and projects."[16] In this way, he concludes, "postsecular narratives affirm the urgent need for a turn toward the religious even as they reject (in most instances) the familiar dream of full return to an authoritative faith."[17] As Kathryn Ludwig explains, in postsecular narratives "the religious is not reaffirmed so much as it is engaged."[18] Ludwig's point reiterates that postsecularism is not necessarily a refutation of secularism as such. Rather, postsecularism denies the universality of secularism; it seeks to conditionalize, not erase. In McClure's terms, postsecular literature "interrogates secular constructions of the real."[19] Thus, to read from a postsecular position means attending not only to postsecular narratives amend ostensibly secular environments with mystical moments or idiopathic events, but also how they present nonsecular ways of knowing.

Postsecular Wallace

Critics like McClure consider postsecularism a close cousin to postmodernism; according to McClure, "some of the very features of fiction which secular theorists have singled out as definitively postmodern must at least in some cases be understood in terms of a post-secular project of resacralization."[20] This suggests that Wallace's work is well suited to a postsecular reading, given that critics frequently read Wallace's writing as both an evocation of and a response to literary postmodernism. In postsecularism's elucidation of a partial and flexible sense of the religious—comprised of both faith and doubt—there is a resemblance to the sincerity critics like Adam Kelly have highlighted in Wallace's fiction. For Kelly, this "New Sincerity" aspires toward ethical seriousness in paradoxical and mysterious ways. He writes that "New Sincerity fiction ... articulates a desire for contamination,"[21] and the resultant sincerity is stuck always in a state of "aporia," of unknowability.[22] Mączyńska, likewise, argues that postsecularism "valu[es] messiness over order and ambiguity over certainty."[23] As critics have already established Wallace's work as preoccupied with the in-between and unknowable, it seems that postsecularism, also attuned to these concerns, might be especially qualified to trace Wallace's spirituality. Amy Hungerford makes this tie between sincerity and postsecularism explicit, writing that "sincerity overshadows irony as a literary mode when the ambiguities of language are imagined as being religiously empowered."[24]

Chris Fogle and postsecular conversion

To explore these connections, we turn first to Chris Fogle, whose vocational conversion to accounting in *The Pale King* is one of the most famous moments of religious significance in Wallace's work. By considering Fogle's conversion as an injection of religious meaning into nonreligious forms (the apparently secular context of actuarial tables and tax schedules), we can add Fogle to the collection of postsecular characters who, as McClure writes, "in varied ways synthesize sacred and secular ways of seeing."[25] In a postsecular sense, Fogle's religious understanding is hybrid; it consists of both religious and secular images and symbols, including some that are both at once. As McClure describes, a postsecular "conversion is in part a matter of coming into community. But the communities founded or discovered by postsecular pilgrims are dramatically small, fragile, and transitory."[26] Likewise, Fogle's conversion means his introduction into a community of wigglers, the low-level tax reviewers who serve as financial clergy. Like clergy, the wigglers conduct work that is ritually stylized, as depicted in the chapter of *The Pale King* devoted to the tiny, shared actions of the examination room. But Fogle's decision to answer his "call to account" is one of three conversions in his narrative, and the other two—Fogle's story of Obetrolling and his roommate's girlfriend's evangelicalism—are examples of failed conversions that do not induct their subjects into these communities. Specifically, Obetrolling offers no experience of community, while evangelicalism represents an exclusivist community that denies flexibility and complexity.

Fogle's other euphemism for Obetrolling, "doubling," reveals his attraction to the religious feeling it offers; the term suggests the sensation of another presence, of intimacy. Obetrolling invokes the idea of community but in a false form; under its influence, Fogle tends to stay in his room, alone. While doubling, Fogle achieves a sort of enlightenment that has "something to do with paying attention," and he realizes he possesses "depths that blazed in an almost sacred way" (*PK* 187). But while Obetrol enables Fogle's awakening to the sacred, his newfound attention only looks inward; he is captivated only by his own "depths." However, it is important to note that the novel complicates a simple reading of Obetrolling as merely false spirituality or idolatry. Although we might at first (and perhaps justifiably) reject the notion of a misused drug as a way to spirituality, the novel suggests that, though problematic, Obetrolling nevertheless encourages Fogle's eventual conversion. We are asked to treat seriously Fogle's recollection of Obetrolling as an experience that feels blazing and sacred. That is, the novel demands we reconsider what we think is "valid" or "appropriate" religious practice. In a postsecular sense, the nature of the sacred is redefined.

We can juxtapose Fogle's Obetrolling narrative with Fogle's reflections on his roommate's girlfriend, whose evangelical "testimony" is the chapter's other failed conversion story. The conversion story of the evangelical Christian—the "testimony"—becomes a sign of identity, marking membership in the church and eventual access to heaven. The testimony's rhetorical goal is the conversion of the listener. If Obetrolling is insufficiently external, the evangelical practice of narrative testimony is *objectifyingly* external. It reduces other people to potential converts. As Fogle notes, these sort of Christians consider "everyone else outside their sect to be—lost and hopeless and just barely clinging to any kind of interior sense of value" (*PK* 211). As Ludwig reminds us, postsecularism interrogates "grand narratives and ... religious establishments," including American evangelicalism.[27] Exclusive forms of evangelical Christianity can be as unyielding and totalizing as the secularization narrative; neither manages to capture the complexity of religion in its various forms, as social practice and personal experience.

Unlike these other conversion narratives, Fogle's "call to account" is more successful, and it is best described in postsecular terms. The substitute Jesuit whose taxation class Fogle stumbles into describes tax workers in both heroic and ecclesiastical terms, figuring them as a Levitical caste inhabiting a "denomination of joy" invisible to the public eye (*PK* 230). Though the Jesuit mingles religious and secular rhetoric, the effect on Fogle is unequivocally spiritual. He feels "unusually aware and alert," but in a way unlike Obetrolling and which he can neither "analyze" nor "rationally explain" (*PK* 216–17). As the Jesuit closes with an exhortation—"Gentlemen, you are called to account," a phrase that presents accounting as both a vocation and a divine judgement—Fogle has a sudden vision of "something lying in its crib and waving its limbs uselessly in the air, its mouth open and wet," and so Fogle has been reborn (*PK* 233).

Significantly, Fogle's conversion relies at least partially upon the Jesuit's sense of "authority," which Fogle comes to realize might be "actually something real and authentic" (*PK* 227). However, the Jesuit's authority does not emerge from his location within the institution of the church. Nor is his authority political, established through the relationship between taxation and national government, which we might consider the secular analogue to the institutional church. Instead, it is the interpersonal, even mysterious encounter between the Jesuit and Fogle from which the Jesuit's authority stems. The authority, the power, is cooperative: Fogle defines it as "a certain kind of power that he exerted and that I was granting him" (*PK* 227). Thus, Fogle's postsecular awakening involves power and authority, but not in traditional ways. Rather than hierarchically imposed, religious authority is mutually created.

Given that postsecular conversions commingle faith and doubt in ways difficult to explain, it is unsurprising we can further complicate Fogle's story. The editorial afterword to *The Pale King* includes one of Wallace's working notes that imagines Fogle possessing a certain phrase or string of numbers that, when recited, induces a trance-like state of intense concentration. This numerical recitation constitutes an enchantment of speech that resembles Allen Ginsberg's mantra making, which according to Amy Hungerford epitomizes postsecular prayer. She writes that Ginsberg's poetry mimics "a resonant chanted mantra, in which the words produce a sound meant to transform the listener into a person of peace."[28] This is language chanted and *enchanted*. On one hand, Fogle's string of numbers suggests a similar intent. On the other, however, to give Fogle numbers rather than words might suggest that Fogle's numbers do not form a mantra but an algorithm, which would make Fogle not a mystic but a program operating with the blankness of a computer.

From a postsecular perspective, though, it might be incorrect to suggest the algorithm is secular and the mantra sacred; a postsecular reading suggests there may be no sacral difference between the two. Fogle is a postsecular character because of these ambiguities, not in spite of them. His narrative suggests we can tell ourselves different stories—of complexity and expansive possibility.

Don Gately and postsecular belief

Like Fogle, Don Gately is a postsecular figure. He performs a postsecular understanding of religious practice through his participation in Alcoholics Anonymous (AA), a community established outside of traditional religious institutions. But while Fogle remakes the sacred through supposedly "secular" taxation, Gately redefines religious practices—like prayer, for example—in less obviously religious ways. Gately's prayer is an expression, an expression of doubt and surrender rather than conviction. This uncertain prayer has antecedents in postsecular fiction. Hungerford stresses speech and language as a primary method by which postsecular characters build religious identities, and she cites Franny, from J.D. Salinger's *Franny and Zooey*, as an example. According to Hungerford, Franny recites a prayer, like Gately's, devoid of prior conviction—what Hungerford calls "belief without meaning."[29] Her description of Franny speaking the Jesus prayer "as a ritual practice leading to religious enlightenment, not as the result of existing belief" also applies to Gately, whose prayer illustrates "meaning without belief."[30] In other words, his prayer does not signify prior belief. Instead, it becomes an embodied religious practice that makes belief itself more complex. As Gately is told, "it doesn't yet matter what you believe or don't believe" (*IJ* 350). He prays, we might say, in-between belief.

Even as Gately's prayer, in typical postsecular fashion, redefines belief, it also rethinks the nature of prayer. While Gately prays, following the AA coda, to some indistinctly imagined Higher Power, that prayer does not follow a traditional, intercessory model. (Nor is that Higher Power necessarily a deity in the traditional sense; AA member Glenn K. prays to Satan) (*IJ* 352). Gately subscribes to no traditional concept of prayer's relationship to godly omnipotence; he asks, "how can you pray to a 'God' you believe only morons believe in, still?" (*IJ* 350). But he prays nevertheless: Gately falls "on his big knees" to pray to "something he still didn't believe in" and asks "for his own sick Spider-bit will to be taken from him" (*IJ* 359–60). It is, however, the act of prayer itself that realizes this inner change. Thus, for Gately, prayer is not an entreaty to the omnipotent deity. It is instead a useful practice, a bodily discipline, and thereby an extension of his routinized social habit, the AA demand he "keep coming and coming, nightly," to meetings for fellowship (*IJ* 350). Thus, Gately's prayer is meant to realize some effect on the material world, and while it does not call out for divine intervention its methodology is as mysterious as any "traditional" prayer. It gathers together in ritual his body, his will, and his participation within a community—what Hungerford calls "a way of living."[31]

In the same way that the nontraditional context of tax work offers Fogle a positive spiritual vitality that Obetrolling cannot, AA reworks religious and secular forms to create a new, postsecular practice that is both meaningful and mysterious. Indeed, for its members AA is as inscrutable as any catechism or koan: "it seemed to be impossible to figure out just *how* AA worked" (*IJ* 349). Likewise, Gately's sobriety is presented as literally miraculous. At one point he realizes his addictive urges have "been mysteriously magically removed" (*IJ* 466). We should note that the novel suggests that AA's mimicry of more traditional religion carries a certain danger: "But and plus in Boston AA there is, unfortunately, dogma, too ... some of it both dated and smug" (*IJ* 360). But there remains a crucial difference between the productive restraint of discipline or habit and the uncritical reiteration of dogma. While a more conventional church or religious body acts as a conduit for a dispensation of grace and power from its singular origin—God—the efficacy of AA is dispersed and always unknowable. Neither Gately nor the reader is sure if his prayer, or the AA meetings, or his service at Ennet House, or his will to abstention, or even his messianic sacrifice provide the key to his sobriety. Even as *Infinite Jest* stresses the treatment of addiction (chemical, digital, or otherwise) as at least partially a spiritual problem, the spiritual answers it gestures toward are multiple, fragmented, and social—we can never extricate one from another. Prayer possesses no more claim to spiritual power than the apparently humbler act of sitting in a meeting and drinking bad coffee.

Elsewhere, *Infinite Jest* makes meaning through the sudden intrusion of the mystical and supernatural. The novel's world is rife with fissures through which the miraculous seeps—a hallmark of postsecular fiction. For example, faced with Gately's telepathic conversations with the ghost of the deceased James Incandenza, the reader must make interpretative claims regarding the nature of this ghostly visitation; delirious from pain, Gately *might* be dreaming, but we cannot be sure. Either way, the world Gately inhabits becomes suddenly and fantastically unloosed, inhabited by presences that deny easy (or entirely secular) explanation. Likewise, the reader must interpret Gately's vision of digging up James's body with Hal, another scene rife with religious meaning.[32] The scene is familiar: the two male protagonists, like Leopold Bloom and Stephen Dedalus in *Ulysses*, finally meet and reach the end of the prodigal journey: the return to James, the godlike father figure (whose absence drives the personal and political havoc of the novel's plot) and the origin of the samizdat (the sacred text capable of transforming lives, in a dark sense, and also a sort of grail). But, occurring beyond the end of *Infinite Jest* proper, the scene is ambiguous. It is ghostly, a haunting possibility—a return that might or might not occur. McClure identifies this pattern of partial or uncertain returning as a quintessentially postsecular narrative structure. If Hal and Gately are moving toward the center of original power, the first mover from which the events of the novel flow, it is fitting that their arrival appears outside the central narrative, shown only in fragmented flashback and dream. Though ambiguously told, this story reiterates that *Infinite Jest* deploys religiously significant patterns that resist an easy, allegorical religious template while remaining meaningful.

"Octet" and postsecular reading

Finally, we should examine the ways Wallace's postsecular narratives are also metafictional. While much postsecular scholarship has addressed the religious possibilities apparent in postmodern novels, there has also been an attempt to show how those novels' postmodern and metafictional techniques might themselves be postsecular. As Paul Corrigan asserts, "[c]ontemporary literature contains not only postsecular themes but also postsecular forms."[33] Given what Kaufmann calls "the innate circularity of the relationship between the secular and the religious," and the fact that "the tension between the two terms generates an endlessly recursive narrative," perhaps it is no surprise that the form of postmodern fiction, which is often self-referential and circular, seems to embody postsecular themes so well.[34] Mączyńska agrees, suggesting that "[o]ne fruitful direction for future postsecular criticism might be to offer more focus on the textual mechanisms involved in contemporary encounters between religious and novelistic discourses."[35] This approach aligns well with attempts to explore and explain how metafictional structures work. But while postmodern narratives often present piecemeal and fragmented religious patterns, or include religious concerns among many other themes, a few of Wallace's texts attempt to encourage (and maybe even demand) the reader's *participation* in religious forms. As Lee Konstantinou asserts, Wallace attempts to "demonstrate that the form of metafiction can produce ... belief."[36] In other words, Wallace attempts to make sacred the act of reading.

This sacralization of reading is most overt in "Octet," in which metafiction serves to pose questions of faith and doubt directly to the reader.[37] A series of "quizzes," the story presents a series of vignettes that conclude with impossible, ethically fraught questions. This quiz format, designed as "a certain sort of '*interrogation*' of the person reading," lends "Octet" a catechistic likeness (*BI* 123). The final quiz, "Pop Quiz 9," positions the reader as the author of "Octet," struggling to shape the collection of quizzes into a form that will "*transmit* or *evoke*" a feeling of intimacy (*BI* 131 fn 7, emphasis original). The reader is thereby placed on both sides of the text, present at writing and reading—while, of course, also metafictionally reading *about* this doubling. The reader is dislocated, and this disintegration of singular identity appears frequently in postsecular texts; for example, Hungerford argues that in *Franny and Zooey* it is "the capacity to act—to assume the identities of others and occupy them for a time, returning then to some other state of consciousness—that represents the religious understanding at work in the novel."[38] As the primary site of this empathetic acting, literature enacts a sort of consubstantiality, making identity multiple. In this way, "[t]he play and the novel are incarnations of the divine word" as they make possible this "divine performance."[39] But rather than only depicting this multiple identity, "Octet" asks the reader to participate in it.

By assuming a double identity—reader and writer, addresser and addressee—the reader experiences a self-alienation; the reader's sense of self is divided and displaced. This is the spiritual heart of "Octet," an attempt to awaken a sense of intimacy in the reader. But intimacy itself is simultaneously redefined. No longer something occurring only *between* individual subjects but also among the pieces of a subject's multiple identity, intimacy is made more mysterious. Paradoxically, to feel multiple and fragmented is, claims "Octet," common and familiar; it is "some sort of weird ambient *sameness* in different kinds of human relationships, some nameless but inescapable *price* that all human beings are faced with having to pay if they ever want truly 'to be with' another person" (*BI* 131–2). This language imbues intimacy with the harrows of sacrifice and points toward its ineffability. Phrases like "some sort" and "nameless but inescapable" and the quotes around "to be with" signal that the text arrives at the limits of language. Intimacy cannot be spoken, but it must be spoken.

Another way to read this intimacy is through the story's invocation of the literal author. Though he conducts a pessimistic reading of "Octet," Iain Williams argues that "Wallace has attempted what is—in the wake of poststructuralism—almost unthinkable, attempting to carve out a space for the authentic author that lies beyond the page."[40] In this way Wallace resembles Ginsberg, who, writes Hungerford, considered "the evacuation of authorial control and intention … devastating."[41] The reintroduction of Wallace as present author would similarly establish a possibility in language to realize intimacy over great gaps in time and space.

Either way, "Octet" pursues an *enchanted reading experience*, during which human intimacy is not only referred to or depicted but actually invoked, manifested—a sort of transubstantiation. As "Octet" warns its reader–writer, "if you go ahead and do it (i.e. ask [the reader] straight out), this whole 'interrogation' thing won't be an innocuous formal belletristic device anymore. It'll be *real*" (*BI* 133, emphasis added). But this "reality" is not easily defined. This making real occurs when something is "felt" or "palpated" that the text tries to "*transmit* or *evoke*" or "*limn*" through its "weird psychospiritual probing" (*BI* 126, 131 fn. 7 emphasis original). Reading "Octet" becomes ceremonial, a rite; like Gately's prayer and Fogle's string of numbers, "Octet" is a ritual meant to enact change, exert a force. It resembles Ginsberg's mantra chanting. In this postsecular vein, "Octet" does not demand the reader observe or adhere to a particular dogma, but it attempts to coerce the reader into a confrontation with the possibility of enchantment; hence the story's final line: "So decide" (*BI* 136). "Octet" does not demand the reader agree that human intimacy is necessarily spiritual, but it urges the reader to seriously consider that possibility. Likewise, the story asks the reader to make judgements regarding the ability of texts to carry and create spiritual experiences. In other words, can symbol and language do the mysterious work of encapsulating not only meaning but also phenomena, personality, or revelation? This fundamental mystery lies at the center of both literature and religion.

Conclusion

While we might read religious and spiritual concerns into Wallace's work through any number of lenses or methods, postsecularism is a particularly generative option. Postsecularism treats seriously the spiritual possibilities of fiction while also remaining rigorous and incisive. As McClure writes, "attending to these preoccupations, investments, and discursive urgencies will make the experience of reading them richer and more productively troubling."[42] At the same time, however, current notions of postsecularism are not without error. For example, various critics, including Mączyńska, have worried that the "weakening" and "expansion" of spiritual practice under postsecularism might lead to a self-serving, à la carte spirituality— charges that might also be levelled at Wallace. Mączyńska notes that the postsecularism of Zadie Smith's *The Autograph Man* "opens itself to accusations, not entirely unmerited, of superficiality and facile textual consumerism."[43] We might read Wallace's emphasis on the restriction of the individual will through membership in a community and the adherence to habit as responses to this vulnerability. Wallace's fiction suggests that more dogmatic and traditional religious forms are insufficiently flexible to assist contemporary people who are caught within the recursive patterns of their psyches and popular culture. At the same time, it asserts that freedom, meaning, and intimacy can emerge from the structures created through reformed and remixed religious practices. And like other postsecular fiction, Wallace's work presents an enchanted world rife with possibility—a reminder that even amidst absurdity and pain, we might still make space for the miraculous.

Notes

1. Tom Bissell, "Everything About Everything: *Infinite Jest*, Twenty Years Later," in *Infinite Jest* (New York: Back Bay Books, 2016), xi.
2. Lee Konstantinou, "No Bull: David Foster Wallace and Postironic Belief," in *The Legacy of David Foster Wallace*, ed. Samuel Cohen and Lee Konstantinou (Iowa City: Iowa University Press, 2012), 86.
3. David Evans, "'The Chains of Not Choosing': Free Will and Faith in William James and David Foster Wallace," in *A Companion to David Foster Wallace Studies*, ed. Marshall Boswell and Stephen J. Burn (New York: Palgrave Macmillan, 2013), 182.
4. Allard den Dulk, "Boredom, Irony, and Anxiety: Wallace and the Kierkegaardian View of the Self," in *David Foster Wallace and the "Long Thing,"* ed. Marshall Boswell (New York: Bloomsbury, 2014).
5. Jonathan Franzen, "Farther Away," *The New Yorker*, April 18, 2011.
6. Bissell, "Everything About Everything," xiii.
7. Jose Casanova, "Rethinking Secularization: A Global Comparative Perspective," *The Hedgehog Review* 8, no. 1–2 (2006): 8.
8. Jurgen Habermas, "Notes on Post-Secular Society," *New Perspectives Quarterly* 25, no. 4 (2008): 18.
9. Michael Kaufmann, "Locating the Postsecular," *Religion & Literature* 41, no. 3 (2009): 68.
10. Michael Kaufmann, "The Religious, the Secular, and Literary Studies: Rethinking the Secularization Narrative in Histories of the Profession," *New Literary History* 38 (2007): 610.
11. Gregor McLennan, "The Postsecular Turn," *Theory, Culture & Society* 27, no. 4 (2010): 3.
12. Judith Butler, "Marx on Ruthless Critique," *PMLA* 31, no. 2 (2016): 467.
13. Magdalena Mączyńska, "Toward a Postsecular Literary Criticism: Examining Ritual Gestures in Zadie Smith's 'Autograph Man'," *Religion & Literature* 41, no. 3 (2009): 76.
14. Kaufmann, "Locating the Postsecular," 68–9.
15. Mączyńska, "Toward a Postsecular Literary Criticism," 76.

16 John McClure, *Partial Faiths: Postsecular Fiction in the Age of Pynchon and Morrison* (Athens: University of Georgia Press, 2007), 3.
17 Ibid., 6.
18 Kathryn Ludwig, "Don DeLillo's 'Underworld' and the Postsecular in Contemporary Fiction," *Religion & Literature* 41, no. 3 (2009): 83.
19 John McClure, "Postmodern/Post-Secular: Contemporary Fiction and Spirituality," *Modern Fiction Studies* 41, no. 1 (1995): 143.
20 Ibid., 144.
21 Adam Kelly, "David Foster Wallace and New Sincerity Aesthetics: A Reply to Edward Jackson and Joel Nicholson-Roberts," *Orbit: A Journal of American Literature* 5, no. 2 (2017): 25.
22 Adam Kelly, "David Foster Wallace and the New Sincerity in American Fiction," in *Consider David Foster Wallace: Critical Essays*, ed. David Hering (Los Angeles: Sideshow Media Group Press, 2010), 140.
23 Mączyńska, "Toward a Postsecular Literary Criticism," 81.
24 Amy Hungerford, *Postmodern Belief* (Princeton: Princeton University Press, 2010), xix.
25 John McClure, "Post-Secular Culture: The Return of Religion in Contemporary Theory and Literature," *Cross Currents* 47, no. 3 (1997), 332
26 McClure, *Partial Faiths*, 4.
27 Ludwig, "Don DeLillo's 'Underworld'," 83.
28 Hungerford, *Postmodern Belief*, 37.
29 Ibid., xiii.
30 Ibid., 10.
31 Ibid., 130.
32 Perhaps Hal's recollection of the same event during his interior monologue that opens *Infinite Jest* encourages us to read Gately's vision with credulity, although this rational appeal to corroboration does little to explain from where, exactly, Gately receives his mysterious vision/dream.
33 Paul T. Corrigan, "Whispers of Faith in contemporary American Literature," *Christianity and Literature* Vol. 63, no. 4 (Summer 2014), 526.
34 Kaufmann, "The Religious, the Secular, and Literary Studies," 615.
35 Mączyńska. "Toward a Postsecular Literary Criticism," 76.
36 Konstantinou, "No Bull," 93.
37 Wallace adopts a similar strategy in "Joseph Frank's Dostoevsky," which, while ostensibly a review of Frank's biography of the Russian writer, also puts forward a notion of fiction's relationship to ethics and religion; like "Octet," the essay includes asides directed toward the reader that demand a straightforward confrontation of complex questions: "What exactly does 'faith' mean? As in 'religious faith,' 'faith in God,' etc." (*CL* 259).
38 Hungerford, *Postmodern Belief*, 12.

39 Ibid., 12.
40 Iain Williams, "(New) Sincerity in David Foster Wallace's 'Octet'," *Critique: Studies in Contemporary Fiction* 56, no. 3 (2015): 310.
41 Hungerford, *Postmodern Belief*, 39.
42 McClure, "Postmodern/Post-Secular," 160.
43 Mączyńska, "Toward a Postsecular Literary Criticism," 81.

11

"There's Always a Mormon Around When You Don't Want One": What Wallace Can Teach the Church Media Machine

Jessica E. Sagers

Near the beginning of David Foster Wallace's "Westward the Course of Empire Takes Its Way," protagonist Mark Nechtr becomes fascinated by a young, well-dressed man sporting a beard and holding an overfull clipboard. The man is interrogating strangers in the Avis rental car line, offering them cash if they are willing to reveal to him their "one great informing fear" (*GCH* 283). Mark eyes the bearded man as he works his way over to his ascetic wife, D.L., then approaches him in an effort to "verify the scam," because "he's figured out how these guys are: they're Mormons, it's some irritatingly altruistic Mormon thing" (*GCH* 264). Despite D.L.'s public outburst at being denied the chance to rent a car, which prompts the bearded man to offer assistance, Mark insists that "they *don't* need Latter-Day charity, Reunion or no. There's always a Mormon around when you don't want one, trying your patience with unsolicited kindness" (*GCH* 276). After a brief interaction, Nechtr is shocked to realize that the bearded man "isn't a practicing LDS [Latter-Day Saint], but rather works for J.D. Steelritter Advertising in some research capacity" (*GCH* 276). Well-groomed, helpful, and inquisitive though he may be, the young man working the line is not a Mormon. He works for an advertising company.

By the 1980s, for both Wallace and Mark Nechtr, the distinction between a Mormon missionary and an advertising representative had grown increasingly easy to miss, especially for a person who, like Wallace, spent "many slack-jawed, spittle-chinned, formative hours" in front of the television (*CW* 24). Fundamentally American and unapologetically peculiar, the Church of Jesus Christ of Latter-Day Saints represents a fascinating test case in the marketing of American religion. The doctrines and practices of Mormonism have attracted public curiosity since the religion's genesis in 1830, leading journalists to claim that "no religion in American history has aroused so much fear and hatred, nor been the object of so much persecution and so much misinformation."[1] As a result, Mormon self-consciousness around the public image of their religion is "perhaps more [intense] than the members of any other religious sect."[2] This self-consciousness reached a U.S. peak following the social turmoil that accompanied the newly progressive politics of the counterculture and Civil Rights era, which seemed to oppose the more traditional values espoused by conservative members and LDS Church leadership.

To counteract the negative press the Church was beginning to attract for ultraconservative positions on racial equality and the Equal Rights Amendment, Latter-Day Saint leaders founded the Church's inaugural Public Communications Department. This department intended to leverage television and radio media campaigns to package and market the religion as a consumer product, refocusing the public image of Mormonism on central tenets calculated to appeal to a larger fraction of the American public, primarily the importance of the nuclear family. By the 1980s, the Church had poured tens of millions of dollars into its award-winning "Homefront" advertising campaign, and microcosmic Mormon family dynamics flooded screens all over the United States. Often featuring morally didactic interactions between adults and children, and always culminating in the logo and phone number of the LDS Church, these ubiquitous advertisements and their potential for parody did not elude Wallace. In James Orin Incandenza's infamous filmography, presented as footnote 24 in *Infinite Jest*, Wallace details a short film known as "Wave Bye-Bye to the Bureaucrat," a 19-minute, black-and-white "possible parody/homage to B.S. public service announcement cycle of Church of Jesus Christ of Latter-Day Saints" in which "a harried commuter is mistaken for Christ by a child he knocks over" (*IJ* 990). Saccharine but sincere, the LDS foray into television advertising proved both memorable and effective, and led thousands of earnest, young, well-groomed missionaries to answer inquiries at potential converts' doors complete with smiling faces, helping hands, and copies of *The Book of Mormon*, a Christ-centered religious text that Mormons revere alongside the Bible.

The capitalistic mindset that underlies advertising a religion like a product did not go unquestioned by thinking Mormons. In a 1983 commencement speech, prominent LDS apologist and professor Hugh Nibley cautioned Brigham Young University graduates that "Those who have something to give to humanity revel in their work, and do not have to rationalize, advertise, or evangelize to make themselves feel good about what they are doing. It is only when their art and their science become business oriented that problems of ethics ever arise. Look at TV. Behind the dirty work is always money."[3] Convincing people that Christianity is a viable life choice by paying smiling actors to act like happy families creates an almost Wallaceian double bind. And this phenomenon is not unique to LDS media. Broader Christian-produced movies and music provoke the same mix of morbid curiosity and low-level distrust in an average viewer as any other as-seen-on-TV product.

In 2010, Mark Willes, CEO of LDS Church-owned media conglomerate Deseret Management Corporation,[4] compared selling religion to selling bottled water:

> [Advertising companies have] done it because they have found a need you didn't realize you had until they offered it: convenience, taste, shape, color, properties inside. They have found that you don't necessarily think water in the tap is safe. Sometimes it was, sometimes it wasn't ... By finding what you are interested in, they have been able to sell a huge amount of bottled water. Well, let me ask you, if they can grow at a compound rate of 8 percent by selling water, shouldn't we be able to grow by selling relevant, compelling, emotional content in print, on the radio, on TV, and yes, on the Internet? My view is, if they can sell water, we can sell what we do and have a whole lot more fun in the process.[5]

Willes's argument, shocking in its pragmatism, relies on the escalation and alleviation of human fears. Water, like personal access to God, is a resource available to everyone for free, no middleman required. So it becomes the advertising man's job to isolate and manage a potential risk: here, that tap water, though free, is somehow suspect, simply not as safe as professionally managed water. Willes's perspective mirrors that of J.D. Steelritter, the cutthroat advertising maverick in "Westward the Course of Empire Takes Its Way," who believes that the best way to sell a thing to someone is to excavate and play upon their fears:

> J.D. eventually figured out that anybody who'd buy a box of baking soda out of fear of refrigerator odor wouldn't hesitate one second to shell out for another box to prevent *drain* odor. He laughs a marvelous laugh. *Drain* odor? What's that, for Christ's sake? It's just fear. Very careful research, fear, and the vision of a genius. The man is a legend. (*GCH* 285)

This is why the well-dressed man with the overfull clipboard pressing the Avis line to reveal their most significant fears is so easily mistaken for a missionary—on the surface, the marketing is the same.

In Nibley's words, "The early Christians called *Christemporoi* those who made merchandise of spiritual gifts or church connections. The things of the world and the things of eternity cannot be thus conveniently conjoined."[6] That may be why a minute-long advertising spot depicting a principle like "integrity" and branded with the logo of the Church of Jesus Christ of Latter-Day Saints can come off as inauthentic. Given the complexities of human life and the difficult ways our desires, vices, and personalities intersect with religious practice, watching inoffensively packaged moral dilemmas conveniently resolve after a few minutes on screen feels practically unethical. More pertinently, it does not make for believable art. To Alyssa Wilkinson, evangelical film critic and professor at The King's College in New York, the gaping chasm between Christian-produced media and meaningful art is a travesty. She argues that

> Christian theology is rich and creative and full of imagination, broad enough to take up residence among all kinds of human cultures. It contains within itself the idea that art exists as a good unto itself, not just a utilitarian vehicle for messages.... There is no reason Christian movies can't take the time to become good art. Each one that fails leaves me furious.[7]

So where is the disconnect between the feel-good productions of the Church media machine and engaging, decent art? In his 1993 interview with Larry McCaffery for the *Review of Contemporary Fiction*, David Foster Wallace offers an explanation for and a corrective to this disparity. Wallace explains that "the big distinction between good art and so-so art lies somewhere in the art's heart's purpose, the agenda of the consciousness behind the text. It's got something to do with love" (*CW* 50). He continues, "What's engaging and artistically real is, taking it as axiomatic that the present is grotesquely materialistic, how is it that we as human beings still have the capacity for joy, charity, genuine connections, for stuff that doesn't have a price? And can these capacities be made to thrive? And if so, how, and if not why not?" (*CW* 50).

Whether through televised media campaigns or next-level engagement with U.S. fiction, at the end of the twentieth century, David Foster Wallace and the Church were attempting to address the same fundamental questions. For members and evangelists of the Christian church, LDS or otherwise, it is Jesus Christ and the contingent promises of Christianity—faith, repentance, baptism, atonement, rebirth—that constitute the reason human beings still have "the capacity for joy, charity, genuine connections, for stuff that doesn't have a price." In language similar to Wallace's, the prophet Nephi in *The Book of Mormon* explains, "Behold, doth [Jesus Christ] cry unto any, saying, Depart from me? Behold, I say unto you, Nay; but he saith: Come unto me all ye ends of the earth, buy milk and honey, *without money and without price*" (2 Nephi 26:25, paraphrase of Isaiah 55:1; emphasis added).[8] Christians believe that it is through living in accordance with the principles of the restored gospel of Jesus Christ that these human capacities are best encouraged to thrive, and therefore feel a "great ... importance to make these things known unto the inhabitants of the earth" (2 Nephi 2:8). Consider the introduction to *Preach My Gospel*, the how-to manual given to all LDS missionaries:

> You are surrounded by people. You pass them on the street, visit them in their homes, and travel among them. They are all children of God, your brothers and sisters. God loves them just as He loves you. Many of these people are searching for purpose in life. They are concerned for their future and their families. They need the sense of belonging that comes from the knowledge that they are children of God, members of His eternal family. They want to feel secure in a world of changing values. They want "peace in this world, and eternal life in the world to come" (Doctrine and Covenants 59:23),[9] but they are "kept from the truth because they know not where to find it" (Doctrine and Covenants 123:12). The gospel of Jesus Christ as restored by the Savior through the Prophet Joseph Smith will bless them and their families, meet their spiritual needs, and help them fulfill their deepest desires.[10]

These high-minded promises are dutifully conveyed by Mormon missionaries, who spend eighteen months to two years as walking advertisements for the religion, their presence and bodies "a unique medium inextricably bound to the social, historical and institutional structures of the Church's mass media."[11] As early as 1951, LDS Church President David O. McKay issued the following advice to missionaries, which still features prominently in *Preach My Gospel*:

> True Christianity is love in action. There is no better way to manifest love for God than to show an unselfish love for your fellow men. This is the spirit of missionary work ... Christlike service should be offered as a sincere expression of love for those around you, without the expectation of people listening to a gospel message or accepting a teaching visit.[12]

Given that the driving ideological goal of any organized religion that urges members to convince others to subscribe is for all people to experience the love and mercy of the Divine, it is inarguable that the "agenda of the consciousness" behind religious outreach efforts genuinely has "something to do with love." Religion is one of the sincerest expressions of humanity. But given the way Wallace depicts the "probable Mormon" in "Westward" and the tongue-in-cheek way he characterizes LDS advertising campaigns in *Infinite Jest*, how and why do LDS and broader Christian media initiatives fail to clear the bar Wallace establishes for sincerity in art? What disqualifies Church-made art and media from being the "really good work [that] comes out of a willingness to disclose yourself, open yourself up in spiritual and emotional ways that risk making you really feel something" (CW 50)?

Wallace uses television to draw a distinction between "low art" and "serious art" that illustrates exactly how and where Church media fails to engage with this dilemma. Wallace's "low art" encompasses all forms of media produced for mass consumption, aimed toward making money and calculated to lead viewers into easy satiation of the most basic human hungers. This kind of art "recognizes that audiences prefer 100 percent pleasure to the reality that tends to be 49 percent pleasure and 51 percent pain" (CW 22) and leads the U.S. public to gorge itself on input that is morally and intellectually empty. Canonical LDS rhetoric casts similar displeasure toward the idea of a pleasure-maximizing, pain-minimizing approach to religion. Elder Joseph B. Wirthlin preaches, "You cannot approach the gospel as you would a buffet or smorgasbord, choosing here a little and there a little. You must sit down to the whole feast and live the Lord's loving commandments in their fullness."[13] In the LDS tradition, observing "the Lord's loving commandments in their fullness" is wildly nontrivial, requiring total abstinence from commonly enjoyed substances like coffee, tea, and alcohol; adherence to archaic social roles and dress standards (particularly for women); and the swearing off of sex outside of marriage. Strict and total adherence to these commandments is the sacrifice required to obtain blessings from God, if not in this life then in the next, and to demonstrate one's devotion and commitment to the Savior, Jesus Christ.[14] Joseph Smith, the founder of Mormonism, preached sacrifice as "the first law of heaven," the principle upon which every meticulous observance required by Mormon doctrine is predicated. Most famously, Smith argued that "A religion that does not require the sacrifice of all things never has power sufficient to produce the faith necessary unto life and salvation."[15] Wallace's description of "serious art" echoes Smith's description of sacrifice as the ultimate salvific power of religion. "Serious art," Wallace explains, is "more apt to make you uncomfortable ... forc[ing] you to work hard to access its pleasures, the same way that in real life true pleasure is usually a byproduct of hard work and discomfort" (CW 22). Buffet fiction is no more expected to produce lasting change in an individual than buffet television programs or buffet Christianity. Wallace continues:

> If writers care enough about their audience—if they love them enough and love their art enough—they've got to be cruel ...."Cruel" the way an army drill sergeant is when he decides to put a bunch of raw recruits through hell, knowing that the trauma you're inflicting on these guys, emotionally, physically, psychically, is just part of a process that's going to strengthen them in the end, prepare them for things they can't even imagine yet. (CW 24)

This kind of programmatic gauntlet, in which an omniscient but steely creator drives His loved ones through life-changing traumas to produce in them a lasting strength, is a fundamental principle of nearly every faith. The feeling is captured in an oft-quoted metaphor: the "refiner's fire," a phrase lifted from the third chapter of the book of Malachi that describes how in the process of purifying gold or silver, impurities are commonly removed by immersing a precious metal in fire to burn them out.[16] In Malachi 3:1–2, the Messiah (who Mormons believe to be Jesus Christ) is himself described as a refiner's fire:

> But who may abide the day of his coming? and who shall stand when he appeareth? *for he is like a refiner's fire*, and like fullers' soap: And he shall sit as a refiner and purifier of silver: and he shall purify the sons of Levi, and purge them as gold and silver, that they may offer unto the Lord an offering in righteousness.

In 1979, LDS Church leader James E. Faust offers a more explicit reading of this metaphor:

> In the pain, the agony, and the heroic endeavors of life, we pass through a refiner's fire, and the insignificant and the unimportant in our lives can melt away like dross and make our faith bright, intact, and strong. In this way the divine image can be mirrored from the soul. It is part of the purging toll exacted of some to become acquainted with God.[17]

Just as a religion that does not require the sacrifice of all things cannot generate the power sufficient to produce the faith required for salvation, a piece of fiction that does not require its "raw recruit" to pass through unfiltered trauma cannot generate power sufficient to catalyze lasting change. And thus both Wallace's readers and active Christians have no choice but to worship and fear the great Creator and His fiery-furnace love, as truly "it would take an architect who could hate enough to feel enough to love enough to perpetuate the kind of special cruelty only real lovers can inflict" (*GCH* 332).

The LDS history of government-sanctioned persecution,[18] combined with a belief in sacrifice as the first law of heaven, makes Mormons intimately familiar with the principle that God can and will burn His children alive in the refiner's fire in order to elevate them to a higher plane of life and salvation. The Christian tradition chalks this up as one reason that bad things happen to good people: to develop in them the hard-wrought human attributes that will purify them and make them more like Jesus Christ, who the prophet Isaiah describes as "a man of sorrows, and acquainted with grief" (Isaiah 53:3). If this is true, if Christian doctrine instills in Church members a deep, emotional connection with the divine that is sincerely founded in love and sacrifice, then why does Church-produced media, which at heart and in purpose subscribes to Wallace's ideology of "serious art," fail so totally in its execution?

T. Leonard Rowley, LDS professor of Theater Arts, answers this question in an insightful 1969 essay in which he subjects the Church's then-popular drama program[19] to serious critical analysis. Although Rowley intended his arguments to address the rash of Mormon-written, Mormon-produced, Mormon-performed theatrical plays published by the Church in the 1960s and 1970s, I find that his rhetoric applies as well to Church commercial media, both LDS productions and those of mainstream Christianity, where his observations seem even more astute. Rowley notes that a careful examination of dramatic works published by the Church reveals that two general categories of media standards developed as the drama program grew, which he terms Ethical Standards and Artistic Standards. Rowley describes these standards, to which all Church-produced dramatic works adhere, in the following numbered points:

Ethical Standards: Official Church publications instruct that (1) evil must never triumph; (2) that which belittles the race, color, or creed of others is unacceptable; (3) while scenes which refer to the use of tea, coffee, liquor, or tobacco may be necessary to the fabric of the play, they are never to be portrayed on the stage, but only referred to; (4) death is to be treated tastefully, and may never be without direct bearing on the play; (5) vulgar, obscene, or suggestive language, costumes, or actions are to be avoided. Suicide and divorce were originally forbidden subjects.

Artistic Standards: According to these standards, a good play should (1) be entertaining; (2) provide insight and understanding of humanity, both local and distant; (3) provide food for thought and a widening of intellectual horizons; (4) be expressed in language that is pleasing and challenging esthetically; (5) contain the dramatic elements of action, conflict, variety and contrast, strong dramatic structure, and carefully defined characterization.[20]

A cursory viewing of any LDS Homefront advertisement or Church-produced film of the same era will make it clear that these works adhere at least as strictly to Rowley's Ethical Standards as the theatrical productions produced for the Church's drama program. For example, one memorable spot stars a tiny Alfonso Ribeiro, the actor who would go on to play Carlton Banks in *The Fresh Prince of Bel Air*. The scene opens with police sirens and children running from a baseball game. We close in on an angry white male in his 60s or 70s, yelling variations on "Who broke my window?" in a minor-key refrain. Ribeiro's character (who as a young black male is the only noticeably nonwhite character in this story) timorously ponders his options over lyrics like "Telling the truth isn't gonna be easy! / Why is my stomach so nervous and queasy?" Eventually, Ribeiro confesses: "Mr. Robinson! Mr. Robinson! I broke your window with my ball. And I've come to confess!" The man increases in fury as he advances on Ribeiro, eventually grabbing him by the arm (an alarming gesture to the contemporary viewer given the climate of violence toward black Americans): "You knew I'd be angry! Aren't you afraid? You have to pay for this mess you've made!" Then the music suddenly changes to a series of triumphant chords and the old man breaks into a smile, singing "But I'm proud of you, child, for you have displayed honor, the stuff from which heroes are made!" Ribeiro smiles widely and shouts "I told the truth!" His childlike voice is then heard in voiceover: "From the Mormons! The Church of Jesus Christ of Latter-Day Saints." Indeed, "Bye Bye to the Bureaucrat," JOI's parody described in *Infinite Jest*, would fit into this campaign without significant alteration.

The core problem with these Church-produced narratives is that they cannot or choose not to engage with genuine elements of the human story without indulging an overwhelming tendency toward camp. Pretending that life is a series of cute vignettes in which every problem can be fixed with a smile and a scripture may preserve the shining Christian image, but by the 1980s, this image had successfully overshadowed the Church's capacity to produce meaningful art. Instead, by depicting superficial solutions to consequential problems, these simplistic narratives create "a fundamental dishonesty of treatment which seems to destroy rather than enhance our understanding of humanity."[21] I believe that this gaping artistic deficiency is explained by an overzealous adherence to Rowley's Ethical Standards, and that it is precisely that adherence which causes Church-produced media to fail to satisfy Rowley's Artistic Standards. No man can serve two masters, and our strict commitment to ethical rigor at the expense of artistic value categorically excludes Church media from Wallace's definition of "serious art." Rowley laments the dullness that such sanitization induces in stories that otherwise might feel alive, explaining:

> One of the greatest dulling influences to this kind of understanding is the straining for a happy ending. In some cases, the happy ending comes with such great effort as to destroy the impact of the suffering within the play. In others, the assurance that all will be well is so implicit within the action as to destroy the comprehension of the enormity of the threat. At best, the constant striving for the happy ending leaves many of the plays only innocuously pleasant rather than profoundly moving.[22]

Alyssa Wilkinson agrees, arguing that

> Christians ought to *especially* value exploration and truth-seeking, wherever it's found. We ought to be making fabulous movies that raise religious questions: who are we? Why are we? Where did we come from?

Where are we going? What should we do while we're here? And since Christians believe in God's very aliveness—since our theology suggests that people don't save others' souls, God does—and since we don't have anything to lose, we shouldn't think we have to swoop in and answer the question before the credits roll.[23]

LDS writer Mary Lythgoe Bradford takes this argument one step further, explaining "a misunderstanding many Mormons share about the purpose of fiction":

> We have not always understood that fiction has been and must always be about sinners and their struggles, those struggles between good and evil which Dostoevsky described as joined on the battleground of the human heart. We have not always understood that fiction writers must stand aside from that which most engages their personal lives, looking to a deeper engagement with their art. Even if this hurts those most engaged with their own lives, it may lead to a deeper understanding of that which must engage us all in the end.[24]

If Mormons cannot or will not infuse LDS-produced art with the painful and traumatic things that make us human—divorce, addiction, death, sexuality, profanity—for fear of besmirching the squeaky-clean image of the Church of Jesus Christ of Latter-Day Saints, then we consciously disqualify ourselves from the production of real and meaningful stories. Rowley correctly notes that such denial of pain and trauma is actually antithetical to Mormon doctrine, as one of the most fundamental tenets of our religion is that man cannot know pleasure without pain, light without dark, or good without evil.

David Foster Wallace famously explained that "Fiction's about what it is to be a fucking *human being*" (CW 26, emphasis original). In attempting to erase conflict and pain from its public-facing art, the Church has forgotten that that the adjective—a *fucking* human being—is as necessary as the rest of the sentence. To reframe Rowley's Standards, we must understand and confront the fact that evil sometimes triumphs; that that which belittles the race, color, or creed of others is ever-present in our own lives and the lives of friends; that the use of tea, coffee, liquor, and tobacco is sometimes as therapeutic as it can be scary; that death is rarely treated tastefully and always has direct bearing on any timeline of events; that vulgar, obscene, and suggestive language, costumes, and actions are intentionally used and should be attempted to be understood in context. Suicide and divorce are here with us to stay. Even so, good Christian lives and the art we make can and should be entertaining; provide a balanced understanding of humans who look and act like us as well as those who do not; work to widen intellectual horizons by questioning strongly held beliefs; be expressed in language that is sometimes pleasing to the ear but always challenging to the spirit; and contain the dramatic elements of action, conflict, variety and contrast alongside real conflicts and characterization that strenuously avoids stereotype.

Although the performance art of our missionary program, the pageantry of television advertisements, and the zealous tradition of Christian-themed music and film may genuinely originate from a place of love, to Wallace and to most Americans, these campaigns look and feel a bit too much like advertising. Artists and writers devoted to the faith can and must do better. By stripping our narratives of the qualities that make them most human, we rob them of the ability to make "heads throb heart-like" the way only "serious art" can. And once again, our missionary is mistaken for a J.D. Steelritter employee.

Notes

1. Richard N. Ostling and Joan K. Ostling, *Mormon America: The Power and the Promise* (New York: HarperCollins, 2007), xvi.
2. Stephen W. Stathis and Dennis Lythgoe, "Mormonism in the Nineteen-Seventies: The Popular Perception," *Dialogue: A Journal of Mormon Thought* 10, no. 3 (1977): 95–113; 95.
3. Hugh Nibley, "Leaders to Managers: The Fatal Shift," *Dialogue: A Journal of Mormon Thought* 16, no. 4 (1983): 12–21; 20.
4. The formal mission statement of Deseret Management Corporation is "We are a trusted voice of light and knowledge reaching hundreds of millions of people worldwide."
5. Mark H. Willes, "To All the World: Reinventing the Church's Media Business," *FARMS Review* 22, no. 2 (2010): 1–13; 13.
6. Nibley, "Leaders to Managers," 20.
7. Alyssa Wilkinson, "I'm a Christian and I Hate Christian Movies," *Thrillist*, March 30, 2016. Available online: https://www.thrillist.com/entertainment/nation/christian-movies-why-gods-not-dead-and-faith-based-films-hurt-religion#.
8. *The Book of Mormon* (Salt Lake City: The Church of Jesus Christ of Latter-Day Saints, 2000).
9. *The Doctrine and Covenants* (Salt Lake City: The Church of Jesus Christ of Latter-Day Saints, 2000).
10. *Preach My Gospel: A Guide to Missionary Service* (Salt Lake City: The Church of Jesus Christ of Latter-Day Saints, 2004), 1.
11. Ibid., 47.
12. Ibid., 14.
13. Joseph B. Wirthlin, "Choose the Right," *BYU Speeches*, September 4, 1994. Available online: https://speeches.byu.edu/talks/joseph-b-wirthlin_choose-right/ (accessed January 12, 2019).

14 As Jesus instructs, "If ye love me, keep my commandments" (John 14:15).
15 Joseph Smith, "Lectures on Faith: Discourse 6," (1835). *The Joseph Smith Papers*. Available online: https://www.josephsmithpapers.org/paper-summary/doctrine-and-covenants-1835/68#facts, 69.
16 Malachi occupies a special place in the LDS canon, as Joseph Smith maintains that this was the text read to him in an angelic visit on September 21, 1823, during which he received instructions regarding the forthcoming translation of the Book of Mormon (*Book of Mormon*, Joseph Smith-History 1:36).
17 The "refiner's fire" metaphor was particularly popular during Wallace's formative writing years; a search of the LDS General Conference Corpus, which comprises over 25 million words from over 10,000 addresses given by LDS Church leaders at the Church's semi-annual General Conference meeting between 1850 and 2010, reveals that fully 52 percent of all references to the "refiner's fire" were made between 1960 and 1980. See, James E. Faust, "The Refiner's Fire," *LDS.org*, April, 1974. Available online: https://www.lds.org/general-conference/1979/04/the-refiners-fire?lang=eng.
18 For example, Missouri governor Lilburn W. Boggs's issuance of the infamous 1838 Missouri Executive Order 44, in which the governor, threatened by the influx of immigrating Mormons likely to form a voting bloc, emphasized, "The Mormons must be treated as enemies, and must be exterminated or driven from the State if necessary for the public peace." On spurious charges associated with this patently unconstitutional Order (for which the state of Missouri offered a formal ceremony of apology in 1976), Joseph Smith was captured by a mob and thrown into jail to await trial in in Liberty, Missouri. Sick, hungry, and without the opportunity to bathe, he lamented his circumstances and inscribed his appeal to God for mercy in the Doctrine and Covenants, a record of Church history later canonized as Mormon scripture.
19 "From the formation of the Nauvoo Dramatic Company by Joseph Smith to the appointment of the Church Drama Committee which now supervises dramatic activity throughout the Church, Mormons have been actively engaged in the theatre. Original plays have been considered an important contribution to the cultural growth of the Church membership since pioneer times. Various contests and incentive programs have encouraged the native playwright. Most of these plans have been Church-sponsored ... Eventually, original works became abundant enough for the Church to publish an anthology of plays expressly written for the Church drama program." See, T. Leonard Rowley, "The Church's Dramatic Literature," *Dialogue: A Journal of Mormon Thought* 4, no. 3 (1969): 129–38; 129.
20 Rowley, "The Church's Dramatic Literature," 130.
21 Ibid., 132.
22 Ibid., 131.
23 Wilkinson, "I'm a Christian and I Hate Christian Movies."
24 Mary Lythgoe Bradford, "Virginia Sorensen: A Saving Remnant," *Dialogue: A Journal of Mormon Thought* 4, no. 3 (1969): 56–64; 56.

12

Zen Buddhist Philosophy Lurking in the Work of David Foster Wallace

Krzysztof Piekarski

Buddhism is still mostly a strange practice on American and Western shores, and it remains either exotic or misunderstood. Even people whose cultural roots are Buddhist have misunderstandings since Buddhism is both ancient and geographically vast, comes in all kinds of varieties, and is difficult to genuinely understand because the core teachings are deceptively simple and paradoxical. Most people do not progress far beyond Buddhism's pop cultural clichés and David Foster Wallace was no exception. He did, however, begin to intuit that Buddhist practices offered much of what he was struggling to embody as an artist.

This essay is not interested in the technicalities of Buddhism, nor scholastic minutiae about this or that sutra and how it compares to this or that line in Wallace's writing, nor in any kind of argumentative proof that Wallace was a Buddhist: he was not. Rather, I am foremost interested in the spirit of Buddhism and the value of that spirit—what does it offer that other systematic and cultural ways of thinking do not? To what extent did Wallace write from this unique Buddhist spirit? And what happens to Wallace's writing and to our experience of Wallace's work when we read him through a Buddhist lens?

Lurking behind this question is my own hypothesis: Wallace became and has remained one of the most important—widely read, intellectually accomplished, and deeply beloved—American authors of the last thirty years because he implicitly stumbled his way into a Buddhist way of thinking, and unbeknownst to his reading audience, a lived, experiential, Buddhist philosophy is what they themselves were starved for in the realm of literature.

More precisely, Wallace seemed to be concerned with two forms of diagnosis, just like Buddha was: what are the stubborn realities of modern life as we human beings live it, and how *ought* we live it instead. The gap in between is all the pain and suffering that we unnecessarily create for ourselves, which both Buddha and Wallace diagnosed with astonishing clarity. Although times change, human nature and experience have not; suffering is still an integral part of what it means to be alive. Recognizing this truth as part of his awakening to the fundamentals of reality, the Buddha tried to teach us ways to avoid adding any extra unnecessary suffering on top of the minimum we are sure to get as our human birthright. Since *Infinite Jest* serves as the center of Wallace's cosmology, and is in essence a catalogue of the ways in which modern humans heap piles of suffering on ourselves, it is reasonable to suggest that Wallace had a practical interest in Buddhism: how to make our ancient, but modern-flavored suffering go away and how to deal with the suffering that remains.

Buddhism differs from other religions because it rests its fundamentals on a spirit of psychological inquisition and curiosity rather than on overt dogma. *Of course* the stories of the Old Testament and about Jesus can be read metaphorically and poetically with an openness of interpretation—but that burden rests on the spiritual intelligence of the reader not to get bogged down in dogmatic tendencies. And *of course* Buddha's teachings can also be read too literally, but those kinds of readings explicitly defy the teachings themselves. "Do not believe me. Go see for yourself," the Buddha taught.[1] This approach to life is emphatically different from "I am the Lord your God ..., you shalt have no other gods before me,"[2] or "Believe in the message I have sent down confirming what you already possess. Do not be the first to reject it."[3] Buddhism does not require belief; in fact, it emphatically implores against it, urging us instead to cultivate our capacity to pause, to reflect, to notice, to be with, to turn toward, and to find out for ourselves what our momentary truth is. In many ways, at least in the ways in which Wallace was intrigued, Buddha was more of a profound psychologist than a religious figure in need of worship.

And so, as a writer deeply steeped in postmodernism, there was a natural alliance for Wallace with the teachings of the ancient mystic who made his bread and butter warning us against fixed views, while at the same time showing people that what is in our heart truly does matter and that a noble life is a compassionate one, lived with upright nobility predicated on generosity, morality, patience, wakeful energy, meditation and wisdom in the face of all our shortcomings.

Postmodernism, after a few decades of deconstruction, turned nihilistic, bleak, and dangerously relativistic; Buddhism, however, is like postmodernism in its capacity to see through the essence of things and to break those essences down into interlocking, interdependent parts, but it does so with a moral heart because it is grounded in an ethical structure which the Buddha always taught alongside his other revolutionary insights. Postmodernism says everything is relative; Buddhism says do not get stuck on any one particular view, but keep looking around to see whether your life has wholesome outcomes or unsavory ones.

Wallace was a postmodernist with heart. In other words, a writer with Buddhist inclinations, who intuited the impermanent interdependence of things and the consequent need to consistently and vigilantly watch our minds and how they construct our realities.

In the 1993 interview with Larry McCaffery, Wallace said:

> The big distinction between good art and so-so art lies somewhere in the art's heart's purpose, the agenda of the consciousness behind the text. It's got something to do with love. With having the discipline to talk out of the part of yourself that can love instead of the part that just wants to be loved. (CW 50)

In an overarching sense, Wallace's artistic manifesto above might be adopted by any religious interpretation: after all, is not there only one Peak on the Mountain of Love and multiple paths to get there? And yet, there is a subtext here in Wallace's aspirational confession that feels implicitly Buddhist because the attention he places on the nature and qualities of consciousness are Buddhism's essential qualities.

To wit: Wallace intuits that consciousness is made of "parts" which are by definition not the whole thing—not *you* as a totality—and that some of these parts are more self-centered than other parts. This is a profound insight on par with a fundamental insight taught by the Buddha: that what people refer to as an "I" or their "self" is not actually a solid, irreducible entity and does not exist in the way our linguistic constructions suggest it does. Instead, what we have is a misleading sense of an "I" which is the cumulative effect of our bodies, feelings, perceptions, ideas, and big-view consciousness. Like a really powerful optical illusion, when we superimpose all those things on top of one another, we feel as though there is a single "I" sitting at some kind of steering wheel. Wallace's acknowledgement of parts is to a considerable degree a negation of this illusion out of which all kinds of other profound insights follow. The Buddha compressed all this into his teachings about Anatta, or "not-self."[4]

We have all kinds of thoughts—chattering monkeys, in the parlance of sophisticated meditation teachers, who throw verbal bananas for sport. And if you act out or speak from those parts like we usually do—meaning, without any form of Buddhist practice as a way to ground and parse the mind's activities—your life will be limited to the perspectives of those particular parts, which are often immature in all kinds of ways, as Wallace would say, and confused for being equal to this larger sense of an "I." But if you can notice that there *are multiple parts*, then it gets a little easier not to take any particular one as The Truth, and that way lies release from your mind's complex web of reactive habits that get you in serious trouble. It is as the sign in a rehab house in *Infinite Jest* says, "My best thinking got me here" (*IJ* 1026 n135). Recognizing we have parts is how we recognize that our thinking isn't our salvation but more often than not, our curse. The implicit paradox—I need to think in order to realize my thinking is a problem—is not really a true paradox because there's a false equivalency between what I would call Buddhist "awareness"—which is sometimes referred to as "Big Mind" or "Buddha Nature" and thinking of the analytical kind, which is more in our "small mind's" wheelhouse. When we are "aware" of our "thinking" we are not really doing more thinking. So, "My best thinking got me here" can be more accurately rephrased from a Buddhist perspective as "Awareness of my thinking habits help me understand that my best thinking is limited in its understanding."

Furthermore, what your "parts" tend to tell you is rooted in their own psychological genesis, their own understanding of the world based on the causes and conditions that gave rise to them, including things like abuse, neglect and severe criticism. Since we are children before we are adults, often many of the parts that run our lives are actually psychological children in a proverbial sense, and many of Wallace's characters are young or adolescent, growing up in severe conditions of abuse (like Hal Incandenza and Don Gately, *Infinite Jest*'s two central protagonists). These young psychological parts that continue to live on as patterns of thought are the reason so many adults continue to make a mess out of their lives. What naturally follows is their need to medicate themselves with addictions and defense strategies to avoid dealing with the consequences of their psychological children having taken over their lives' steering wheel.

But with the kind of artist's reflective creed that Wallace offers us here, we can intuit a path to liberation in the classic Buddhist sense: free from the reactivity of our habitual, self-centered mind's parts—which continuously crave things and cause us to suffer—we can live in a way that is more spacious, more mysterious, more free, and not have to suffer psychologically on top of the suffering we are going to get anyway by simply being alive. Wallace's conclusion is therefore this: spending our time with fiction that gives us an opportunity to reflect upon and recognize these troublesome psychological fractals is extremely valuable in tangible, nontheoretical ways and is his definition of art made out of love.

Instead of monolithic Buddhism, however, I want to focus specifically on Wallace's implicit relationship with Zen, which is a form of Buddhism that means "meditation."[5] It is this embodied practice that Wallace was slowly struggling toward and the one that offers readers of Wallace's writing a genuine payoff.

Because Buddhism is not a set of beliefs (especially not in terms of gods that require worship), it is much more accurate to call it a set of practices. And the particular form Wallace became engaged in and curious about, via correspondence with Christopher Hamacher,[6] to name one concrete example, was Zen Buddhism, a tradition which stripped Buddhism of all the cultural and mythological baggage it had accumulated over the centuries, and returned to meditation as its fundamental core: the embodied, real-time, nonanalytic, nontheoretical experience of sitting still and watching your mind do what it does with no goal and with as little manipulation as possible.

If you do this practice you will notice, eventually, that there is something "behind" your thoughts. Which implies that, despite all previous evidence to the contrary, you are not your thoughts. For those like Wallace who have a quick and restless mind that secreted thoughts one after another, experiencing this insight is a form of awakening and freedom—if your best thinking got you to the rehab house, and all you ever felt and experienced up to then were an endless stream of thoughts and anxiety inducing beliefs, then maybe whatever you find lurking "behind" them can provide an alternative way of being.

Wallace brings this burgeoning recognition of a more fundamental form of consciousness not made of thoughts wonderfully and earnestly to life in a Chris Fogle section of *The Pale King*, which is worth quoting at length as a microcosm of Wallace's Buddhist understanding:

> [T]he CBS daytime network announcer's voice would say, '*You're watching* As the World Turns', which he seemed, on this particular day, to say more and more pointedly each time—'*You're watching* As the World Turns'—until I was suddenly struck by the bare reality of the statement. I don't mean any sort of humanities-type ironic metaphor, but the literal thing he was saying, the simple surface level. I don't know how many times I'd heard this that year while sitting around watching *As the World Turns*, but I suddenly realized that the announcer was actually saying over and over what I was literally doing .... It could not have felt more concrete if the announcer had actually said, '*You are sitting on an old yellow dorm couch, spinning a black-and-white soccer ball, and watching* As the World Turns, *without ever even acknowledging to yourself this is what you are doing.*' This is what struck me. It was beyond being feckless or a wastoid—it's like I wasn't even there. The truth is I was not even aware of the obvious double entendre of '*You're watching* As the World Turns' until three days later ... " (PK 224)

"Until I was suddenly struck by the bare reality of the statement" is the kind of insight a beginning meditation practitioner might have; bare reality is what "consciousness" is *before* all our thoughts start parading down its boulevard and clogging up the view. In fact, this entire passage can be read as an allegory about meditation, and what happens when a person's thoughts finally settle down long enough for the presence of bare consciousness to peek through. You hear Zen teachers from across millennia say the same thing: what you're looking for is so obvious and is so much in front of your nose, you're missing it because you're busy hunting for something bigger and shinier, a sentiment reflected here by Fogle: "I don't know how many times I'd heard this that year while sitting around watching *As the World Turns*, but I suddenly realized that the announcer was actually saying over and over what I was literally doing" (*PK* 224). This is Chris Fogle's (i.e., Wallace's) mini-satori, or small moment of awakening.

There is precedence for this idea, of course, in Wallace's *This Is Water* speech, in which he uses two fish swimming in water to ask, "What the hell is water?" (*TIW* 4). But coming from an author who so maddeningly and accurately described an anxious person's thought patterns—see "The Depressed Person" for a fine example—the Wallacean reader knows how suffocating it is to feel as though there is nothing *but* thoughts. So the value of seeing *through* one's thought-fog should under no ethically responsible circumstances be understated. In fact, I would like to risk overstating it: anyone who reads Wallace has to some extent identified their own suffering as coming from their endless thought parade and is looking for an alternative. Buddhist meditation provides exactly that, and like Chris Fogle's story suggests, requires absolutely nothing to get started, except for maybe a kind of stillness, however accidental.

What is Chris Fogle awakening from? Commercials selling things he doesn't need; entertainment that renders him addicted and immobile; a fog of endless thoughts, coming from his unmotivated parts, imploring him to keep vegetating in order to avoid any greater risk of trying to do something much harder and consequently more worthwhile. Put another way, Fogle is waking up from literally not having any perspective on his life: "it's like I wasn't even there" (*PK* 224). So the first step on the Zen path of awakening is one of recognition, because you can't do what you want—freedom—if you don't know what you're doing—sitting in front of a T.V., zoning out.

Wallace also importantly discerns between alternate states of consciousness and meditation: "I was not Obetrolling at this moment of awareness, I should add. This was different. It was as if the CBS announcer were speaking directly to me, shaking my shoulder or leg" (*PK* 224).[7] Buddhism has as one of its precepts, or descriptions of what awakened behavior looks like in real life, this injunction: "A noble disciple gives up wines, liquors, and intoxicants, the basis for negligence, and abstains from them."[8] In an attempt to move beyond our burdensome everyday thoughts, many people turn to drugs to experience an alternate reality. For some, this glimpse provides enough of a shock of an alternative way of seeing things to inspire them on a genuine path of awakening without further chemical assistance. For most, tragically, drugs end up being a deeper form of hell because of their initial pleasurable qualities, something Wallace understood in both theory and practice. Therefore, when Chris Fogle offers us this disclaimer, it is not a throwaway line; what meditation offers us is not merely an alternate state of consciousness that replaces one pair of glasses with another. "I was not obetrolling at this moment of awareness" (*PK* 224) suggests that awareness itself is something different from any particular state of consciousness and is more like a blank canvas on which our states of consciousness paint their pictures. The paintings made of words are the most common; those in which time loses its linearity, is another. But bare awareness is a foundational "something else."

Buddhism's eightfold path of awakening—the fourth of Buddha's Four Noble Truths—has right action (to protect life and be compassionate), right effort (to end unwholesome states and strengthen wholesome ones), and right livelihood (not artificially dividing our work from our morality) as its ethical foundations. By having Chris Fogle focus on the literal awakening first, and the "double entendre" of the awakening's meaning second, Wallace wisely implies that awakening, by itself, does not actually *do anything*. Another way of saying this more crudely is that meditation and its fruit of clean awareness, in and of itself, is useless, something Zen masters have been known to say *ad infinitum* to their goal-oriented students.

Zombies, like the pre-awakened Fogle and a meditator who does nothing but sit and meditate, do nothing for the world in equal measure. "The show's almost terrifying pun about the passive waste of time of sitting there watching something whose reception through the hanger didn't even come in very well, while all the while real things in the world were going on and people with direction and initiative were taking care of business in a brisk, no-nonsense way" is Fogle's awakening moving toward some kind of aspiration.

This is a theme Wallace had been exploring long before *The Pale King*, even in his *Infinite Jest* years: "It's snowing on the goddamn map, not the territory, you dick," (*IJ* 333) says Michael Pemulis, foreshadowing Wallace's increasingly careful and sustained effort to differentiate between conceptual thought and the real-world reality of actions and their consequences.

A final exam in American Political thought is Chris Fogle's destination. Can you even begin to imagine the difference between the Chris Fogle taking this exam before his awakening experience and the Chris Fogle after it? You do not have to, because the narrative of the *Pale King* traces that very trajectory, and is in a sense what Wallace was most concerned with: how to give our lives direction, beyond our self-centered delusions. You could do worse than argue that is what the Buddha was up to in his teachings as well.

When you have a Buddhist hammer, everything looks like a Buddhist nail. So it is easy to find Buddhism everywhere in the books of what George

Saunders called our "great American Buddhist writer."[9] But knowing that Wallace was undergoing an authentic exploration of Buddhist practice and understanding gives the nails extra dignity. For example, in the handwritten draft notes after the Chris Fogle section above, Wallace wrote (to himself) what reads like a seemingly literal key to Chris Fogle's state of consciousness[10]:

10–06 This is a deeper level of surrender:

1. ID a bad feeling. Fear, lack of confidence, despair, jitteriness, urgency/hurry. Observe it. Pay attention to it.
2. Realize that it's in me, not in reality. Remind myself of this.
3. Realize that it's in "me," not in the real "I." It's in the construct. It feels bad, but I can also observe it feeling bad. I can sit there and pay attention to it and not do anything about it. Can let it "be as it is." The "I" is what observes it, without judging or acting.
4. Detach from the feeling. Don't identify with it. What-ever "I" is, it's not my body, job, success, prestige, reputation, or what others think of me. It's the part that can pay attention. The part that's so worried about career, reputation, and writing is part of the construct, the "conditioned self." The culture teaches me to value what it calls achievement. I've bought into this teaching, deeply—I cannot change this fact, or the way my thorax feels. But I can watch it, try to be aware of it. I cannot change it by force of will. But I can exert will trying not to let it think for me, take me over, make me see reality through its filter.
5. Pray for awakening. Awareness is not the same as knowledge. God, please let me wake up. Please let me feel the truth. True-for-me instead of just a proposition I assent to. I want to know it, not just "know" it like a principle of abstract math.

Wallace's sincerity is staggering in its authenticity and humility, and was palpable to his readers because it offered spiritual guidance beyond all the entertaining aesthetic–linguistic fireworks. It was practical, in other words, in much the same way Buddha was a practical teacher.

Therefore, prayer in Buddhist terms should be understood not as supplication to a more omnipotent being with power to alter the course of one's life, but a focusing of one's aspirations. But to "pray for awakening" as Wallace writes to himself, is to realize that unlike Chris Fogle, awakening needs some help. However, it is not a one-to-one utilitarian correspondence; if it were, the self-help genre would be where it is at, and busybody achievers would be the most enlightened among us. But as Flint Sparks, my own Zen teacher once told me, "Enlightenment is an accident; zazen meditation practice makes you accident prone."

Wallace's Buddhism went as far as genuine curiosity and inconsistent meditation practice. He read Paramananda's *Practical Guide to Buddhist Meditation*,[11] and scribbled marginalia. I spoke to Karen Green, Wallace's widow, about his practice briefly and informally, and she told me he would sneak off at odd hours to "sit" with varying "results."[12] In more concrete evidence, we also have his correspondence with Christopher Hamacher, including this letter:

> I do like your letters. I'm not sure why. People send me all kinds of letters—you can imagine. A few get in me. Yours do ... Sitting [i.e. meditating] is weird ... Some days I sit enthusiastically, enjoy it, am sorry when time's up. Other days I feel a visceral distaste for it, extreme reluctance ... If I were to read one book or pamphlet about Z[en], sitting, etc., what one would you recommend?[13]

So it is clear from both his life and his writing that Wallace had begun walking the bare-bones Buddhist path and that tragedy cut his explorations far too short. But for those of us still here, what next steps might *we* take?

The Buddhist concept of "not-self" and the practice of meditation help us see that we are all philosophers with dysfunctional views of reality. Purifying our water—letting the silt settle on the bottom—is the first step, but what will we see at the bottom once we have a clear view? And how might Wallace's work further focus our reflections? These questions possess Taoist flavors that Zen incorporated into its own form of Buddhism when it reached China and began to ferment there.

There are essentially four Buddhist practice principles out of which everything else flows[14]:

1. Caught in a self-centered dream, only suffering.

    Speaking from our self-centered parts, as Wallace called them, is the recipe we use to bake our individual and collective cakes of misery. Unfortunately, this is the only recipe we know in the opening arcs of our lives and it is inescapable.

2. Holding to self-centered thoughts, exactly the dream.

    This is how Chris Fogle describes his life as a "nihilistic wastoid," "the passive waste of time of sitting there watching something whose reception through the hanger didn't even come in very well." In more precise Buddhist terms, it's the craving for pleasure and the aversion from pain that gets us addicted to these unwholesome states of mind, and the consequence is sleepwalking through life, as the world turns.

3. Each moment, life as it is, the only teacher.

    Awakening is realizing, like Chris Fogle, that you are not your thoughts, and that staying present to what is, rather than what was or what will be, brings us closer to our lives. In doing just this practice, in this moment, we are all Buddhas—awakened ones.

4   Being just this moment, Compassion's Way.

Instead of chasing happiness or running away from boredom, life teaches us to encounter each of life's things more fully, and a permanent sense of ease begins to arise knowing that there are nothing but teachers everywhere. This way is the beginning of a greater sense of living life morally for the benefit of others rather than just for yourself.

Buddha had three profound insights after he settled his mind: The sense of "I" is not what we think it is; everything is impermanent and change is the fundamental structure of the universe; and if we fail to understand that everything is inextricably linked to everything else in an interdependent web of oneness, we will suffer.[15] Out of these three insights about life and how we can best live it, a practical and philosophical revolution began its slow crawl through humanities' karmic jungles.

For most of his writing career, until he started researching and composing *The Pale King*, Wallace circled these fundamental Buddhist ideas. Postmodern thinking, for example, lends itself to the deconstruction of all categories, including the "Self." The structure of *Infinite Jest* invokes a world in which nonlinear, interconnectivity feels more appropriate than a straightforward teleological plot. And the impermanence of all things heightens our sense of compassion for them, a quality which was obvious in all of Wallace's work, but increasingly so as he matured from a wounded young man trying to prove his intelligence, to a man who wanted to describe our wounds so we might better care for each other. Having finally arrived at meditation and awareness as the gate through which these insights come fully alive, anyone with a Buddhist practice will recognize in Wallace's writing our birthright of suffering and our way out.

Notes

1   Anguttara Nikaya 3:65. See *In the Buddha's Words: An Anthology of Discourses from the Pali Canon*, trans. Bhikkhu Bodhi (Boston: Wisdom Publications, 2005). The actual quote is: "When you know for yourselves, 'These things are unwholesome; these things are blameable; these things are censured by the wise; these things, if undertaken and practiced, lead to harm & to suffering'—then you should abandon them" (89).

2   Exodus 20:3. *The New Oxford Annotated Bible: Revised Standard Version* (Oxford: Oxford University Press, 2001).

3   Qur'an 2:41. *The Qur'an: English Translation and Parallel Arabic Text*, trans. M.A.S. Abdel Haleem (Oxford: Oxford University Press, 2010).

4   This concept is found in abundance in a vast number of Buddhist sutras in the Pali canon. Samyutta Nikaya 22:82 is a good example. Note that "not self" is a better understanding than "no self." See also Thanissaro Bhikkhu, "There Is No Self," *Tricycle Magazine*, Spring 2014. Available online: https://tricycle.org/magazine/there-no-self/.

5   Buddhism traveled East to China where it flourished in more ideal Taoist conditions than what was available in India. There it was called Ch'an. When it spread to Japan, Ch'an was translated as "Zen." The practice of sitting meditation in Japanese is called "Zazen": sit + meditation. It was Japanese priests who brought Zen to San Francisco in the 1960s and started the U.S. chapter, which eventually made its way to Wallace's curiosity.

6   See D.T. Max, *Every Love Story Is a Ghost Story: A Life of David Foster Wallace* (New York: Viking, 2012), 291.

7   Obetrol was an amphetamine produced by Obetrol Pharmaceuticals and marketed as a weight loss drug in the 1960s and 70s, but later branded as Adderall, and used to treat attention-deficit/hyperactivity disorder. In *The Pale King*, Fogle uses it to induce a state he calls "doubling"—a heightened sense of self-awareness.

8   Anguttara Nikaya 8:39. *In the Buddha's Words*, 173.

9   "I don't know much about Dave's spiritual life but I see him as a great American Buddhist writer, in the lineage of Whitman and Ginsberg. He was a wake-up artist." See, "Informal Remarks from the David Foster Wallace Memorial Service in New York on October 23, 2008," in *The Legacy of David Foster Wallace*, ed. Samuel Cohen and Lee Konstantinou (Iowa City: University of Iowa Press, 2012), 53–5; 54.

10 David Foster Wallace, *The Pale King*, handwritten drafts, Box 38.5. David Foster Wallace Papers. Harry Ransom Humanities Research Center, Austin, TX.

11 *Paramananda, A Practical Guide to Buddhist Meditation* (New York: Barnes & Noble Books, 1996). Wallace's annotated copy is available in the Harry Ransom Center.

12 Personal conversation with the author, April 5, 2012.

13 David Foster Wallace to Christopher Hamacher, shared via email correspondence with the author, May 2, 2012.

14 These are American Zen teacher Joko Beck's poetic translations of Buddha's Four Noble Truths. For an annotation by a contemporary Zen teacher Peg Syverson, Available online: https://appamada.org/application/files/2915/1412/9354/Daily_chants_annotated_2017.pdf.

15 See *The Dhammapada: A New Translation of the Buddhist Classic with Annotations*, trans. Gil Fronsdal (Boston: Shambhala Publications, Inc., 2005), 72. "'All created things are impermanent'/Seeing this with insight/Once becomes disenchanted with suffering./This is the path to purity" (Verse 277).

Conclusion: The Religious Worlds of David Foster Wallace—Both Fiction and Not

Michael McGowan

I never met David Foster Wallace, but I was in Claremont, California on the night he died. I was a first year Ph.D. student studying philosophy of religion and theology, and I had not read Wallace before then. I learned later that he and I shared some of the same friends. After his death, I immersed myself in his writings and found them not only intellectually stimulating, but also deeply moving. My experience with Wallace's writing is surely not unique: most of us begin as fans, and then we use our scholarship to unpack why his work is appealing, how his writing works, and how it works *on us*.

When I discussed this book with a colleague, I was asked whether Wallace and religion is too specific a niche to warrant an entire book dedicated to it. This seemed like a reasonable question, because Wallace is known more as a philosophical writer than a religious one. His writings do not deal with religious concepts as overtly or in the same way as he wrestles with metaphysical (e.g., *Fate, Time and Language*) or ethical ones (e.g., "Consider the Lobster"). While it is true that metaphysical issues are often related to issues in philosophy of religion, there are issues and methodologies unique to philosophers of religion that metaphysicians as such do not address. And while it is also true that Wallace's work directly addressed metaphysical problems to a greater degree than religious issues, careful readers know he was certainly not silent on the latter in print. One reason for this lacuna may be that Wallace was thought to have a set of multifarious "attitudes toward" religion but not a fully developed or enunciated "philosophy of" religion per se.[1]

But the essays in this volume argue that Wallace offers much *more* than philosophical reflection on the nature of ultimate reality. He also asks profound existential questions of religion, spirituality, and faith, an interest that grew the older he got. From its inception, I wanted this book to present a variety of approaches to reading Wallace through a religious lens, and I wanted the collection to include not only tenured scholars, but also those at the start of their careers. We included contributors who see in Wallace a fellow traveler, probing the religious dimensions of human existence for ultimate meaning. Some of the contributors to this volume see in Wallace *more* than a fellow traveler, however. They see Wallace functioning as a modern-day Virgil to the de-churched generation's Dante.[2] The de-churched generation in America and Europe has lost confidence in institutional religion and craves for a creative rethinking of old problems, or at least the creative expression of the search itself. And Wallace gives these things to them, breathing life into their stagnant faith's dry bones. Wallace helps them push through the painful reality of selfishness on their way to Truth, Goodness, and Beauty.

Notes from the archive

One way to evaluate where a particular author stood vis-à-vis religion is to look at the ways in which s/he was shaped by or had knowledge of specific religious beliefs and practices. The case for reading Wallace as a religious writer is bolstered by study of the material he consumed, the sources that shaped his art and life. Wallace's personal library, now housed at the Harry Ransom Center at the University of Texas at Austin, allows us to peek into the mind of an author whose work resonates with religious seekers today, providing us with a window through which to view Wallace's own processing of religious issues. In addition to personalizing the author we never got a chance to meet, we learn a lot by seeing (a) which books Wallace had in his collection, (b) which passages he found worthy of underlining, starring, or checking, (c) which concepts prompted him to reflect in the comments he wrote in the margins, (d) which ideas made their way into Wallace published work, and (e) which books were vehicles for Wallace's self-reflection. In what follows, I'll give some examples of each of these windows into Wallace's mind.

First, the specific books Wallace thought were worth including in his library (or at least not discarding) are illuminating, and they show that Wallace grew more interested in religion the older he got. In the books the young Wallace likely read in college, he does not underline or otherwise mark up sections dealing with religion. But in the books he received later in life, his interaction with the religious parts of them grew considerably. The HRC collection now stands as testimony that the mature Wallace was cognizant of and immersed in information about the world's great wisdom traditions.

The HRC houses over three hundred books from Wallace's personal library, of which roughly three dozen deal with explicitly religious themes or were written by authors whose goals were religious. (Another several dozen contain material that is religious in nature even if not explicitly.) The subjects of these religious books range considerably: from Amir Aclef's *The Mystery of the Aleph* to Curtis White's *Anarcho-Hindu*; from John Shae's *Stories of Faith* to Catholic-convert, Dorothy Day's, autobiography, *The Long Loneliness*; from Huston Smith's introductory survey, *The World's Religions*, to Richard Rohr's *Everything Belongs*, a guidebook on "contemplative prayer"; from C. S. Lewis's fictional kid-lit *Narnia* series to Paramananda's *A Practical Guide to Buddhist Meditation*; from Anthony DeMello's series of short reflections in *Awareness* to a book on demon possession and exorcism (Malachi Martin's *Hostage to the Devil*).

There are more books in Wallace's library on religion than there are on the IRS and taxation, which is striking considering the research Wallace conducted for *The Pale King*. There are nearly as many books on religion in his library as there are on literary criticism and the craft of writing, which is remarkable considering Wallace's teaching career. So, based on the list of books now at the HRC, Wallace grew increasingly interested in religion, and he thought and read widely about it.

Second, we can get a glimpse of Wallace's thinking by seeing the ways in which he interacted with these books. Many of Wallace's books have portions underlined, starred, checked, or circled, indicating that Wallace found a particular passage meaningful or worth remembering. This adds a new level of importance to religious traditions and themes in Wallace's thinking. For example, in Annie Dillard's *For the Time Being*,[3] Wallace noted portions dealing with Buddhism, Taoism, Judaism, Hinduism, Christianity, and Islam (these same faiths are interacted with in other books, too). The stories Dillard discusses that caught Wallace's attention are from great figures in the history of religions (e.g., Augustine and Aquinas), serious scholars and theologians (e.g., Karl Rahner and Paul Tillich), mystics (e.g., Thomas Merton), cutting-edge or *avant-garde* religious thinkers (e.g., Teilhard de Chardin), and lay people (e.g., someone who saw Jesus in a Mexican tortilla). Wallace resonated with many of Dillard's comments, as he underlined, circled, and put three check marks by a passage that reads: "In any instant the sacred may wipe you with its finger. In any instant the bush may flare, your feet may rise, or you may see a bunch of souls in a tree. In any instant you may avail yourself of the power to love your enemies; to accept failure, slander or the grief of loss; or to endure torture."[4]

Even in books that are not explicitly religious, Wallace finds and gravitates towards the religious core of the text. In a book dedicated to the craft of writing, Bonnie Friedman's *Writing Past Dark,* Wallace underlines the section in which Friedman connects writing to Jung's comments about religion: "Only the living presence of the eternal images can lend the human psyche a dignity that makes it morally possible for a man to stand by his own soul, and be convinced that it is worth his while to persevere with himself."[5] In preparation for his book about infinity, *Everything and More,* Wallace read a biography of Georg Cantor by Joseph Warren Dauben. Notably, Wallace does not mark up much in the book about the underlying math or philosophy of the infinite; rather, Wallace notes Cantor's religious upbringing, relationship with his father, and how Cantor's work was influenced by his religious commitments.

Third, we can see from Wallace's library that some things he read prompted not only underlining, but also handwritten comments in the margins. "Why are we aware?" he asks in Dillard's book. At times, Wallace argues *against* the author's point of view, even displaying hostility to the work or author he is reading,[6] but there are other times when Wallace's comments reveal a deep connection to the religious idea under consideration. In Joseph Campbell's *Myths to Live By,* Wallace writes "spirituality > religion" in the margin, which could explain why the Kenyon speech did not advocate for one particular religion but rather the value of them all.[7] In Rohr's book on prayer, Wallace writes "discipline = acceptance of pain." In Lawrence Gonzales's *Deep Survival,* Wallace resonates with the author's description of struggle: "fatigue = spiritual collapse."[8]

In Leo Tolstoy's *What Is Art?,* Wallace asks "All religions OK?" and "One?" in response to Tolstoy's assertion that there is "a religious sense."[9] Wallace cautions himself to "look out for TS intentions about 'true' religion." Broadly, Wallace uses Tolstoy to help him understand the search for faith itself: "'religion' = wisdom about good + evil," Wallace writes. Wallace also reflects on the meaning of life in Tolstoy's book, writing, "Today it's not Church Christianity but Science as Meaning that's been debunked—and we've nothing to replace it." Wallace also read about the problem of pain and suffering and religious responses to it (i.e., theodicies) in Rabbi Harold Kushner's famous, *Why Bad Things Happen to Good People.* Wallace writes "Do not assume God 'causes' or 'allows' suffering," and that perhaps "G. chooses to limit His control." Elsewhere in the margins, Wallace asks whether God "wants us to be happy?" and then asks himself, "Who are you to ask Why?" Wallace learns from Kushner that he needs to work on "accepting randomness," because "mankind is broken. We ascribe meaning where there is none" (Wallace's words). And in Flannery O'Connor's collection of short stories, Wallace writes in the margins, "What does 'redeemed' mean?" only to answer later in the story, "Redemption is accepting Christ."[10]

Fourth, one can see how important an idea was to Wallace by looking at the concepts that made their way into Wallace's published work. This is nowhere as prevalent as in the material that made its way into Wallace's Kenyon Commencement speech, where he synthesizes several authors into one coherent whole. In this book, Bolger notes the impact of Rohr on Wallace, but there are other notable influences from whom Wallace gets inspiration. In Anthony DeMello's *Awareness*, for example, DeMello insists that "Good Religion" is "The Antithesis of Unawareness."[11] Wallace notes, too, the perils of "sleepwalking"[12] through life, or "losing the rat race."[13] When Wallace admonishes the students to detach from fleeting idols (beauty, intellect, money), he is repackaging DeMello's insistence that "The world, power, prestige, winning, success, honor, etc., are nonexistent. You gain the world but you lose your soul … There is nothing there."[14] And the crucial distinction he draws between "knowledge" and "awareness" is found in DeMello's chapter on "Hidden Agendas,"[15] much of which Wallace starred, circled, *and* underlined. DeMello's book stays lodged in Wallace's mind, too, as evidenced by his writing "DeMello" in the margins of Huston Smith's *The World's Religions*.

The Kenyon speech was also influenced by Timothy Wilson's *Strangers to Ourselves*, in which Wilson discusses what Wallace would later call the "default setting,"[16] i.e., an innate tendency toward self-centeredness. Wallace's assertion that we are unable to talk about the things that are most real and essential likely comes from Tor Nørretranders, *The User Illusion*, in which the author argues that "*Most of what we experience, we can never tell each other about,*"[17] which Wallace underlines and writes "Loneliness— can't talk about it" in the margin. Wallace also notes in this book that we are "able to choose focus of attention." And Wallace's suggestion that students not prejudge the motives or experiences of others (e.g., the lady who yells at her child in the checkout line) is likely informed by Malcolm Gladwell's *Blink*, which was released a few months before his speech by a Little, Brown subsidiary. Wallace underlines the section in which Gladwell talks about overcoming the "fatal mistake" of "rapid cognition," i.e., forming snap judgments about others. Instead, Gladwell recommends "that we take active steps to manage and control those impressions."[18] Wallace's speech, it could be argued, provides the Kenyon students with precisely those steps.

Fifth and finally, there are several books in Wallace's library in which he interacted with the text on a *personal* level. He wrote notes to and about himself, reflected on his progress as a writer or the development of his character, or simply wrote "DW" or "DFW" next to a passage that speaks truth to his situation. Often, these writings give Wallace permission to express his self-doubt. For example, in Jacob Needleman's *Money and the Meaning of Life*, Wallace finds a list of self-critical vices like "fear, self-deception, vanity, egoism, wishful thinking, tension, and violence."[19] Wallace writes next to Needleman's list, "I have them all (so does everyone else)." Wallace had two copies of Dostoevsky's *The Idiot*, and in both copies he makes marginal comments about the desire to create original work.[20] In Richard Schacht's *Alienation*, Wallace writes "DW" next to passages that talk about depression and insecurity that he will ever make it as a writer. In R. D. Laing's *The Divided Self* (a book that was originally Mark Costello's) Wallace writes "Yes" next to a section that describes severe isolation, and "DFW" next to passages having to do with living in fantasy (i.e., not accepting reality at all costs, as AA would say) or his difficulty being in front of people. Wallace also reflects on his mental state: "I AM NOT PSYCHOTIC. I DO HAVE SCHIZOID TENDENCIES" (capitalization original). He writes about how strong his emotions are, how they overpower his reasoning capacities and logic: "Emotions so powerful that reasoning systems are perverted and subordinated to them—hence not vulnerable to persuasion by logic or argument."

In Rohr's book on prayer, Wallace writes "DW" next to a section in which Rohr discusses momentary plateaus in our spiritual journeys that give us a false sense of security or superiority. In Philip Wylie's *Generation of Vipers*, Wallace writes "DW" next to a passage in which Wylie discusses the breakdown of Christianity's witness to others in the form of "dogmatic perfectionism" and a host of "you must" commandments. Wallace underlines and presumably resonates with the post-Reformation sentiment Wylie criticizes in Christianity, namely, that "you had to be spiritually perfect—or else. Or else you would go to hell."[21]

There are some books in the HRC collection that directly relate to religious concerns but are not yet available to researchers. If one of Wallace's book notations mentions someone specific (other than himself) in an unflattering way, the HRC and the Wallace Estate has rightfully decided to wait until those mentioned in the margin pass away before the book is viewable by visitors to the archive. For example, Wallace owned a book on Jesus's Sermon on the Mount,[22] in which remarks are made in the margins, but that book is not open to public viewing until Sally Foster Wallace's death. Seeing how Wallace reacted to the New Testament accounts of Jesus, the Lord's Prayer, and the Beatitudes will be helpful in the future to get a further handle on Wallace's views of religious issues.

The exploration of Wallace's thinking on religion is likely not finished, and in this book we have only scratched the surface. But as these essays and the HRC archives suggest, what can *not* be said is that Wallace was ignorant of or unconcerned with religious questions. As this admittedly brief and grossly oversimplified list of Wallace's library illustrates, Wallace was actively seeking for answers to the ultimate questions, and he sought those answers in the world's great wisdom traditions. He used the material he found to examine himself and the world around him in religious ways. He did not shy away from naming God or writing about God in his comments in the margins of these works. So, rather than religion being only a peripheral concern of his, and rather than his experience being one of faux-religiosity, Wallace was on a serious search for faith.

Wallace and paradox

Mary Karr couldn't "name the gods" Wallace "worshipped at the end, if any."[23] Perhaps Wallace couldn't name them himself. It may be that Wallace understood belief in God like one of his most memorable characters, Don Gately: somehow beyond comprehension, beyond systemization, and full of paradoxes. Gately prays to a God he does not believe in, even on bended knee. Presumably, Wallace did the same. But paradoxically, even fabricated higher powers really work to alleviate the suffering of addicts.

Wallace was no stranger to drawing our attention to a paradox when he found one. Despite the scarcity of scholarly attention to paradoxes in Wallace's writing, they are a recurring feature of his work, both in fiction and nonfiction. Indeed, one of the books in Wallace's library was R. Mark Sainsbury's *Paradoxes*,[24] in which Sainsbury defines a paradox as

> an unacceptable conclusion derived by apparently acceptable reasoning from apparently acceptable premises. Unlike party puzzles or brain teasers, many paradoxes are serious in that they raise serious philosophical problems, and are associated with crises of thought and revolutionary advances. To grapple with them is not merely to engage in an intellectual game, but to come to grips with issues of real import.[25]

These "serious philosophical problems" made their way into Wallace's writing irrespective of genre: paradoxes are found in his novels, interviews, nonfiction journalistic pieces, and short stories.

In *Infinite Jest*, for example, Wallace mentions some seemingly trivial paradoxes, e.g., the ETA class on double-binds with a midterm exam that asked students to discuss how a kleptomaniac with agoraphobia might feed the desire to steal if s/he cannot leave the house (*IJ* 306–8). But there are also serious paradoxes, like the "paradox of Substance addiction" (*IJ* 201), where newly sober addicts quit their drug and alcohol use to save their lives and mental health only to find that quitting makes them *want* to lose their minds. There is also the paradox of using clichés to address serious problems. In *Infinite Jest* and *The Pale King*, Wallace discusses the paradox of plagiarism: while it initially seems a good way to avoid the hard work of composition and research, to plagiarize well requires hard work. *The Pale King* also discusses the paradoxes of ceding autonomy, conformist nonconformity, and feeling good about feeling bad. In his "Author's Forward," Wallace claims veracity, but only under the legal protection of the clause at the beginning of the book that describes it as a work of fiction.

Wallace thought in terms of paradoxes,[26] as his many interviews indicate. In his Bookworm Interview of 2006, Wallace says that *Consider the Lobster* was a paradoxical book of sorts: some of the essays require requisite knowledge of their publishing organs to make sense of the essay, but the publishers of the book wanted to remove the references to those publishing organs, thereby making them less comprehensible. In his Terry Gross interview of 1997, Wallace discusses the paradox of expensive vacations, like his cruise experience: the greater the expense, "the more potentially anxiety-producing it is … A big part of [professional fun managers'] job is to assure you that you're having a good time."[27] In Wallace's interview with Charlie Rose, he mentions several paradoxes: by studying modal logic and semantics, he both followed in his father's footsteps by studying philosophy but also "did the required thumbing the nose at the father" thing; people are hired to teach but are only given tenure if they publish; and writers want to not be bothered while at the same time seeking adulation and praise. This paradoxical sentiment also occasioned Wallace's writing "DFW" next to Joseph Frank's description of Dostoevsky's underground man, whose "vanity convinces him of his own superiority and he despises everyone; but since he desires such superiority to be *recognized* by others, he hates the world for its indifference and falls into self-loathing at his own humiliating dependence,"[28] which Wallace also underlined.

And then there are the paradoxes Wallace mentions in his nonfiction, the pieces themselves blending into some sort of paradoxical hybrid of nonfiction reporting and literary performance. Not only on cruise ships was Wallace faced with paradoxes, but also in his political reporting. In *Up, Simba!,* Wallace's reflections on John McCain's presidential campaign of 2000, Wallace mentions paradoxes large and small. Hotel chains give the appearance of hospitality without cultivating the feeling that one is welcome there. The specific era in which Wallace was following McCain had, after Clinton's scandals and impeachment, made feigning noninterest in getting elected a political commodity that might help a candidate get elected. And most notably, the fact that the important things to talk about in politics require trite and overused cliché words. Or that a public servant can be personally genuine and politically savvy at the same time. His essay ends on the ambivalent note of indecision, directing the reader to embrace the paradox and see what it portends about his own state of mind.

In Wallace's "Big Red Son," Wallace describes a paradox facing the pornography industry: as it becomes more mainstream and "respectable," it loses the very *un*acceptability that drove its viewers to the films in the first place (which Wallace argues will need to go *further*, into dangerously and shockingly new territory). Wallace's lifelong friend, Mark Costello, notes that the creation of Wallace's porn piece was itself paradoxical: Wallace wanted to write intelligently and artfully about that which is ultimately dumb and unartistic. Wallace's and Costello's book about rappers dealt with two sorts of paradoxes: the individuality required for rappers to set themselves apart and gain notoriety was undermined by their rapping over sampled tracks from earlier musicians, and cutting-edge rap was becoming mainstream to the point of negating its very *raison d'etre*, a similar criticism of the porn piece (*SR* ii).

Or consider the paradoxes mentioned in "Good Old Neon," in which Neal (the narrator) mentions them at every turn. Costello tells me that Wallace's "great fear" with religious questions was "infinite regression, both the meaninglessness of egocentric circles and their infinitude, their inescapability." Costello says "Good Old Neon" actually "captures very well his lifelong feeling of the overactive ego feeding forever on itself."[29] Some of the paradoxes in "Good Old Neon" are minor—e.g., how one can see better with low beams than high, whether pills "worked" or just gave the impression that they worked, etc.—and they seem thrown into the story without a clear reason for being there other than the highlight the importance of paradoxes.

But "Good Old Neon" has larger, more significant paradoxes, like Neal's "fraudulence paradox," according to which the more time a person spends attempting to feel genuine, the more s/he feels like a fraud, and the more a person felt fraudulent, the more s/he attempts to remedy the situation by attempting to be genuine. Time also functions paradoxically in "Good Old Neon," as thoughts race so fast as to not really qualify as "fast" but rather immediate sense impressions, which need to be expressed in words though words are hopelessly inadequate to express them. Or the paradox of measuring time itself: how does one chronologically measure the passage of time? And then there is the whole paradox of going to therapy: Neal *needs* therapy but spends his time mentally jousting with Dr. Gustafson; he questions whether a fraud can be a fraud without knowing he is a fraud. In Wallace's handwritten drafts of "Good Old Neon," he shows how paradoxes emanate and return, expand and contract, creating a plurality of paradoxes which are just functions of the first paradox. Wallace writes in the margins of his own handwritten manuscript, "So there were more like two paradoxes, the second being that seeing the first paradox didn't keep me from continuing to do the fraudulent stuff that got me into the first paradox in the first place."

Suffice it to say, paradoxes are not peripheral to what Wallace wrote about in his all-too-short career. Rather, they play a central role in elucidating those elements of the human experience that transcend understanding. As he describes them, Wallace not only considers what he is considering, but also considers himself in relation to what he is considering; further, he considers others considering him in relation to himself as the one doing the initial considering.

Realizing that many parts of the human experience lack a coherent center around which to orient oneself, Wallace qua author "was often to chart and stack the paradoxes, creating ever more elaborated mazes." But, Costello says, "This was writing as compulsion, not as pleasure" (*SR* xii). And it can lead to some very dangerous places. Costello elaborates on Wallace's fear of the vicious infinite regress and its relationship to the ego Wallace continually strove to suppress:

> No real believer is ever in danger of thinking they are the final measure or meaning of anything. Other measures, other meanings might be mysterious or agonistic, and it is very likely I can't do much more than posit them—treat them as true on earth—but the radically self-centered viewpoint has no appeal, and is not terribly persuasive. In the end, there are a million ways to defeat the self-referential spiral and almost all of them lead back to God. [Wallace] was fascinated that anybody could hold to this viewpoint and he was very interested in knowing how it worked for even a bad believer.[30]

Costello says Wallace had to treat religious beliefs "as true," i.e., he had to rely on the very clichés he initially found untenable. He did this "to save his own life ... to not kill himself." One of those clichés is "Fake it 'till you Make it," that is, act *as if* it is the case that a higher power loves you and has good plans in store for your future.

This idea, acting "as if" such and such is the case, has a long history in modern moral philosophy, stretching back at least to Kant's categorical imperative. Wallace would no doubt have known that Kant framed morality in terms of what is *universalizable*, that is, able to be applied ubiquitously without contradiction. "So act *as if* the maxim of your action were to become through your will a universal law of nature," Kant writes in the *Groundwork for the Metaphysics of Morals*.[31] Or, as expressed in recovery literature with which Wallace was likely familiar,

> The majority of us are very aware of our defects of character, but often it isn't until we are 'sick and tired of being sick and tired' that we become willing to change... Acting 'as if' the choice is already made and the changes in our lives are already in place put the power of our will in line with the power of the universe so that we can move forward more gracefully into living without defects unchecked... Will it work? About as well as we surrender. Will it change our lives? Yes, without question... The more willing we become, and the more we practice acting "as if," the more active our surrender becomes and the more we are able to live "as if." ... Authenticity is being true to a vision and purpose. We are authentic when we choose to act and feel and choose to behave in balance with the higher values and principles we've chosen for our lives. If those principles and values are not fully in place and manifested, it doesn't make us phony. *It makes us human*. If we feel the conflict between who we are and who we would become, it is good. It signals that we understand the difference between reality and fantasy, and are moving toward reality.[32]

Wallace likely saw the value of a religious belief system qua way of life: in the end, it *worked* to save his life from alcohol and drugs, whether he believed it ontologically corresponded with reality or not.

Perhaps Wallace, like Emerson, resisted overt speculation on religious matters because of the paradoxical nature of it. "A foolish consistency is the hobgoblin of little minds," says Emerson, "adored by little statesmen and philosophers and divines. With consistency a great soul has simply nothing to do."[33]

What might all this mean for Wallace's take on religious issues? I would submit that Wallace's attraction to AA as his "church" was a natural fit for a mind who regularly saw the absurdities of life, its inconsistencies, its absolute lack of coherence. AA recognizes this, and so as to be most welcoming to the most people, it speaks in Steps Two and Three of a "God of one's understanding." The members of AA can *choose* their higher power, a paradoxical notion, indeed. In Dillard's *For the Time Being*, Wallace underlines, "Only some deeply grounded and fully paradoxical view of God can make sense of the notion that God knows and loves each of 5.9 billion of us."[34] Paradoxes stretch our logic and language to the breaking point, but seemingly contradictory assertions may both still be true. "What wonder is it if you do understand?," Augustine asks and Wallace underlines, for "If you do understand, it is not God."[35]

But lack of knowledge and understanding is not cause for great concern, and one can still lead a meaningful life. The Serenity Prayer recited by Wallace and other recovering addicts worldwide is actually a longer prayer written by the great twentieth-century theologian, Reinhold Niebuhr.[36] In addition to the part that is recited at the end of AA meetings—"God, grant me the serenity to accept the things I cannot change, the courage to change the things I can, and the wisdom to know the difference"—Niebuhr's original prayer extends the meditation to pray for peace in the middle of an ultimately incomprehensible world:

> Living one day at a time, Enjoying one moment at a time, Accepting hardship as a pathway to peace, Taking as Jesus did, this sinful world as it is, not as I would have it, Trusting that You will make all things right if I surrender to Your will, So that I may be reasonably happy in this life, and supremely happy with You forever in the next.

Despite the tragic end to Wallace's story, he was not alone in this journey. He was surrounded by countless fellow addicts who highly value the Big Book. The chapter, "How it Works," consistently sounds the alarm against the overactive ego that constantly tries to make matters about the self, and the chapter, "We Agnostics," convinces its reader that the overactive ego manifests in intellectual superiority, even to the point of worshipping it: "Yes, we had been faithful," it reads, "abjectly faithful to the God of Reason."[37] That is to say, disbelief in God is not synonymous with not worshipping. In one of Frank's books on Dostoevsky, Wallace writes in the margins "Atheism is a religion." Wallace is also not alone in embracing a paradoxical faith.

There are others, like de-churched former evangelical, Frank Schaeffer, who now honestly and contradictorily claims to be "an atheist who believes in God."[38] Maybe that is the only way to "give love, create beauty, and find peace," as Schaeffer says.

God, in Wallace's view, is somehow, paradoxically, both fiction and not. Wallace, like all of us, struggles to speak meaningfully about that which is ultimately ineffable. But to give up on the search is to abandon the power of *asking for help*. In Gately's moment of greatest vulnerability, Ferocious Francis G. mumbles as he walks out the door, "Might want to Ask For Some Help" (*IJ* 889). Wallace religiously capitalizes AA's trite clichés because here and throughout *Infinite Jest* they are worthy of reverence, just as a proper name would be capitalized. The renunciation of the ego by asking for help gives us a sense of the divine, which St. Ignatius had "a nice expression for … He calls it tasting and feeling the truth—not knowing it, but tasting and feeling it,"[39] which was underlined by Wallace. In another book, Wallace notes "What seems a paradox is simply the act of living: Never stop struggling. Life itself is a paradox, gathering order out of the chaos of matter and energy. When the struggle ceases, we die."[40]

In Tolstoy's meditation on art, Wallace repeatedly makes note of Tolstoy's connection of aesthetics to food, so he may appreciate what Barbara Brown Taylor says about the value of seeking faith through asking for help. In *When God is Silent*, she says:

> In a way that surpasses understanding, our duty in this time of famine is not to end the human hunger and thirst for God's word but to intensify it, until the whole world bangs its forks for God's food. That is what the famine is for, according to scripture. That is why God has hidden God's face: to increase our sense of loss until we are so hungry and lonely for God that we do something about it—not only one by one but also as a people who are once again ready to leave our fleshpots in search of real food.
>
> Whatever preachers serve on Sunday, it must not blunt the appetite for this food. If people go away from us full, then we have done them a disservice. What we serve is not supposed to satisfy. It is food for the journey. It is meant to tantalize, to send people out our doors with a taste for what they cannot find in our kitchens. When they find it, they understand why we did not say more about it than we did. It was not that we didn't. It was that we couldn't.
>
> Our words are too fragile. God's silence is too deep. But oh, what gorgeous sounds our failures make: words flung against the silence like wine glasses pitched against a hearth. As lovely as they are, they were meant for smashing. For when they do, it is as if a little of God's own music breaks through.[41]

Notes

1. See Matthew Mullins, "Wallace, Spirituality, and Religion," in *The Cambridge Companion to David Foster Wallace* (Cambridge, UK: Cambridge University Press, 2018), 190–203.
2. Skye Jethani, "Who are the De-Churched?" *Christianity Today* (March 2010). Available online: https://www.christianitytoday.com/pastors/2010/march-online-only/who-are-de-churched-part-1.html.
3. Annie Dillard, *For the Time Being* (New York: Alfred A. Knopf, 1999).
4. Ibid., 89.
5. Bonnie Friedman, *Writing Past Dark: Envy, Fear, Distraction, and Other Dilemmas in the Writer's Life* (New York: HarperCollins, 1994), 137.
6. For example, in response to John Gardner's *On Moral Fiction*, Wallace presents a short counterargument to Gardner's assessment about what makes art good or poor: "Because this is always implicit, or else historical, asshole. This is fascism." Elsewhere in the book, Wallace writes "No!" and "Oh, come on!" in the margins.
7. He also underlined in Campbell, *Myths to Live By* (New York: Random House, 1984), 261: "Essentially the same mythological motifs are to be found throughout the world. There are myths and legends of the Virgin Birth, of Incarnations, Deaths and Resurrections; Second Comings, Judgments, and the rest, in all the great traditions."
8. Lawrence Gonzales, *Deep Survival: Who Lives, Who Dies, and Why: True Stories of Miraculous Endurance and Sudden Death* (New York: Norton, 2003), 169.
9. The early Wallace has an ambivalent relationship with Tolstoy. After *Broom of the System* but before *Infinite Jest* was published, the young Wallace expressed admiration for Tolstoy in his 1993 interview with Hugh Kennedy and Geoffrey Polk. Wallace says he "absolutely worships Leo Tolstoy," but only "if you edit out the heavenly Christian stuff." See Stephen J. Burn, *Conversations with David Foster Wallace* (Jackson: University Press of Mississippi, 2012), 18–19.
10. This is not to suggest that Wallace is always asking himself these existential questions. It is likely that some of these marginal comments were for use this as a teaching tool in a seminar. But these comments *do* show that Wallace was steeped in religious literature and theological reflection.
11. S.J. Anthony DeMello, *Awareness: A de Mello Spirituality Conference in His Own Words*, ed. J. F. Stroud (New York: Image Books, 1990), 64.
12. Ibid., 86.
13. Ibid., 103.
14. Ibid., 136.
15. Ibid., 144–6.

16 Timothy O. Wilson, *Strangers to Ourselves: Discovering the Adaptive Unconscious* (Cambridge, MA: Harvard University Press, 2004), 38: "People who grow up in Western Cultures and who have an independent view of the self tend to promote their sense of well-being by exaggerating their superiority over others."

17 Tor Nørretranders, *The User Illusion: Cutting Consciousness Down to Size* (New York: Viking, 1998), 145 (emphasis in original).

18 Malcolm Gladwell, *Blink: The Power of Thinking Without Thinking* (New York: Back Bay Books of Little, Brown, 2005), 98, 194.

19 Jacob Needleman, *Money and the Meaning of Life* (New York: Doubleday, 1994), 87.

20 Interestingly, one of *The Idiot's* passages seems to have struck a cord with Wallace on another level, providing a glance at the thought process behind *Infinite Jest*. Wallace writes "1990s" next to a passage that reads: "It appears from the snatches of conversation that Radomsky had long ago announced his forthcoming resignation from the army, but that every time he had spoken of it in so jesting a manner that it had been impossible to take him seriously. Indeed, he always talked in a jesting manner about the most serious manners, so that it was quite impossible to make out whether he meant it or not, especially if he did not want people to be sure."

21 Philip Wylie, *Generation of Vipers* (New York: Pocket Books, 1959).

22 Emmet Fox, *The Sermon on the Mount: The Key to Success in Life* (New York: HarperCollins, 1989).

23 Mary Karr, "Suicide's Note: An Annual," in *Poetry* (September 2012). Available online: https://www.poetryfoundation.org/poetrymagazine/poems/55744/suicides-note-an-annual.

24 R. M. Sainsbury, *Paradoxes*, 2nd ed. (Cambridge: Cambridge University Press, 1995).

25 Ibid., back cover.

26 Even in his comments in the margins of his books, Wallace thought in terms of paradoxes and contradictions. In *Deep Survival*, he writes in the margin: "The phrase 'maximally concise' is less concise than the more modest claim: 'concise.'"

27 Terry Gross, "David Foster Wallace: The Fresh Air Interview," on *National Public Radio*, March 5, 1997. Available online: https://www.npr.org/2015/08/14/432161732/david-foster-wallace-the-fresh-air-interview.

28 Joseph Frank, *Dostoevsky: The Stir of Liberation, 1860–1865* (Princeton, NJ: Princeton University Press, 1988), 334.

29 Personal Correspondence, January 2019.

30 Ibid.

31 Immanuel Kant, *Groundwork for the Metaphysics of Morals*, trans. and ed. A.W. Wood (New Haven, CT: Yale University Press), 38 (emphasis added).

32 Bill Pittman and Todd Weber, *Drop the Rock: Removing Character Defects* (Center City, MN: Hazelden Publishing, 1999), 16–18.
33 Ralph Waldo Emerson, *The Selected Works of Ralph Waldo Emerson*, ed. B. Atkinson (New York: Random House, The Modern Library, 1950), 152.
34 Dillard, *For the Time Being*, 132.
35 Ibid., 47. See also Wallace's notations about paradoxes on pages 146 and 197.
36 For the story behind its composition and efforts to find its original author, see Fred R. Shapiro, "Who Wrote the Serenity Prayer?" *The Chronicle of Higher Education* (April 28, 2014). Available Online: https://www.chronicle.com/article/Who-Wrote-the-Serenity-Prayer-/146159/.
37 Bill W., Alcoholics Anonymous: *The Story of How Many Thousands of Men and Women Have Recovered from Alcoholism*, 4th ed. (New York: Alcoholics Anonymous World Services, 2001), 54.
38 Frank Schaeffer, *Why I Am an Atheist Who Believes in God: How to Give Love, Create Beauty, and Find Peace* (North Charleston, SC: CreateSpace, 2014).
39 DeMello, *Awareness*, 168.
40 Gonzales, *Deep Survival*, 206.
41 Barbara Brown Taylor, *When God is Silent: The 1997 Lyman Beecher Lectures on Preaching* (Lanham: Rowman and Littlefield, 1998).

INDEX

Abraham 76, 77
absolute, the 76
acedia xiii, 114–23
addiction 4, 8, 14, 17, 19, 21, 46, 52,
    83, 84, 85, 94, 102, 105, 110,
    126, 128, 133, 138, 156, 172,
    178, 193
Alcoholics Anonymous (AA) xii, 2–9,
    13–23, 26, 27, 33, 37, 41, 53–4,
    74, 86, 102–4, 117, 126, 128,
    135, 138, 146, 155, 156, 197
  Alcoholics Anonymous (Big Book)
    xii, 14, 15, 16, 20, 21, 197
"All That" 3, 8, 123 n.15
All Things Shining xii, 44 n.36, 45, 48,
    50, 58, 59, 88
Anatta ("not self") 177
Anderson, R. Lanier 51
Arden, Patrick 3, 5, 127
atheism xiv, 3, 8, 69, 139, 197
Aubry, Timothy 14

Baker, Lynne Rudder 30
Balthasar, Hans Urs von 90
baptism 86, 127, 166
Barth, Karl 89
Beadsman, Lenore 70–2, 77–81
Bell, Robert H. 87
Bernard of Clairvaux 27
Bible
  1 Corinthians 97 n.25
  2 Corinthians 96 n.9
  Ephesians 85, 86
  Galatians 85
  Isaiah 87, 96 n.24, 169
  James 23 n.14, 87, 136 n.10
  John 87, 89, 90, 96 n.20, 96 n.22
  Luke 91

  Malachi 169
  Matthew 86, 87
  Romans 85
"Big Book". *See Alcoholics
    Anonymous*
"Big Red Son" 194
Bissell, Tom 13, 149
Bolger, Robert 11 n.26, 38, 191
boredom xiii, 3, 7, 26, 46, 51, 54,
    55, 114–16, 125, 128, 130,
    132–4
Boswell, Marshall 72, 73, 77
Both Flesh and Not 4
Bradford, Mary Lythgoe 172
Brinkley, Douglas 138
Broom of the System, The xii, xii, 32,
    46, 69–81, 102, 103, 199 n.9
Buddhism xii, xiv, 2, 4, 7, 34, 110, 133,
    175–85
  Buddha 176, 181, 182
  Buddha nature 178
  Buddhist postmodernism 177
Burn, Stephen J. 101
Bustillos, Maria 10 n.12, 148
Butler, Judith 151

*Cambridge Companion to David
    Foster Wallace* xii
Campbell, Joseph 190
Carlisle, Clare 77
Carlisle, Gregory 113
Casanova, Jose 150
Casey, Michael 118
Cassian, John 116
Catholic/Catholicism 1–6, 87, 95 n.3,
    127, 131
Christian/Christianity xi, 6, 27, 49–51,
    69, 73, 74, 84–94, 99, 108,

114–18, 120, 121, 123 n.13, 139, 142–3, 154, 165, 173, 189, 190
Consider the Lobster 137, 187, 193
Corrigan, Paul 157
Costello, Mark 5, 192, 194, 195
Critchley, Simon 50

Dauben, Joseph Warren 190
David Foster Wallace: Presences of the Other xi
Dean, Lane Jr. 114–18, 121, 122 n.7, 123 n.13
"default setting" 3, 31–3, 35, 38–9, 56, 144, 191
Deleuze, Giles 69
DeLillo, Don 47, 95 n.2, 99, 101
DeMello, Anthony 53, 111 n.4, 189, 191
den Dulk, Allard 64 n.70, 74, 77, 89, 149
"Depressed Person, The" 180
"Derivative Sport in Tornado Alley" 138
Derrida, Jacques 73, 76
Descartes, Renee 25
Desert Fathers, the 114–16
Dillard, Annie 189
Dionysius the Areopagite 27
Dostoevsky, Fyodor 9, 38–40, 60 n.7, 79 n.2, 172, 191, 194, 197
Doubting Thomas 89–90
Douglass, Christopher 11 n.33
Dowling, William 87
Dreyfus, Hubert. *See All Things Shining*
Drinion, Shane 46, 55, 119, 121, 132

eightfold path of awakening 181
Eliot, T.S. 9, 33
Emerson, Ralph Waldo 197
Ennet House 4, 7, 19, 52, 85, 88, 94, 102, 106, 156
epistemological humility 35
"E Unibus Pluram" xii, 2, 56, 99, 109, 135
Evagrius Ponticus 114–16
evangelical/evangelism 8, 11 n.33, 118, 123 n.17, 130, 131, 153–4

Evans, David 63 n.34, 70, 149
Everything and More 190

Fate, Time, and Language 3, 187
Faust, James E. 169
Federer, Roger 2
Fogle, Chris xii, 6, 8, 54, 55, 120–2, 125, 130–5, 153–6, 159, 179–84
Four Noble Truths 183–4
Franny and Zooey 155, 158
Franzen, Jonathan xi, 54, 99, 127, 138, 149
Friedman, Bonnie 190

Gaddis, William 99
Garner, Brian 13
Gately, Don xii, xiii, 4, 6, 7, 19–20, 40–1, 53–4, 84–8, 90, 92–4, 102–4, 106, 109, 126, 128, 155–7, 159, 178, 193
Gesturing Toward Reality xi
Gilbert, Matthew 4
Ginsberg, Allen 155, 158, 159
Girl With Curious Hair, The 99
Gladwell, Malcolm 191
G. O. D. (Great Ohio Desert) xiii, 69–81
Gonzales, Lawrence 190
"Good Old Neon" 57, 195
"Good People" 8, 107 n.10, 117–18
Gospel According to David Foster Wallace, The xi, 45–6
grace xiii, 8, 38, 84–94, 118, 156
Granada House 102
Green, Karen 183
Greene, Graham 79 n.6

Habermas, Jurgen 150
Hamacher, Christopher 7, 147, 179, 183
Hamilton, Robert 136 n.15
Harris, Charles 5, 135 n.5, 138
Harry Ransom Center (DFW Archive) xi, 5, 46, 138, 141, 145, 188–92
"higher power" xii, 2, 4, 7, 14, 15, 19, 27, 41, 53–6, 70, 74, 117, 126, 130, 155, 193, 196–7

INDEX

Holley, David 32
Hungerford, Amy xiii, 151, 152, 155, 156, 158
hypostatic union 89

Ignatius of Loyola 27, 198
Imago Dei 93
Incandenza, Hal 52, 70, 84, 88, 91–2, 95 n.7, 96 n.14, 102, 157, 161 n.32, 178
Incandenza, James 72, 96 n.16, 102, 106, 156–7, 164
Incandenza, Mario xiii, 7, 70, 84, 88–94, 96 n.16, 102, 106
Incandenza, Orin 72, 75, 102
Infinite Jest 2, 4, 5, 6, 7, 8, 13–23, 40, 41, 43 n.30, 47, 48, 51–5, 66 n.82, 70, 72, 74, 75, 78, 83–97, 99, 112–17, 126, 128, 133, 142, 144, 146, 149, 155, 156, 157, 161 n.32, 164, 167, 171, 176, 178, 181, 184, 193, 198, 199 n.9, 200 n.20
innate selfishness 31, 34
Internal Revenue Service (IRS) 54, 103, 114, 118, 132, 133–4, 189

Jacobs, Timothy 111 n.27
James, William 20, 27, 37, 41, 58, 125–36
Johnston, Mark 30

Kant, Immanuel 30, 51, 55, 196
Karr, Mary 4, 5, 126–7, 193
Kaufmann, Michael 151, 157
Kaufmann, Walter 46
Kelly, Adam 152
Kelly, Sean Dorrance. *See All Things Shining*
Kennedy, Hugh 21
Kenyon Commencement Address. *See This is Water*
Kierkegaard, Søren xiii, 70, 73–7, 107, 149
kinsman redeemer 87
Konstantinou, Lee 149, 157
Kushner, Harold 190

Lacan, Jacques 75
Laing, R.D. 192
Lao-tzu 100
Larkin, Philip 33
Latter Day Saints, Church of xiii, 163–74
  Book of Mormon 164, 166–7
  Doctrine and Covenants 167
Lenz, Randy 19, 85, 88, 106, 109
Lewis, C. S. 99–112
  Abolition of Man xiii, 99, 100, 101, 103, 106
  An Experiment in Criticism 101
  Great Divorce 103
  Screwtape Letters 100, 101
Lipsky, David 1, 4, 17, 51, 53, 101
Loach, Barry xiii, 90–1, 94
loneliness/lonely 22, 37, 51, 54, 101, 106, 110, 122, 183, 189, 191
Loy, David 32, 36
Ludwig, Kathryn 152, 154
Lyle xiii, 92, 103–4

Maczynska, Magdelena 151, 152, 157, 159
Marathe, Remy 21, 53, 102, 107–9
Marilyn Manson 78
Matrix, The 137, 141, 142, 145, 148
Max, D.T. 2, 3, 5, 6, 7, 8, 21, 101–2, 105, 110, 126–7, 130, 133, 138
McCaffrey, Larry 1, 10 n.11, 13, 80 n.13, 89, 166, 177
McCain's Promise. See Up, Simba!
McClure, John xiii, 151–3, 157, 159
McKay, David O. 167
McLennan, Gregor 151
Merton, Thomas 115, 189
metafiction 1, 157–8
Miller, Adam 45
Moltmann, Jurgen 2
Mormons. *See* Latter Day Saints
Mosaic Law 87
Mullins, Matthew xii, 10 n.22, 199 n.1

Natural Law 100, 107
"The Nature of Fun" 13
Nechtr, Mark 73, 163–4

INDEX

Needleman, Jacob 191
New Sincerity 48, 99, 103, 106, 110, 152
Nhat Hanh, Thich 7
Nibley, Hugh 164, 166
Niebuhr, Reinhold 197
Nietzsche, Friedrich xii, 45–67, 88
   The Antichrist 48
   The Case of Wagner 48
   Ecce Homo 48
   The Gay Science 57
   Thus Spoke Zarathustra 47, 50, 51, 57
   Twilight of the Idols 48, 59
   The Will to Power 48, 49, 50
nihilism xii, 8, 45–67, 176
noonday demon. *See* acedia
Nørretranders, Tor 191
Norris, Kathleen 115

Obetrol 153, 154, 156, 180, 181, 185 n.7
O'Connell, Michael 79 n.6, 111 n.26
O'Connor, Flannery 1, 79 n.6, 190
"Octet" xii, xiii, 157–9, 161 n.37
Oxford English Dictionary 6

Pale King, The xii, xiii, 6, 8, 42 n.3, 46, 48, 54, 55, 60 n.7, 101, 103, 113–23, 125–36, 144, 153, 154, 179, 181, 184, 185 n.7, 189, 193
Paramananda 182, 189
Pascal, Blaise 25
Paul the Apostle (St. Paul) 84
Percy, Walker xiii, 80 n.16, 122 n.6
Piekarski, Krzysztof 89, 93, 110
postmodern/postmodernism xii, 2, 9, 21, 26, 48, 56, 84, 99, 102, 103, 109, 110, 126, 135, 151, 152, 157, 176–7, 184
postsecularism xiii, 149–60
practical solipsism 33
prayer 7, 8, 28, 41, 114, 115, 118, 127, 136 n.17, 149, 150, 155–6, 159
   Buddhist prayer 182
   Lord's Prayer 86, 192

Serenity Prayer 147 n.29, 197
   Thankfulness prayer 126
Preach My Gospel 167
process theology 2
Pynchon, Thomas 69, 99, 102

"Quo Vadis" 113 (quote from)

Raban, Jonathan 119
religious stance 38
Richard Rohr 6, 7, 33, 35, 40, 144–5, 189, 190–2
Rowley, T. Leonard 170, 171, 172
Ryerson, James 3

Sainsbury, Mark 193
sanctification 86
Saunders, George 181–2
Schacht, Richard 46, 192
Schaeffer, Frank 198
Severs, Jeffrey 11 n.34
Shakespeare, William 75
Short, Rob 95 n.7
Signifying Rappers 5, 194, 195
Silverblatt, Michael 144
sincerity 83, 89, 92, 103, 106, 110, 126, 135, 152, 168, 182. *See also* New Sincerity
Smith, Huston 16, 18, 189
Smith, Joseph 168
Smith, Warren Cole 8
Smith, Zadie 99, 159
Solomon, Robert 58
soteriology xiii, 83–97
"The Soul is not a Smithy" 7
Spark, Muriel 79 n.6
Sparks, Flint 182
Steeply, Hugh 21, 53, 102, 107–9
Steiner, George 139–41, 143
Streitfeld, David 5
Supposedly Fun Thing I'll Never Do Again, A 137

Tao, Taoism 2, 100, 183
   C. S. Lewis's use of term 99–112
Taylor, Barbara Brown 198
Taylor, Charles 150

This is Water xii, xiii, xiv, 1, 2, 3, 6, 7, 8, 13, 26, 27, 28, 30, 32, 34, 40, 41, 42, 44 n.38, 56, 58, 70, 103, 107, 109, 117, 128, 129, 131–48, 149, 180, 190, 191
Tiebout, Henry 37
Tolstoy, Leo 190, 198

Übermensch/overman 50–1, 56, 110
Ulysses 157
Unamuno, Miguel de 26
Underhill, Evelyn 40
Up, Simba! 194

Van Dyne, Joelle 20, 70
"The View from Mrs. Thompson's" 5, 138

Wallace, James 3, 46
Wallace, Sally Foster 192
Walls, Seth Coulter 138
"Westward the Course of Empire Takes it Way" xii, xiii, 8, 69, 73, 163, 165, 167
Wilkinson, Alyssa 166, 171–2
Willes, Mark 165
Williams, Iain 158
Williams, Rowan 96 n.9
Wilson, Timothy 191
Wittgenstein, Ludwig 2–4, 32, 40, 72, 73
Wood, David 77
Wylie, Philip 192

Zane, J. Peder 100
Zen 143, 145, 178–84, 185 n.5

www.ingramcontent.com/pod-product-compliance
Lightning Source LLC
Chambersburg PA
CBHW052040300426
44117CB00012B/1910